THE
MAN WHO
SAVED
CINCINNATI

BY PETER BRONSON

AUTHOR OF

Not in Our Town

AND

Forbidden Fruit

The Man Who Saved Cincinnati

© 2023 Peter Bronson

National Colors of the Cincinnati Black Brigade courtesy of the Ohio History Connection.

Public domain art courtesy of Wikimedia Commons.

ISBN: 979-8-9885817-1-0

For information, contact the author:

Peter Bronson
1488 Greystone Lane
Milford, Ohio 45150
Pbronson1253@gmail.com
513-287-0001

Published by:

Chilidog Press LLC
pbronson@chilidogpress.com

Chilidog Press
Milford, Ohio
www.chilidogpress.com

Cover design, interior design and typesetting:
Craig Ramsdell, RamsdellDesign.com

For the Queen City of the West—
blessed with beauty, generous in friendship, rich in history.

"May a man tell what he can do until he tries? That, I take it,
is the soul of the Americanism."

—Lew Wallace

CONTENTS

INTRODUCTION

In 1862, Cincinnati was the sixth largest city in the *dis*-United States.

- Four times bigger than San Franciso.
- Twice as big as Chicago.
- Almost five times bigger than Detroit, Pittsburgh or Cleveland.
- By comparison, Atlanta, Columbus and Indianapolis were Hicksville towns of fewer than 20,000.
- Covington, Kentucky was bigger than Toledo and Sacramento.

The reason: German immigrants flooded "Zinzinnati" in the Great Migration of the mid-1800s as refugees fled European wars and revolutions. More than half the population of Ireland came to America in those decades. And Cincinnati's fame as the front door to the Underground Railroad made it the beacon of freedom for slaves set free by the war.

St. Louis was the nearest competitor. But Cincinnati was the Queen City of the West when the real West was still unexplored empty places on the map and the Mississippi River marked the Western frontier.

It was also the largest inland city. The five biggest cities in the 1860 Census were seaports: New York, Boston, Philadelphia, Brooklyn and Baltimore. And that made Cincinnati the center of gravity for the Union in the Civil War.

If the Civil War were a movie, the best actors on the Union side came mostly from Ohio: Grant, Sherman, Sheridan, Buell, Rosecrans, McCook, Lytle, Force, Hickenlooper and future presidents Rutherford Hayes and James Garfield—all from Ohio.

Even George McClellan, the "Little Napoleon" stone in Lincoln's shoe, served in Cincinnati as commander at Camp Dennison near Cincinnati when the war began. (He found residents were "really quite Eastern and civilized.") Gen. Joe Hooker was stationed at Newport, Kentucky.

Another testimony to Cincinnati's pivotal role can be found at Spring Grove Cemetery: A thousand Civil War soldiers are buried there, alongside 41 generals.

Only New York state sent more men to the Union Army than Ohio. And Cincinnati lost more sons, husbands, brothers, uncles and friends than any other city in Ohio.

Gunboats, military supplies, uniforms, cannons, smelted iron and other war supplies came from Cincinnati. It fed the nation, sent its best young men, nursed and healed the wounded, offered hope of freedom to the enslaved and elected and protected an untested, raw new president named Abraham Lincoln.

Much of this history has been forgotten like yellowed, mildewed pages in old books on dusty library shelves.

But once upon a time, the Queen City was on the front lines in the War Between the States. It was the young nation distilled to its raw essence: not solidly South, and not naturally North. Like a few other border cities, Cincinnati was painfully torn in two directions. It had Copperheads who hated Lincoln, and abolitionists who abhorred slavery.

Both could be violent fanatics.

Northern Kentucky was part of the city—in business, social life and culture. But it was also separated by a gap wider than the Ohio River: the institution of slavery.

Some of the following might sound familiar in 2023.

America was split between the industrialized, urban North and the rural, agricultural South—a lot like the electoral maps from 2020 that show cities in blue and the rest of the country in red.

Opinions were hazardous. Abolitionists were shouted down, even stoned. Secessionists were not welcome in polite society. Each side had their own rabidly partisan press, and newspapers warred against each other, fanning the fury that finally spilled rivers of blood in places nobody had ever heard of: Antietam. Gettysburg. Shiloh.

The typical young men who fought and died were under 20; some as young as 10. They came from farms and cities and had never been so homesick or so far from families and hometowns, or less prepared for the plague of diseases that killed twice as many as cannon shells, bayonets and bullets. More than 750,000 died; only 250,000 were killed in combat.

Records are not complete, but among a US population of 31.5 million, the death rate among young men who were eligible to fight may have been as high as 15 percent to 22 percent.[1]

The violent rhetoric of those times is not the only echo heard today. The first time half of the nation refused to accept a national election was the 40 percent plurality victory by President Abraham Lincoln in 1860.

Slavery was not the only issue that split the nation. New immigrants were drawn to northern cities, where they gave the North a majority in Congress. The North used that political muscle to strong-arm the South with tariffs to protect northern industry. The Civil War has been called "A second American Revolution" that married the federal government to Northern industry and orphaned the South's agrarian economy.[2]

The Senate became a battleground, almost evenly divided. The rhetoric was so overheated Sen. Charles Sumner was almost beaten to death in the Senate by Rep. Preston Brooks.[3]

As new states were admitted to the Union, there were violent conflicts over political power. Murderous violence broke out in Kansas and Missouri. "Bloody Kansas" became a battleground to determine if it would join the South as a slave state, or add to Northern political power as a free state.

---

1   Hacker, David, "A Census-Based Count of Civil War Dead," *Civil War Times,* 2011.

2   Historians Charles and Mary Beard, 1925. Industrial capitalists "succeeded in capturing the state and using it as an instrument to strengthen their economic position."

3   In recent years, Rep. Steve Scalise was shot, Sen. Rand Paul was assaulted, and Supreme Court Justice Brett Kavanaugh was nearly killed, all by politically motivated fanatics. Violent threats against members of Congress have increased tenfold in five years.

John Brown, funded by abolitionists, killed five men and was hanged for treason after he seized a federal armory at Harper's Ferry in Virginia in an attempt to incite a slave rebellion.

The South lost trust in the "Northern" government and asserted a constitutional right to be left alone and secede from the Union.

During the war, President Lincoln suspended the Bill of Rights and arrested thousands of citizens for speaking opinions that were "disloyal" to the Union.

Immigration. Abuse of power to punish political enemies. Midnight arrests. Unhinged rhetoric. Refusal to accept an election. Media incitement of violence. Huge segments of the nation alienated and losing trust. Suppression of free speech. A new "outsider" president who is so viscerally hated, his enemies make death threats and plot to overthrow the government....

The echoes from history can be painful and inconvenient.

Our modern "narrative" has conveniently forgotten that Democrats were the pro-slavery party; or that less than a third of Confederate soldiers had any connection to slave ownership; or that Republicans were the party of legal immigration; or that the Great Emancipator, Lincoln, said he would support slavery to save the Union.

The veneer of civilization can look as deep and strong as mahogany, yet be as brittle and thin as bark on a birch tree.

This book is about what happens when it is peeled away.

It's about a nation drawn into the undertow of a Civil War.

It's a story of generational bitterness over race that has roots in the muddy banks of The Bottoms in Cincinnati, where underclasses of blacks and Irish wrestled for a grip on freedom and security in a new land of opportunity.

It's about a city that straddled the quaking fault line of history.

And it's about the remarkable men who fought a savage war, yet somehow held on to their sacred code of honor. They were small men by today's physical standards, but they make us all look Lilliputian next to their courage and achievements.

John Wesley Powell lost an arm at Shiloh, returned to combat and then explored the untamed West, including a harrowing, deadly expedition down the Grand Canyon.

Manning Ferguson Force of Cincinnati was horribly wounded in the face and sent home to die. He recovered, returned to battle and won the Medal of Honor. He came home to be a judge, author and lecturer who helped found the Cincinnati Zoo and Cincinnati Music Hall. He struggled with the deep soul-wounds of the war and turned his anguish into a mission to help other veterans.

Confederate soldier Henry Stanley survived the terror of Shiloh and other battles, then became famous as the reporter who went through seven layers of jungle hell to finally track down Dr. David Livingstone in Africa. He was the man credited with saying, "Dr. Livingstone, I presume."

Ulysses Grant grew up near Cincinnati (Pleasant Plain and Georgetown) and failed at nearly everything he tried, then became the most celebrated Union general of the Civil War—and President of the nation he glued together with blood.

Andrew Hickenlooper fought heroically at Shiloh with his fierce battery of cannons, then fought on through more than 30 battles including Vicksburg, Stone Mountain, Atlanta and Sherman's March to the Sea. He was promoted by Grant to chief of artillery, then chief engineer, and rose to general. After the war he came back to Cincinnati and served as a US Marshal and president of the company that became Cincinnati Gas & Electric. He was elected Ohio Lieutenant governor in 1879.

Lew Wallace was a true renaissance man: self-taught artist, sculptor, musician, military tactician, state senator, outstanding horseman, decorated general, diplomat, governor of New Mexico who captured Billy the Kid and tamed the Apache raids, judge in the Lincoln assassination trial, referee in the disputed presidential election of 1876, inventor of historical novels and the author of one of the most popular books ever written, *Ben-Hur, A Tale of the Christ*.

He was also the "Savior of Cincinnati" who rescued the city from a Confederate invasion—and saved it from itself. For two weeks in September 1862, Cincinnati was united, rich and poor, doctors and dockworkers, Irish and Germans, blacks and whites, men and women, bankers and bricklayers—side by side in a single cause: the Defense of Cincinnati.

"There is no telling what a man may do until he tries," Wallace said. He proved it with his amazing life and showed Cincinnati it was capable of greatness and grace.

It's hard to imagine such men today, when "renaissance man" means a guy who can text and watch TV at the same time. But it's harder to imagine what history would be like without them.

What would they think of us today?

One of them, Andrew Gillespie, was my great-great grandfather, who fought at Corinth and possibly at Shiloh with the 12th Michigan. Otherwise, his adventures here are as fictional as his sidekick Duck and the two outlaws who follow Billy the Kid. Mose of the Black Brigade and Nehemiah the Squirrel Hunter are also fictional. The rest of the names in the book are real, and their thoughts, dialogue and experiences are taken almost entirely from their own words, biographies, letters and memoirs.

The Civil War left us a vast Permian Basin oilfield of stories, records and research. Wherever possible, I used primary sources and deferred to those who lived it rather than those who teach and study it.

I hope you enjoy the story and that you are as surprised as I was at some of the treasures uncovered during a year of research.

This is the Queen City's forgotten past: a legacy to American history.

September 2023

BOOK I:

THE DEVIL'S OWN DAYS

The 9th Illinois at Shiloh, at the Sunken Road near the
Peach Orchard. By Keith Rocco for the State of Illinois, 1862.

SHILOH DAY 1
'My God, we are attacked!'

Dawn: Fraley Field,
near Pittsburg Landing, Tennessee

A voice was telling him "Andrew, wake up! Get up!" It was his mother...
Wait. No, it was not. It was the querulous voice of a crow, dismayed,
complaining... No, it was a scratchy, angry Blue Jay... then a hammering
woodpecker?

"Ahh," he breathed as he slowly drifted like a bubble to the surface
of the deep and gentle river of dreams. "A mockingbird."

The voice stopped. But the hammering continued.

He heard it in the distance. Not a woodpecker. More like a crackling
bonfire deep in the woods. He sat up and felt a few seconds of dreamy
confusion. For the briefest moment, he had no idea where he was or how
he got there. Then it came filtering in like shafts of sunlight through the
opening in his sepia-brown dog tent. He was soaked in sweat, all wound
up like string on a stick in his scratchy green wool blanket, sleeping on
the soggy ground in a small clearing on the hem of the skirts of southern
Tennessee. A long, long way from home in western Michigan.

That crackling noise was building now, and he thought it could be
guns, but there were so many at once it didn't sound like guns, as if they
were canceling each other out. The loud voice of one rifle couldn't be
heard over all of them talking at once. "A great confabulation of fire-
crackers," he whispered, smiling at the sound of the three-dollar word.
"Or pickets shooting at shadows again."

A huge bumblebee flew through his tent at astonishing speed. So
fast it left a hole where it came in, about level with his head as he lay half
sitting up on the ground, leaning on his arms braced behind him. It was
slowly dawning on him that it was not a bee when he heard another one
buzz by and someone outside made a strange animal noise, something

like a grunt and whimper, then an almost comical shout of indignant, alarmed surprise: "I've been SHOT!"

Gillespie found himself on his feet, wrestling up and through the tent, tearing the stakes out of the ground, as if his body knew what was going on before his mind could even form the thought. He pushed his feet into those damned army-issue boots that felt like they were made of tree bark and broken glass, all the while keeping his eyes riveted on the tree line to the south, where the crashing noise was building like a surge of something dark and terrible that was not of this world.

There was lots of yelling now. Sergeant Cross was shouting in his parade-ground voice, "Form up, men! Grab your muskets! Light marching order! For you men from Michigan with mosquitos where your brains should be, that means leave your soldier's trunk, but make sure you have cartridges, caps and bayonets...."

The sergeant seemed pretty calm. That was reassuring. It could not be a real battle. There were no formations, no marching columns, no lines of infantry facing off in an open field.

But over there, behind him among the lines of tents... men in their long johns were skedaddling north, their bare white feet and arms flashing like whitetail deer flushed out of cover. Another bumblebee flew by. "Bullets," he suddenly realized. "My God, someone is shooting at us!"

That was impossible. General Sherman himself had ridden through the camp the day before, rallying the troops. He had promised that the "Butternuts" were all in Corinth, Mississippi, miles and miles south, afraid to come out and fight, scared like whipped pups. General Grant was sure of it, Sherman said. They had been mangled so badly up north at Fort Henry and Fort Donelson, he laughed, they were dang near finished. The war would be over in weeks, if not sooner.

Besides, Gillespie thought, his 12th Michigan Regiment had barely had a chance to get off the steamboats that carried them down here to Pittsburgh Landing. What a sight that was. More than 170 steamboats carrying 40,000 men from Wisconsin, Illinois, Ohio, Michigan, Iowa, Kentucky, Nebraska.... It looked like the biggest invasion armada since the Trojan War.

Until this morning it had rained steadily. Furious, raging thunder and lightning, winds like cyclones, making it feel like this part of the country had its own species of weather, wilder and more ferocious than anything back in Michigan.

And then today... who could choose such a beautiful spring morning for a battle? A clear blue sky, warm sunshine, blooming trees and wildflowers, a perfect April Sunday. Surely the Confederates were not so godless they would march all the way from Corinth, Mississippi to kill their fellowmen on the Lord's Day.

But someone was in those woods and they were getting closer. Maybe they were not so afraid to fight. He could hear strange yelps and high-pitched screams mixed with the popping gunfire, like all the demons in Hell unleashed. It made the hair on the back of Gillespie's neck stand up. Maybe those rumors he had heard about hundreds of Rebel campfires to the south were true.

Private Fritz Ludwig of the 16th Wisconsin had told him that some Rebs had been captured and locked up in a little church nearby. According to the rumor passed by Ludwig, the Reb prisoners had swaggered and bragged that an entire army was on its way to drive them all into the river like field mice running from a barn fire. But what else would defiant prisoners say?

As he scrambled to obey orders, Gillespie never gave a thought to his canvas knapsack "soldier's trunk" that carried his Bible, with room for his blanket and a few personal items – a piece of soap, a little frypan, a straight razor and a brush that he might as well throw away for all the good it did his tangled, shaggy, reddish-brown hair. The pack also contained his ration: some salt pork, a potato, hardtack, split peas and coffee.

He just strapped on his cartridge belt with shaking hands and picked up his rifle. "Is this how it begins?" he wondered. "Am I about to die? Lord, I'm too young. Let me at least get to twenty."

Not even a half-mile farther south, the Battle of Shiloh had begun while Gillespie was still asleep, dreaming of birds and his mother. It was April 6, 1862. Around 5:00 a.m., as the orange sun was peeking over the horizon, patrols sent out by Col. Evert Peabody were stumbling through the thick underbrush and briars, unaware that they were about to bump into 10,000 Confederates led by Gen. William Hardee, who had written the West Point two-volume textbook on *Rifle and Light Infantry Tactics* that was used by both armies.

Colonel Peabody had been approached late yesterday by Capt. Gilbert Johnson of the 12th Michigan. Johnson had been out on picket duty and reported seeing lines of campfires to the south. But when Johnson had reported the disturbing news to the division commander, Gen. Benjamin Mayberry Prentiss, Prentiss scoffed and said it was nothing to worry about.

Captain Johnson was not reassured. He shared his worries with Peabody and got a typical Missouri answer: "Show me." Peabody organized 250 men to go with Johnson on patrol at midnight, all volunteers from his 25th Missouri and Gillespie's 12th Michigan Volunteer Infantry.

Peabody had no trouble rounding up men for the pre-dawn scouting mission. He was a natural leader with a commanding presence that seemed too big even for the broad six-foot frame that made him a giant among men of his time.

As the patrols felt their way through the dark woods under a white apple-slice of moon, they spotted what looked like dense bushes lining a low hill in the dim dawn light. They stood on the edge of the woods, looking south across 40 acres of cleared fields owned and worked by a farmer named Fraley. As they stepped off into the field, they saw something odd and alarming: dozens of rabbits running toward them.

In moments, the most devastating battle of the Civil War up to that time was about to begin.

The "bushes" across the field were Confederates. Suddenly, Johnson and his patrol saw muzzle flashes and heard sporadic shots from the southern edge of the field. Then, almost before they could react, the shots crescendoed to a crashing wave of withering fire from thousands of enemy rifles.

That morning, Confederate Gen. Albert Sidney Johnston had ordered the attack to commence, saying they would drive the Yankees so far back, "Tonight we will water our horses in the Tennessee River."

At 5:15 a.m., overwhelmed by a storm of lead and getting flanked on their left, the Union patrol began to withdraw. A runner was sent to warn Colonel Peabody that a massive attack was coming.

Peabody needed no warning to know what was happening. He could hear the guns and knew the battle had begun. "Nobody should be surprised," he thought. "But they will be. Especially the brass."

As Peabody rallied his command, General Benjamin Prentiss, commander of the Sixth Division, rode up to brusquely demand a report and find out what in hell was going on. What was going on was that Peabody and Johnson, through their own foresight, had prevented complete surprise, and their men were fighting furiously to buy time for the rest of the Union Army and its generals to finally wake up.

But Gen. Prentiss didn't thank Peabody for his initiative. Instead, he scorched him for "initiating an engagement" without permission—in violation of the direct orders from supreme commander Major General Halleck to General Grant, and all the way down the line of command to Prentiss himself: avoid a fight and do nothing.

To Colonel Peabody and his soldiers, "doing nothing" sounded like something the Union generals had almost perfected. If anyone looked afraid to fight, it was not Johnny Reb—not from what he had heard from Fraley Field.

Peabody scowled and stood his ground, telling the general he would soon see for himself what was coming. Prentiss would have none of it. "I will hold you personally responsible," he huffed. Peabody replied, "I am responsible for all of my actions." The insult to Prentiss was implicit: Some commanders make sure they are not held responsible.

As the general rode off, Peabody shook his head. He knew a fool when he saw one, and General Prentiss fit the description: a political appointee, promoted for his connections, not his command abilities.

Those last words from Prentiss were clear enough, though. It would be Peabody, not Prentiss, who took the blame if Grant and Halleck got indigestion over the "unauthorized engagement."

Peabody smiled bitterly and thought, "I sure as hell didn't start this, but I will do what I can to finish it." He ordered the rest of his troops to follow, turned his horse and spurred it back to the sound of guns.

The unprepared Union generals were lucky he did. Peabody and Major James Powell held back the overwhelming tide of Confederates for an hour before they were forced to retreat as the entire Third Army Corps of 9,000 soldiers of the Confederate Army of The Mississippi emerged from the woods and drove the front lines of the Union Army all the way back into the disbelieving lap of General Prentiss.

While Peabody's troops were fighting for their lives, Prentiss had finally sent five companies of infantry from the 16th Wisconsin and 21st Missouri. But by then it was too late, and far too little. His front line was being rolled up like a carpet.[4]

Meanwhile, another spearpoint of the Confederate surprise attack was hitting Gen. William Tecumseh Sherman's camp to the northwest, where the 53rd Ohio from Jackson, Ohio, near Chillicothe, was scrambling out of its tents. Just the day before, Sherman had written to General Grant, "I have no doubt that nothing will occur today other than some picket firing. The enemy is saucy, but ... will not press our pickets far. I do not apprehend anything like an attack on our position."

Gen. William Tecumseh Sherman.
Mathew Brady, 1861-1865.

Sherman still didn't believe it even as wounded pickets stumbled out of the woods warning, "The Rebels are coming! Thicker than fleas on a dog's back!"

As Sherman rode to the sound of guns to see for himself the attack that could not possibly be happening, he paused, unaware that a line of Confederates had burst from the woods to his right. A soldier shouted to warn him, but not in time. Sherman's aide was shot from

---

4   Groom, Winston. *Shiloh, 1862*. National Geographic Books, 2012.

his horse and Sherman was shot by buckshot through his hand.[5] "My God, we are attacked!" he shouted.

He wheeled his horse and spurred it to the rear, shouting to Col. Jesse Appler of the 53rd Ohio, "Hold your position! I will reinforce you."

For Colonel Appler, that was bitter irony. For days, he had been mocked by Sherman for daring to suggest there were Rebels in the woods. When Appler reported Rebel patrols the day before, Sherman had told him "Take your damn regiment back to Ohio! There is no enemy nearer than Corinth." The rebuke stung. Sherman was a West Pointer, a veteran of First Bull Run in July 1861. Appler and his 53rd Ohio were as green as spring grass. They had not "seen the elephant."[6]

But as the US Army Staff Guide to Shiloh says, West Pointers like Sherman were not yet professionals. "Leaders became more professional through experience and at the cost of thousands of lives. General William T. Sherman would later note that the war did not enter its 'professional stage' until 1863."

If West Point training was the key to success, the Confederates would have won the battle. They had five West Point graduates leading their Army of The Mississippi. The Union Army of the Tennessee[7] had just Grant and Sherman on April 6; the rest of the Union generals were lawyers and politicians.

But thanks to a few bold Union officers such as Peabody, Johnson and Powell, their men from Michigan, Missouri, Wisconsin, Iowa, Illinois, Kentucky, Minnesota, Indiana and Ohio held back the gray tidal wave long enough for Grant's Army of The Tennessee to shake off the cobwebs of disbelief and form a defense before they were overrun.

General Prentiss never got a chance to apologize to Colonel Peabody. Before the morning was gone, Peabody was killed. Already wounded four times, he was shot through the head and fell from his horse as he

---

5   Many of the Confederates were issued obsolete flintlocks which were loaded with cartridges that contained powder, a ball and three smaller buckshot, called "ball and buck."

6   For veterans of the Civil War, to "see the elephant" meant to have been in combat. It may have come from circuses that kept their elephant for last, the ultimate experience.

7   Armies on both sides were named after rivers that were the transportation arteries of the 1860s.

rode to rally his troops at about 9:00 a.m. Major Powell also was killed that morning.[8]

"We were like a hungover drunk who was shaken awake, all angry, crapulous and confused," Gillespie recalled later. "I saw Peabody ride off. He had a look like a thundercloud and waved off Prentiss as if the general was a raw private. That man had sand. But that was the last I ever saw of him."

As a few men ran and others scrambled to grab muskets, shoes and cartridge cases, Gillespie lined up with the troops falling in behind Sergeant Cross. He checked his rifle again to make sure it was ready. He touched his 18-inch bayonet that hung like a giant icepick in a sheath at his side. He jiggled his canteen to make sure it was filled and then, too soon, before he felt ready, they all stepped off, quick-timing through the woods, hopping over fallen tree limbs and trampling through the underbrush, running to the roar of battle.

He learned something about himself in those first few moments of panic at the southern tip of Grant's shocked army. As he marched into a tornado of killing and chaos at the northern edge of Fraley Field, things slowed down for him. Part of his mind knew that bullets were flying around him. But another part of his mind pushed that deep into the back of a drawer and closed it, as he focused with almost supernaturally clear vision on what was happening and what had to be done. He took his stand at the edge of the woods, standing sideways, left foot and left shoulder forward, to present less of a target. Some men kneeled. "Wrong," he thought, remembering what Sergeant Cross had told them. "More likely to get shot in the head or upper body."

He could see the musket flashes all across the southern edge of the field, like morning fireworks. He could hear the Minié balls[9] whizz past and thunk into trees with the flat sound of a dull axe. But everything was

---

8   As the battle raged into the afternoon, Gen. Prentiss and his Corps were surrounded, and he was forced to surrender his sword. He was released in a prisoner exchange five months later. Gen. Prentiss fought bravely at Shiloh, but never gave Col. Peabody the credit he deserved. That might have undermined his political career after the war.

9   Introduced in 1847, named after the French inventor, Claude-Etienne Minié.

so clear, almost beautiful—the sky, the rising sunlight falling in shafts through the gentle spring green of new leaves—even those bold flags across the field were pretty, bright red with the giant "X" of blue stars.

The noise was deafening almost to the point where it no longer mattered. He began to see as if through a tunnel, completely focused on those men across the field. They were coming on now, marching across the open field as if they were out for a festive Sunday morning stroll to church, waving those bright flags almost joyfully.

Sgt. Alvin Cross started the commands. "Load!"

Gillespie stood his rifled 1861 Springfield musket butt down between his feet. It weighed almost 10 pounds and was accurate enough to kill a man at 600 yards. At 200 yards it could drive a round through 11 inches of white pine lumber.

"Cartridge!"

He reached back with his right hand, opened the black, hard leather cartridge case on his belt and withdrew one of the 40 tallow-greased paper tubes. Each contained 60 grains of black powder and a cone-shaped lead Minié ball that was hollow at the bottom and weighed about one and a half ounces.

"Tear!" Sgt. Cross shouted over the constant crash of guns.

He tore the cartridge with his teeth and spit out the scrap of paper.

"Charge!"

He poured the powder into the barrel of his Springfield and pushed the Minié ball in last.

"Draw!"

He drew his ramrod and inserted one end into the barrel. His hands shook a bit. He noticed some men were fumbling worse, struggling to match the end of the rammer with the mouth of the gun.

"Ram!" This was all happening too fast. Less than a minute had passed. But the familiar commands helped him ignore the battle around him and concentrate on the task, using the ramrod to push the ball down onto the powder.

"Return!" He fumbled the ramrod back in its slot below the barrel of his gun.

"Prime!"

He reached into his pouch of percussion caps on the left side of his belt and pulled forth one small brass cap filled with fulminate of mercury, about the size of a nail head, shaped like a miniature top hat, and put it on the tiny nipple that sat where the hammer would strike to ignite the cap and the powder in the breech.

When that cap was struck, the flash would explode 60 grains of black powder, and the "skirt" of the soft lead bullet would expand like an opening flower; the compressed gasses would force it through the gun barrel's rifled grooves, spinning the .58 caliber projectile to make it more accurate.

The rifle had a rear leaf sight for 300 yards, and another that was accurate at 500 yards. Both were folded down, flat against the 40-inch barrel, giving him fixed front and rear sights set for a range of about 100 yards or less.

Almost before he could think about it, he heard the last command: "Fire!"

As guns crashed in his ears, he took aim, picked out a man in the front lines who seemed a bit bigger than the rest, pulled the trigger and felt the comforting punch in his shoulder. The percussion cap banged, the black powder ignited, and the explosion sent the Minié ball from the muzzle at 1,000 feet per second.

If it hit a man, the subsonic, soft lead projectile would deform and flatten out on impact, spreading to nearly the size of a half-dollar coin. The heavy acorn-sized bullets left huge exit wounds, but often lodged in the body, carrying shreds of dirty clothing, bone and debris that quickly spawned infections.

As they struck a man, Minié balls caused massive damage. They pulped flesh, shredded organs and shattered bones, forcing bone splinters deep into surrounding tissues. A single bullet could destroy six inches of a femur or humerus, forcing assembly-line amputations on blood-soaked "butcher tables" in unsanitary field hospitals—if the wounded soldier did not bleed to death first.

Exploding bullets filled with black powder or fulminate of mercury

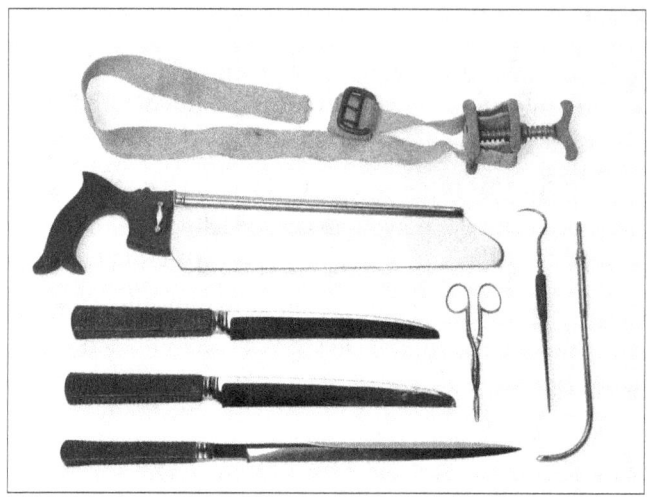

Tools of the surgeon's trade, 1862. Sterilization was unknown.

were also used later in the war, causing more devastating, usually fatal damage.

Surgeons were unaware that germs caused infections. It was not unusual for them to hone their knives on the bottoms of their shoes between patients. Their instruments looked like tools for woodworking and torture: saws, long knives, needlelike probes and hammers. Almost anyone who could stand the gore and screams could qualify to be a surgeon.

Fatality rates varied by the wounds: head, 80 percent; abdomen, 74 percent; chest, 73 percent. Death rates from amputations: foot, 13 percent; leg below the knee, 26 percent; leg at the hip, 85 percent; lower arm, 20 percent; arm at shoulder, 40 percent.

Fast-acting chloroform was used when it was available. Morphine and opium were given during recovery. But when field hospitals were overwhelmed, anesthetics became scarce, especially in the South. Many patients died from shock and sepsis. Surgeons were so hated and feared they avoided battlefields for fear of being shot by their own troops. Some soldiers kept derringers under their pillows to shoot a doctor who tried to take a limb.[10]

---

10   Dr. Gordon W. Jones, Wartime Surgery, *Civil War Times*, May, 1963.

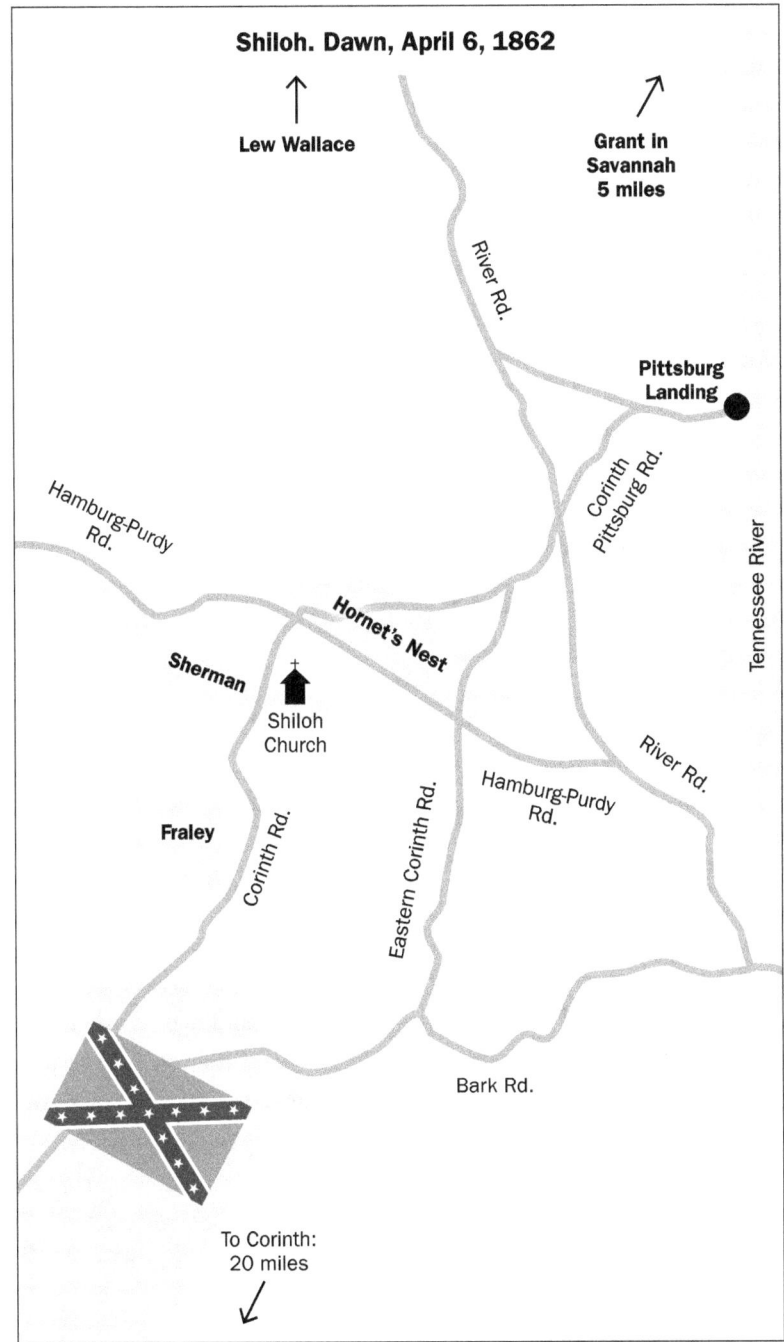

Map 1

'There they are!'

The smoke was too thick for Gillespie to tell if his first shot was true or a miss. He didn't waste any time looking but went right into his reloading routine. This time he stuck his ramrod into the ground to save time and reduce weight on the gun barrel.

He was proud that he could fire almost three times in a minute, but time had become elastic. Seconds felt like hours and hours could pass like minutes. He saw something like an arrow sail off into the smoke out of the corner of his eye. Some panicked soldier had forgotten to remove his ramrod before pulling the trigger.

A man a few yards to his right grunted and toppled backward as if struck by a bolt of lightning. The impact of the bullet made a sound that reminded Gillespie of killing a hog with a sledgehammer. He tried not to think about it.

Snugging the gun tight to his shoulder, he fired again into the gray-yellow, sulfurous cloud where thousands of men in gray seemed almost on top of him. He could make out faces now through gaps in the smoke; could see real men, just like him, their mouths set in grimaces, teeth bared, with wild eyes like madmen.

Many of those men in gray were part of the 1st Brigade of Colonel Robert G. Shaver, which included the 6th Arkansas. Among them was Private Henry Stanley, who described it later:

> We loaded our muskets and arranged our cartridge pouches ready for use. Our weapons were the obsolete flintlocks, and the ammunition was rolled in cartridge-paper, which contained powder, a round ball, and three buckshot.... Within a few minutes, there was another explosive burst of musketry, the air was pierced by many missiles, which hummed and pinged sharply by our ears, pattered throughout the tree-tops, and brought twigs and leaves down on us.
>
> "There they are!" was no sooner uttered, than we cracked into them with leveled muskets. "Aim low, men!" commanded Captain Smith. I tried hard to see some living thing to shoot at, for it appeared absurd to be blazing away at the shadows... My nerves

tingled, my pulse beat double quick, my heart throbbed loudly, almost painfully.... I was angry with my rear rank because he made my eyes smart with the powder of his musket; and I felt like cuffing him for deafening my ears!

Stanley survived the assault and the war, and became the famous *New York Herald* reporter who finally tracked down a lost missionary explorer in Africa in 1871, uttering the words: "Dr. Livingstone, I presume." [11]

As Gillespie kept firing, he found his ramrod was harder and harder to push. The rifled muskets that gave him such an advantage of accuracy over the Confederate smoothbores had a drawback: The rifling grooves would clog with soot and powder. The guns would be all but useless unless they were cleaned, but there was no time for that. He put both hands on the ramrod, jammed home another round and fired again. This time the enemy line was so close he thought he could hear his bullet strike with a crunching smack. But it could have been anyone's shot.

Cherry Mansion, Savannah, Tennessee

About 10 miles away, on the opposite side of the Tennessee River, Maj. Gen. Ulysses Samuel Grant nearly spilled his morning coffee as he heard the first thunder of distant cannons. He was in his headquarters at Cherry Mansion in Savannah, Tennessee. It had been chosen by the previous commander, Gen. Charles F. Smith, as a place to recuperate from an accidental injury. Grant found it very comfortable, in spite of the chilly Mrs. Cherry, whose Confederate sympathies for her brothers serving in the Confederate Army made her a reluctant, grudging hostess.

Unlike Smith, Grant did not have any wounds to keep him away from his army across the river. He had intended to finally move his headquarters to Pittsburg Landing that day, but like so many things in the army, that was delayed.

Truth was, Grant was in a funk. In March, Maj. Gen. Henry

---

11 Probably a myth created by a headline writer. Livingstone's account never mentioned the phrase.

Gen. Ulysses Grant in 1864.
Mathew Brady.

Halleck had demoted Grant and put Grant's subordinate, General Smith, in charge of the Army of The Tennessee. Halleck claimed that Grant had disobeyed orders, but more likely that was a fabricated excuse to yank the leash on a general whom Halleck feared was getting too much acclaim.

Complaining by letter to General-in-Chief George B. McClellan, Halleck even got permission to "arrest him (Grant) at once." But a week later, McClellan was "relieved of command" by President Lincoln,[12] and Halleck let it drop. Grant had no idea how close he came to being booted from the Army.

But the unexpected demotion hurt enough, especially following his recent victories at Fort Henry and Fort Donelson, where the newspapers gave him the nickname of "Unconditional Surrender Grant."

Then Providence stepped in: General Smith slipped and fell into a boat, lacerating his leg after visiting Gen. Lew Wallace at Crump's Landing. Infection set in, and Smith was disabled.[13] President Lincoln overruled Halleck and put Grant back in command—to be pestered relentlessly by Halleck's nagging orders to do nothing: "Avoid an

---

12 West Pointer McClellan was demoted because he failed to pursue the enemy after the Union victory at Antietam, but the distrust of him by Lincoln had simmered for a long time. Lincoln once wrote McClellan a one-sentence letter: "If you don't want to use the army, I should like to borrow it for a while." After being removed, "Little Mac" McClellan ran against Lincoln as the Democratic Party nominee in 1864, but lost. To his credit, he rejected his party's platform promise to negotiate with the South to end the war and create a divided nation.

13 General Smith, respected and admired by soldiers as an honest, fearless, humble and unselfish leader, died from his foot infection and dysentery at Cherry Mansion in Savannah, Tennessee on April 25, three weeks after the battle of Shiloh.

engagement if at all possible."

Halleck was a meddler. As a West Point professor, he was "Old Brains," who knew war on a chalkboard but had never led more than a few hundred men in a skirmish. He knew nothing about real battles, where classroom diagrams and textbook tactics were carried away on the wind like dandelion seeds in a storm. Halleck was afraid to do anything until Maj. Gen. Don Carlos Buell could bring the Army of The Ohio from Nashville to Pittsburg Landing. "Overwhelming numerical superiority," Halleck would have lectured the cadets in class. "The key to victory."

Grant already had 48,000 troops. Buell would bring 18,000 more. The Confederates had 46,000, but Halleck and Grant mistakenly believed the Rebs had at least 80,000 in Corinth.

It never seemed to occur to Old Brains that the enemy had a vote, too. The Confederate commander in Corinth, Gen. Andrew Sidney Johnston, had been fighting battles long before the Civil War and had led his troops with great skill in the Texas War of Independence and the Mexican-American War, among others. He had already outsmarted Halleck by abandoning Nashville ahead of Grant and Buell, taking his Army of The Mississippi to Corinth.

Johnston was celebrated as the greatest general in the South before Robert E. Lee rose to renown. And Johnston had his own key to unlock victory before Grant could be reinforced by Buell at Pittsburg Landing. It was a tactic as old as the Trojan Horse: surprise.

Grant should have known better. He had been caught by surprise at Fort Donelson and nearly lost that battle on the Tennessee River in February, less than two months before.

But there was that demotion, followed by rumors spread by Halleck about his drinking. Bruised by it, he resolved to follow Halleck's repeated orders to adopt a hands-off strategy of stagnation. He sat back in the easy chair of paperwork, regular meetings with his staff and evenings with his whiskey. He saw no need to get involved in the placement of his encampments across the river. He left that to "Cump," his old friend General Sherman. So the Union divisions were heedlessly scattered, placed for access to fresh water and good campsites, with many of the greenest, untested troops in front, facing Corinth.

Grant also saw no need to dig trenches or prepare even a token defense. The Confederates were in Corinth, and that's where the battle would be fought, at the Crossroads of the Confederacy. Confederate deserters captured by his pickets had reported that their army was demoralized by the losses of Fort Donelson and Nashville.

And when Corinth fell, the rebellion would fall with it. Halleck was sure of it, so Grant was sure of it.

Until he heard the distant rumble of guns.

His first impulse was to dismiss it as gunnery practice. But that reassurance lasted only a split second, washed away by the rising roar of battle. He realized he needed to get across the river to Pittsburg Landing immediately. That meant going upriver against the current of a spring flood on his paddlewheel steamboat, *Tigress*. Grant must have felt a brief twinge of alarm: He was miles from his army, on the wrong side of the river, in the wrong place to command a defense that should have been planned weeks ago.

And there was another pang in his gut: He had sent a dispatch telling General Buell there was no need to hurry. A division of Buell's troops under Gen. William Nelson had already arrived, and he had ordered them to stay on the east bank of the swollen river. Now they would have to cross on pontoon bridges he had not built or boats he had not provided. Grant was like a man caught in the privy with his pants around his ankles.

But he pushed all that aside and began issuing orders. He wanted General Nelson to get his troops across the river as fast as possible, by whatever means he could find.

"The ball is in motion," he announced to his staff, slapping the table as he stood up from his breakfast. He ordered them to get his headquarters aboard *Tigress* immediately. They would steam for Pittsburg Landing. On the way, he would swing by Crump's Landing.

There was still General Wallace, held in reserve, far to the rear, above Pittsburg Landing at Crump's Landing. He had been put there to protect the rear and right flank of Grant's army from recent skirmishing attacks by Confederate cavalry and prevent a Rebel flanking maneuver by railroad, from Corinth north to Bethel Station, which was west of Crump's Landing.

Grant considered his youngest Union general, Lew Wallace. Difficult, headstrong, intemperate with his public remarks, no respect for the chain of command, sometimes disregarded orders, vain—and *not* a West Pointer. Self-taught. Too eager for glory. Too touchy about his pride and the honor of his beloved Hoosiers. Immature, perhaps.

But with all that, Grant had to admit that as much as Wallace annoyed him, he was a hell of a leader in a fight. And his Indiana "Zouaves" in their garish baggy-pants copied from French infantry in North Africa, and equally unconventional aggressive tactics, were like mad dogs on the battlefield.

Zouave soldiers are shown in Winslow Homer's painting, 'Briarwood Pipe,' 1864. Homer was embedded with the troops as a correspondent for *Harper's Weekly*. The pants and caps were bright red.

Wallace had said that being a Zouave meant "they were nimble on their hands and knees far beyond the ordinary infantrymen, that they could load on their backs and fire with precision on their bellies, and were instinctively observant of order in the midst of disorder."

At Fort Donelson, it was Wallace who saved the victory by disobeying Grant's orders to stay put. As the Confederates broke out of the besieged fort in a desperate surprise attack, they nearly overran the Union Center, where Gen. John McClernand sent repeated couriers to beg Wallace for help. But Wallace had been ordered by Grant not to move without an order. He waited and waited for orders from Grant to join the battle. But they never came. Grant was on a steamboat, meeting with Commodore Andrew Foote, who had been wounded (ironically) in the foot by splinters from a Confederate cannonball that struck his flagship during a naval bombardment of the fort.

Finally, Wallace would wait no more. He quick-marched his elite troops into battle, set up a tactically brilliant attack on the Confederate flank and turned the tide at the decisive moment. It was Wallace, as much as anyone, who could take credit for repelling the Confederates, and forcing them back into the fort and their collapsing defense. Overnight, Wallace ordered his men to light as many campfires as possible outside the fort to trick the Confederates. It worked. Believing themselves to be trapped and surrounded, the demoralized Rebs surrendered the next day.

That battle at Fort Donelson also spawned a feud between Wallace and Grant's staff. One of Grant's aides asked Wallace to change his report to say that the aide had been in the thick of the fight, delivering orders. Wallace had seen no such thing. He questioned all of his officers, and they said the same. He refused to amend the report. And the seeds of animosity were planted.[14]

Grant knew few of his generals were as bold and creative as Wallace. But to admit Wallace's heroic initiative in his formal reports to Halleck would have also revealed Grant's own mistakes. Grant's staff helped prepare his report, with no love for Wallace. Whatever the reason, the

14 Morsberger, Robert Eustis, and Katharine M. Morsberger. *Lew Wallace, Militant Romantic.* McGraw-Hill Companies, 1980.

Gen. Lew Wallace

heroics by Wallace were left out. And Wallace was not a man to forget that, Grant nodded to himself.

But now he had to go, get aboard his steamboat, get to Pittsburg Landing and organize a battle. And he might have to rely on Wallace again to save the day. In an army infested with obsequious officers who saluted and gladly followed orders to "stay put," he could do worse than Wallace.

Crump's Landing

Gen. Lew Wallace paced in his tent, ready to explode with anger, frustration and humiliation. It was happening again. He was a hunting dog left behind, chained to a fence, straining against his leash as he heard the sound of guns, unable to run to the action and do what he was born and bred for. He was destined for glory, honor, to lead men in battle and preserve the Union—but the West Point fraternity was holding him back again.

He had proved himself by leading his Hoosiers in combat in the Mexican-American War at the Battle of Buena Vista, then watched as his men were slandered with accusations of cowardice because one officer, whose courage wilted in the heat of battle, panicked and ordered a retreat.

He had won a stirring victory at Romney, West Virginia with his elite and colorful Zouaves' aggressive and creative tactics and unmatched fighting spirit. Articles in newspapers and *Harper's Weekly* celebrated his leadership and the courage of his men, who had redeemed their honor with the battle cry, "Remember Buena Vista."

At Fort Donelson, his initiative had won that decisive battle to control the upper Tennessee River, seize Nashville and close that artery to the South. And his thank-you was to be ignored in Grant's reports, then sent back to the rear at Fort Henry.

Now here he was again, pushed back behind the lines, five miles from the rest of the army, separated by swamps and flooded creeks. All morning, almost since sunrise, he had heard the sound of battle, "until it bore likeness to a distant train of empty cars rushing over a creaking bridge."[15]

And still not a word from Grant. No orders. The Third Division was forgotten or deliberately ignored.

No matter how many victories, headlines and dashing displays of courage and leadership, he would never be admitted to the West Point clique. Even Confederates Robert E. Lee and Stonewall Jackson were probably more respected by Grant and others like Zachary Taylor, because they had fought together in Mexico and suffered together through lessons and lectures at West Point.

Lew Wallace was self-taught. While they sat in classrooms, he barely made it to fourth grade before he ran away to escape the teachers' regular beatings and rigid rules. His mother died of consumption when he was 6 and his father lit out to wander all over Indiana like a blind political possum looking for the scent trail that would take him into

---

15   Lew Wallace; An Autobiography. Vol. II - Scholar's Choice Edition. 2015.

the governor's office. When Lew was 10, his father David Wallace was elected as the sixth governor of Indiana.[16]

Lew Wallace had no need for professors like Old Brains Halleck. He had the woods, the rivers, the experience of life all around him. And he had his books. He read about the great battles, the explorers who settled the New World, the classic poets and best military minds of the ages, especially his beloved *Plutarch's Lives of the Noble Greeks and Romans* that he kept with him and read almost nightly, carried off to sleep on stirring stories about honor, courage, glory and ancient heroes.

He had the heart of a warrior and the soul of a poet—a seemingly incompatible combination that coexisted because he was never taught that they could not. For all its mental nourishment, self-improvement and ability to expand the world, formal education also puts a ceiling over the imagination and builds fences in the mind.

The four walls of a classroom represent far more than just bricks and mortar to an intelligent, spirited student. They are also the prison walls of authority. As they show their pupils how to learn and grow in the world, teachers implicitly teach them how *not* to do things. Like the forbidden fruit in the Garden of Eden, the knowledge of good and evil carries the seeds of slow poison that kills dreams and cripples the childlike, romantic imagination.

Lew Wallace at 21.

Not for Lew Wallace. He never *learned* there were limits to what he could do. He made his own fiddle and taught himself to play it so well he could draw a crowd on a busy street. His artistic spirit

---

16 Lew first began to dream of being an artist while watching the artist who painted his father's portrait as governor. His lifelong love of literature was born in a state library near the governor's mansion.

was set loose in drawings and paintings, without a ruler slapped across his knuckles to force him back to his arithmetic. He learned the law by reading it and practiced as an attorney until the stifling rules and courtroom codes drove him to mind-numbing boredom and frustration.

He wrote, "My rating at school was the worst; yet, strange to say, education went on with me, for I was acquiring a habit of reading. Looking back to the thrashings I took stoically and without a whimper, I console myself thinking of the successful lives there have been with not a jot of algebra in them."

In 1850 he was elected as a county prosecutor. In 1852, at age 25, he married the love of his life, Susan Elston, daughter of one of the wealthiest men in Indiana. They had one child, Henry Lane Wallace, named after the US Senator and Indiana governor who was Lew's brother-in-law.

In 1856, he won election to the Indiana State Senate.

Along the way he taught himself military tactics, formed a unit to fight in the Mexican American War, distinguished himself as a leader in battle, and then formed another division of Hoosiers to save the Union from the "traitors" in the South who were tearing his beloved nation apart.

His Montgomery (County) Guards militia, formed in 1856, traveled the state, earning a reputation as elite soldiers—and drawing attention to their commander, Lew Wallace.[17]

While cynics in the West Point fraternity saw nothing but a recruiting slogan in the ancient Roman poetry from Horace, "*Dulce et decorum est pro patria mori*," Lew Wallace believed in his heart and soul that "It is sweet and beautiful to die for one's country."

But his romantic ideals were crushed by commanders who would not let him fight and the horrible diseases that thinned out his division in ways that were anything but sweet and beautiful.

About 750,000 young men were killed in the Civil War. Two-thirds of all the deaths were caused by disease, not combat. In the 12th Michigan Infantry, for example, one officer and 54 men were killed in combat;

---

17 The unit was formed of 65 volunteers from Crawfordsville. When it went to war, 63 volunteered. Source: Tom Meeks, associate director, Lew Wallace Study & Museum, Crawfordsville, Indiana.

375 died of disease. The 20th Ohio of Cincinnati: 89 killed in combat; 271 killed by disease.

The Confederates organized their regiments and divisions by states, cities and towns; neighbors and brothers fought alongside each other. But the Union tossed regiments and brigades from several states together like a salad of contagion.

City boys from Chicago and Cincinnati, who had immunity from a lifetime fighting germs and viruses, were thrown in with farm boys from Indiana, Wisconsin, Michigan and Ohio, who were helpless against the deadly diseases that ravaged their camps.

Typhus, spread through a bacterium carried by body lice, chiggers and fleas, killed tens of thousands. Victims would break out in an angry red rash and become delirious with fatal fevers. The Tennessee woods at Shiloh were also infested with ticks that carried spotted fever.[18]

"These Tennessee chiggers don't like officers," a soldier from the 12th Michigan joked to Gillespie. "They prefer to bite your privates."

Typhoid fever, different from typhus, was called "camp fever." It was caused by salmonella bacteria spread by food and water that was contaminated by animal and human feces, with symptoms of weakness, severe headaches, abdominal pain and red spots. Some who carried it had no symptoms, but infected dozens of others.

Pneumonia, measles, tuberculosis and malaria killed thousands.

Dysentery, called the "bloody flux," was usually caused by the bacteria shigella or parasites. It was a leading killer. Sanitation was mostly undiscovered. Latrines were too close to drinking water, or sources of fresh water were used as latrines; food was often spoiled and contaminated.

Field hospitals could be as fatally dangerous as battlefields. Patients were packed together, spreading more disease and infection. Doctors wiped surgical knives and saws on their aprons with no sterilization between patients. Bandages were taken from the infected dead and applied to fresh wounds.

18　White, David, "Medical Mayhem in the US Civil War?" Open History Society, April 2013.

The average soldier was under age 20 and weighed just 143 pounds. They came from hardscrabble farms and urban slums. Most were malnourished when they enlisted, giving them no reserves or stamina to fight disease, germs and infections.

During tedious hours of chess, reading Plutarch, staff meetings and endless boredom at Crump's Landing, Wallace had watched hundreds of his men fall sick and die, mostly from typhus. He had smelled the stench of sickness and decay at Crump's Landing, and heard the low moans of agony, the gibbering delirium, the heart-wrenching cries for mothers, sweethearts, wives and children. He had seen the eyes go empty of hope, then glassy with the vacant shine of death.

At the same time, he could read a story between the lines of dispatches and paperwork that described Halleck and Grant as they schemed and dithered.

He had written to his wife Susan, "There is no more pure patriotism. Everything is political. Even the blood of soldiers is the subject of political traffic."[19]

Other officers might call that naive. Susan called it his "fierce ethics."

He saw what was so well concealed from the American people by the fog of war and the blood-stirring barking of war-hound newspaper editorials: The West Point fraternity of "experts" was populated by frauds and humbugs. Paralyzed by years of rigid classroom instruction, they were too cautious, fearful and obedient to orders that often made no sense and squandered lives.

The West Point generals had their own diseases: consumptive ambition, gnawing hunger for promotion and attention, and feverish anxiety that one impulsive mistake could saw through the rungs on their red-white-and-blue ladder to the top. They spent more time looking over their shoulders than looking ahead, fretting about promotions and resenting success and medals won by their West Point classmates. They were more careful of their careers than they were with the lives of the men they led.

---

19   Wallace, Lew. *Lew Wallace; an Autobiography ...* New York; London, Harper & brothers, 1906.

And that debilitating germ went all the way to the top, where Halleck was in command, wrapped like a constrictor around the neck of the Union Army, an implacable, devious schemer who saw men like Wallace as dangerous "amateurs" who could expose West Point "experts" as impostors.

"Halleck was sober, deliberate, cautious," wrote Brigadier General Manning Force of Cincinnati, who fought at Shiloh with the 20th Ohio Volunteer Infantry and was awarded the Medal of Honor for gallantry in action. "He had written a book on strategy and logistics and his attention appeared sometimes to be distracted from the actual conditions under which present military operations were to be conducted by his retrospective reference to the rules which he had announced."[20]

Put bluntly: Halleck had the rigor mortis of fatal incompetence.

The young nation was in a transition from the heroic citizen-militia leaders who had won American independence in the Revolutionary War, to a new "professional army." The West Pointers had a fragile perch at the top of the military tree, but the Union desperately needed troops and leaders. President Lincoln welcomed local politicians and citizen officers who could recruit regiments from their counties, towns and cities. Those regiments were named for the states where most soldiers still pledged their allegiance, such as the 12th Michigan, 52nd Ohio and 23rd Indiana.

And Wallace was an Indiana man before he was a federal.

As a wild, untamed boy of 16, Wallace had been told by his father, "Were I to die tonight, your portion of my estate would not keep you for a month. I am sorry, disappointed, mortified; so, without shutting the door upon you, I am resolved that from today you must go out and earn your own livelihood. I shall watch your course hopefully. That is all I have to say."[21]

The son was not wounded. He did not feel like a victim or wallow in self-pity. "There was no argument, no reproach, no entreaty," he wrote

---

20 Force, Manning Ferguson. *From Fort Henry to Corinth*. 1881.

21 Wallace, Lew. *Lew Wallace; an Autobiography* ... New York; London, Harper & brothers, 1906.

later. "The affair was merely as if one party were making the other a present; and such in fact it was—he had given me my freedom."

At age 16, Lew Wallace was a free man—free to paint his own life, without compromise.

His "West Point" was the western Indiana wilderness. "When I was a boy, I ran wild in the great woods of my native state," he would say. "I hunted, fished, went alone, slept with my dog, was happy, and came out with a constitution."

His constitution had no clause for caution, no paragraphs for political calculations, no articles of insincere flattery, blind obedience and the other oily arts of ambition. He wanted romantic glory, recognition and respect, but he had no patience for the small "p" politics of the West Point crowd.

He was not a team player.

On the morning of April 6, he was stuck at Crump's Landing, cut off from the rest of the Union Army, a racehorse still locked in the gates while the bell rang and the derby was off. His only order from Grant, issued weeks before, was to wait and be ready for orders.

At one point, soon after they arrived, it looked like something would happen. Grant had issued orders to prepare to march to Corinth. But then a day later, on March 20, those orders were rescinded, vetoed by Halleck. "Wait, wait and wait some more" was Halleck's strategy—and therefore Grant's.

Aboard the *Tigress*

Before leaving Savannah, Grant wrote orders to General Nelson and General Buell of The Army of the Ohio: Cross the Tennessee River and join the battle as soon as possible. But poor planning and spring floods delayed their arrival until late afternoon and evening, when the first day of battle was over.

As the *Tigress* steamed upriver to Pittsburg Landing, Grant stopped at Crump's Landing and told Wallace to get his troops ready to march "in any direction." From the deck of his own riverboat, Wallace shouted back that those orders had already been given. He was a step ahead of Grant.

Expecting to be called to the front, Wallace was told to wait.

As Grant's steamboat churned upriver for Pittsburg Landing, another boat was spotted approaching from the south. It was the *Warner*, rushing to find Grant. It carried an urgent dispatch from the other Wallace at Shiloh, Gen. William H. Wallace of Illinois, who was fighting alongside General Prentiss, taking the brunt of the Confederate assault at Fraley Field. Grant was told that the camps south of Pittsburg Landing were being overrun by massive numbers of Confederates and "a battle had commenced."

Reinforcements were needed, but Grant did not order Wallace to march south. Rather than send the *Warner* back to Crump's Landing with urgent orders for Wallace, he ordered the steamboat to follow him to Pittsburg Landing.

Critics would later wonder why Grant wasted 30 minutes aboard the *Tigress* without sending an order to mobilize the Third Division of nearly 6,000 men and artillery batteries sitting idle near Crump's Landing. If he had carefully reviewed his army in person, on horseback, he would have known the landscape and the roads available and might have seen a tactical opportunity offered by the position of Wallace and his Third Division.

Wallace had told Grant about a road to Sherman's right that had been improved by his men, with "corduroy" logs and a bridged dam to support his infantry and artillery. Wallace had ridden the length of the Shunpike Road to make sure it was ready.

Sherman also knew about that backdoor road to his right flank. He told Grant it was the best route south to Corinth for Wallace and his Third Division. And he stationed a regiment to guard the final bridge so that Wallace could come quickly in support.

Battles and empires can slip and break a hip on the slick steps of missed opportunities and blunders in the fog of war. If Grant had been better informed, he could have seen an almost miraculous opening: As Wallace and his Third Division came down the Shunpike Road, they would be in perfect position to strike the Confederates on their rear left flank as Sherman's Fifth Division fell back to Pittsburg Landing.

Instead, Grant played Halleck's overcautious chess game, and left a critical knight stuck on the board, missing his opening for a checkmate.

After the war, Wallace resolutely refused to criticize Grant, but blamed the tragedy of Shiloh on Grant's staff and the incompetence of Halleck, "who had no genius except as a marplot, in which he was incomparable." (The archaic "marplot" means plot spoiler: a meddler who ruins everything.)

Finally, after arriving at Pittsburg Landing, Grant gave verbal orders to his staff, who dictated them to a messenger. Lew Wallace was ordered to "come up to Sherman's right flank."

Grant's staff would claim later that he ordered Wallace to take the River Road along the Tennessee River. But Wallace insisted for 30 years—along with his own staff—that Grant named no route. The written order was lost in the heat of battle, but Wallace's claim remained consistent; the versions by Grant's staff were not, and Grant remained silent—an implicit admission.[22]

Also incriminating was Sherman's silence. He knew very well that Wallace had scouted and improved the Shunpike Road and planned to use it. But like his close friend Grant, Sherman chose silence.

Years later, Grant's staff (and Sherman) would also claim that his army was not surprised, despite firsthand newspaper accounts of abandoned weapons and the vivid, undisputable testimony of soldiers and officers who were routed by the Confederates. Grant's aides rallied around their leader and rewrote the history of Shiloh to protect his reputation as he ran for President.

As Wallace prophetically said, "Even the blood of soldiers is the subject of political traffic."

Most likely, Grant didn't remember or care what route Wallace took to support Sherman. The River Road to the east was muddy and flooded after recent heavy rains; the Shunpike was improved and ready.

The two roads made a block "A," with River Road running southeast along the Tennessee Riverbank, and Shunpike running southwest. They

---

22 Beemer, Charles G. *"My Greatest Quarrel with Fortune."* 2015.

were crossed in the middle by Snake Creek and, just north of the creek, an unnamed road that ended just north of Pittsburg Landing.

The Hornet's Nest

Gillespie had no idea how long he had stood in the line firing, but knew his rifle was red hot by the burns on his fingers as he held the muzzle steady for his ramrod to load again. It seemed like days, years—or maybe mere minutes. The smoke around him was a living thing, a hellish cloud of sulfurous, eye-stinging chaos.

He caught glimpses of the dead and dying, moaning or screaming, writhing or lying completely still in twisted, unnatural positions on the bloody ground.

Even the blooming dogwoods and redbud trees that had made the woods so beautiful and reminded him of Michigan springtime, had disappeared in the thick gouts of gun smoke and noise from rifles and thundering cannons.

He could hear the enemy bullets whizz by, filling the air with angry buzzing like someone had whacked a beehive with a stick. The strange chorus made a continuous roar that seemed to swell and recede like crashing waves of death.

Lt. Ephraim Dawes, fighting on the right with the 53rd Ohio Infantry in Sherman's division, described it years later: "All around was a roar of musketry; immediately about us was the silence literally of death, for the ground was strewn with the slain of both armies."

Gillespie saw Rebs march across the field bravely, but they fell by the dozens like children playing war, with great drama, outflung arms, twisting gyrations or hurled backward off their feet, as if some giant hand had yanked a string in their backs. Some just stopped suddenly and collapsed in a heap, struck senseless by an invisible club.

Gradually, then all at once, the Rebel line fell back. Gillespie didn't know it, but his line had just driven back Confederate Gen. Adley Gladden's Brigade—but not before a shell fragment tore away Gladden's right arm. He died as it was amputated on the battlefield.

As the first wave of attackers receded like a falling tide, there was no time to celebrate. Within moments the roar of guns and high-pitched Rebel yells grew impossibly louder. Confederate cannons turned loose a barrage on the woods where Gillespie stood, and here came another, much larger line of men in gray. It looked a mile wide.

He heard Sergeant Cross shout hoarsely, "Fall back!" Gillespie stepped back, firing, but saw men all around him turning to run. Gillespie found himself running too, unable to stop his pumping legs that acted on their own, as if they belonged to a stranger. He pushed through the trees and brambles then fell headlong, his left foot snagged on a fallen log. He hit the ground hard, paused a second to catch his breath and began to gather himself. He focused on a brown leaf in front of his eyes, each vein visible like delicate bones in a tiny leaf skeleton, slowly rotting to join the forest floor's carpet of mulch. *Earth to earth*, he thought.

As he looked down at his feet to see what tripped him, he saw a bloody stump and realized it was not a log, but a leg, severed at the hip—still wearing uniform pants and a muddy boot. A small crater smoked nearby. Where the rest of the unfortunate body could be he had no idea. He felt sick for a moment and dizzy. Then those angry bees came swarming closer and he knew he had to move.

Some of the men who ran past him would run all the way to Pittsburg Landing and arrive there at about the same time as General Grant, forming a seething, hopeless mob of 5,000 "shirkers" who refused to return to the battle, even when they were threatened with cannons on nearby gunboats.

A private in the Volunteer Infantry of Ohio from Cincinnati described the scene that greeted the arrival of reinforcements that evening:

> "At the landing—but how shall I attempt to set the picture forth? I have never yet seen told in print the half of the sickening story. Wagons, teams and led horses, quartermaster's stores of every description, bales of forage, caissons—all of the paraphernalia of a magnificently appointed army—were scattered in promiscuous disorder along the bluff side. Over and all about the fragmentary

heaps, thousands of panic-stricken wretches swarmed from the river's edge ... a heaving, surging herd of humanity, smitten with a very frenzy of fright and despair, every sense of manly pride, of honor, and duty, completely paralyzed, and dead to every feeling save the most abject, pitiful terror.

"A number of officers could be distinguished amid the tumult, performing the pantomimic accompaniments of shouting incoherent commands, mingled with threats and entreaties. There was a little drummer boy, I remember too, standing in his shirt sleeves, pounding his drum furiously, although to what purpose we could not divine. Men were there in every stage of partial uniform and equipment; many were hatless and coatless, and but few retained their muskets and their accoutrements complete. Some stood wringing their hands, and rendering the air with cries and lamentations, while others, in the dumb agony of fear, cowered behind the object that was nearest them in the direction of the enemy ... There was a rush for the boat when we neared the landing, and some, wading out breast deep into the stream, were kept off only at the point of a bayonet."[23]

The swelling crowd of deserters must have been a disturbing sight for Grant. As he stepped off the *Tigress* and climbed into a boat, he twisted his ankle badly, an accident ironically similar to the one that disabled and finally killed Gen. C.F. Smith, giving Grant command.

Grant usually wore an ordinary dark suit and shapeless slouch hat, so poorly dressed he was sometimes mistaken for a loitering, cigar-smoking civilian. But today, expecting to greet General Buell, he was in his full-dress uniform.

Grant had finally arrived—limping into battle like his confused, disorganized, leaderless army.

It was 8:45.

As Gillespie and the remnants of Peabody's brigade fell back past their own camps, retreating north, he was surprised that the enemy's firing slowed, then stopped. They were not being followed. Later he would

---

23   US Army Staff Ride Handbook, Battle of Shiloh.

learn that the Butternuts, after days marching on muddy roads, were tired, thirsty and hungry. The Union camps and tents were irresistible.

As they stopped to wolf down food that was still cooking over Union campfires, they also looted the tents and knapsacks left behind. The battle paused and the Confederate momentum was lost. There seemed to be no one in charge. The command structure had collapsed. It was now a soldier's fight.

Confederate Sergeant Horatio Wiley, of the 22d Alabama Infantry, wrote in a letter to "My Dear Josie":

"On both sides the slaughter was heavy until the command to charge was given & as soon as our columns began to move the enemy fled & our forces took possession of their camp. Here was a perfect curiosity shop. Everything in the eating & wearing line, in fact every tent told of high & extravagant living."[24]

As the Confederates "shopped" through the abandoned tents and discovered the marvels of the industrialized North, the battle paused for nearly an hour. In the sudden quiet around him, Gillespie could

The Hornet's Nest, illustration by Thure De Thulstrup for *Harper's Weekly*, 1862.

24   US Army Staff Ride Handbook, Battle of Shiloh.

Shiloh Church as it looked on April 6, 1862, the first day of battle. It became a field hospital. Unknown illustrator. Library of Congress, 1862.

hear a great roar to his right, in the east, where General Sherman and his Fifth Division were camped near Shiloh Church.

Just that morning, Sherman had refused to believe what was happening until he was personally informed by a piece of buckshot through his hand. Now he was fighting a desperate battle near the Shiloh Church, a tiny, rustic log cabin that looked as if it were hand carved out of the wilderness with axes, saws and chisels. The Hebrew name from the Bible meant "Place of peace."

Lieutenant Dawes, an 1861 graduate of Marietta College in Ohio who became a member of the Literary Club of Cincinnati after the war, described that morning years later in an essay for Civil War veterans:

A Confederate regiment came through the line of our officer's tents; Colonel Appler gave the command to fire; there was a tremendous crash of musketry on the whole front... The battle was fairly on.

The hour marked by the first cannon shot was seven o'clock. The first fire of our men was very effective. The Confederate line fell back, rallied, came forward, received another volley, and again fell back, when our colonel, who was behind the left wing, cried out, "Retreat, and save yourselves."

35

Dawes saw the urgent need to reinforce a regiment on the right that was taking brutal punishment.

> I ran to where the colonel was lying on the ground behind a tree, and stooping over said, "Colonel, let us go and help the Fifty-seventh; they are falling back." He looked up. His face was like ashes. The awful fear of death was on it. He pointed over his shoulder with his thumb in an indefinite direction, and squeaked out in a trembling voice, "No. Form the men back here."
>
> Our miserable position flashed upon me. We were in the front of a great battle. Our regiment never had a battalion drill. Some men in it had never fired a gun. Our lieutenant colonel had become lost in the confusion of the first retreat, the major was in the hospital, and our colonel was a coward! I said to him, with an adjective not necessary to repeat, "Colonel, I will not do it!" He jumped to his feet, and literally ran away.[25]

Colonel Appler, the butt of Sherman's taunt for being "badly scared" by "phantoms" that morning, had bravely repulsed waves of Rebel attacks, then lost his nerve and proved Sherman right about his lack of courage.

The same fight in Sherman's camp was described by veterans of the 6th Mississippi that attacked the 53rd Ohio.

> The two regiments charged bravely into the camp of the enemy, but were sent reeling back in retreat by the withering fire... Though the attack surprised Sherman's men, they nonetheless gave a good account for themselves. Cleburne records that the Twenty-third, having been driven back, "was with great difficulty rallied about 100 yards in the rear." The Sixth however, charged again and again unaided. Despite the Sixth's unflagging courage, it eventually had to retreat "in disorder over its own dead and dying," of which there were many.

---

25 Ephriam Dawes papers. Written for the Cincinnati Chapter of the Military Order of the Loyal Legion of the United States, 1896.

Artillery Battery in the Hornet's Nest.

The men from Mississippi had been shot to shreds. Of the 425 who attacked, 300 were killed or wounded. The shocked survivors bravely joined other regiments and continued fighting until they finally took the camp.

Dawes described a Union soldier who was shot in the shin and was ordered to "Go to the rear." The man answered, "Cap, give me a gun. This blamed fight ain't got any rear."

Hickenlooper's battery

To the east, Gillespie and the remains of the Union line formed a ragged defense deep in tangled woods and underbrush, in a low spot that became known as the Sunken Road and the Hornet's Nest, because it was filled with the hum from swarms of buzzing bullets.

Capt. Andrew Hickenlooper and his 5th Ohio Light Artillery formed the center of their line on a salient of higher ground, giving him and his battery of four six-pound cannons a devastating field of fire on the attacking Rebs.

After the war, he described the scene:

Soon the shells gave warning, and the skirmish fire grew stronger and deeper. Then came long triple lines of bristling steel whose stern-faced bearers, protected and yet impeded by the heavy undergrowth, came pressing on, until our cannon's loud acceptance of their challenge and the infantry's crashing volleys caused the assailants to hesitate, break in confusion and hastily retire.

The ear-piercing and peculiar Rebel yell of the men in gray, and answering cheers of the boys in blue rose and fell with the varying tide of battle and, with the hoarse and scarcely distinguishable orders of the officers, the screaming and bursting of shell, the swishing sound of canister, the roaring of volley firing, the death screams of the stricken and struggling horses and the cries and groans of the wounded, formed an indescribable impression which can never be effaced from memory.[26]

Between 10:30 and 3:30, Confederate Gen. Braxton Bragg ordered eight suicidal charges against the Hornet's Nest. Again and again they were torn apart and driven back by Union rifles and artillery concealed in the woods.

Field artillery on both sides was about even. Both armies used four types of ammunition fired from various smoothbore canons, howitzers, siege guns and rifled guns: Solid shot was a cast-iron ball weighing from 6 to 12 pounds, effective for battering enemy cannons and bouncing through the ranks of massed troops, with devastating results. New, rifled canons used an elongated solid shot called a "bolt." Rifled Parrott Gun projectiles could weigh 20 or 30 pounds.

---

26 After Shiloh, Hickenlooper was promoted by Grant to engineer the siege at Vicksburg. After the war, he was president of what became Cincinnati Gas & Electric and also was a lieutenant governor of Ohio. He is buried in Spring Grove Cemetery in Cincinnati.

Shells and explosive shells were packed with powder ignited by a fuse timed to the second, causing the shell to fragment into sharp pieces of molten metal like shards of broken glass, tearing into troops or spreading panic and death by detonating over their heads.

Case shot shells contained round lead or iron balls propelled by a bursting charge.

Canister was an empty can filled with iron balls in sawdust, or sometimes rocks, nails, whatever could be found. It turned a canon into a giant shotgun. It was only effective to about 400 yards, but it was tremendously lethal in close combat, where it could mow down enemy soldiers by the dozens.

At Shiloh, both sides discovered a flaw in their tactics: The nine-man crews serving canons could be cut to pieces by the latest rifled muskets, neutralizing the effect of close-support artillery. Artillery horses made favorite targets to disable the guns and pin down their crews, who could then be shot, one by one.

Captain Hickenlooper of Cincinnati described what it was like in his artillery battery during charges at the Hornet's Nest:

> Quickly came the orders sharp and clear: "Shrapnel," "Two seconds," "One second," "canister." Then, as the enemy made preparations for their final dash, "double canister" was delivered with such rapidity that the separate discharges blended into one continuous roar. Then the supporting infantry, rising from their recumbent position, sent forth a sheet of flame and leaden hail that elicited curses, shrieks, groans and shouts, all blended into an appalling cry... Again and again, through long and trying hours, this dance of death went on, at frequent intervals, from 9 in the morning until 4 in the afternoon, thus gradually sapping the energies of these heroic men, who had borne the heat and burden of the fateful day with a courage unparalleled in the annals of the Civil War.

The South never smiled again

On the Confederate side of the battle, General Johnston saw that his carefully laid plans were among the first fatalities. Johnston had begun

Gen. Albert Sidney Johnston

the day in an argument with his subordinate Gen. Pierre Gustave Toutant Beauregard, a West Pointer from New Orleans who had become famous for ordering the cannon barrage at the Battle of Fort Sumter that ignited the Civil War.

As they marched up the final mile of the Corinth Road and approached the Union Army, Beauregard wanted to call off the assault because he feared surprise was lost; all the noise made by the marching Confederate Army must have surely alerted the Yankees, he insisted. Several other generals nodded and agreed.

Then Johnston rode up on his horse, Fire Eater. "Gentlemen, we attack at daylight tomorrow," he ordered. Beauregard and the others knew by Johnston's tone that it was futile to argue. It was settled. As they returned to their divisions to prepare, Johnston growled to an aide, "I would fight them if they were a million."

Gen. Johnston was leading 45,000 men who were determined to resist the "War of Northern Aggression," inflamed by the bluecoat invasion of their states, farms and homes. Fewer than a third of them came from families that owned slaves. But Gen. Manning Force noted an unusual story that said a lot about the plantation economy and culture of the South.

When Johnston arrived in Corinth, he was unable to get the reinforcements he needed. But he calculated that he could build another fresh brigade if all of his cooks and teamsters were freed from their labor to fight.

"He sent messengers through the surrounding country, urging citizens to (loan) their negroes as cooks and teamsters for ninety days, or even sixty days. But the messengers returned with the answer that the planters would freely give their last son, but they would not part with a negro or a mule."[27]

Johnston abandoned the idea and planned his attack. He was nothing like Halleck. He had an army and he intended to use it.

Respected as a military genius even by the Union West Pointers, Johnston had predicted that the Western Theater of the Civil War would be determined near the Shiloh Church. He planned to bully Grant's left flank back with brute muscle and force the Union Army away from its boats on the Tennessee River; Grant would be trapped in the swamps of flooded creeks behind Pittsburg Landing and forced to surrender.[28]

But because of the rugged terrain and communication problems, the Confederate lines that extended more than three miles across their front quickly became separated and spread out. The result was that General Beauregard attacked in columns that struck first at Fraley Field and near Shiloh Church.

"Thus opened the battle of Shiloh," Gen. Manning Force of the 20th Ohio and Cincinnati recalled. "A combat made up of numberless separate encounters of detached portions of broken lines, continually shifting position and changing direction in the forest and across ravines, filling an entire day, is almost incapable of a connected narrative."[29]

---

27 Force, Manning Ferguson. *From Fort Henry to Corinth.* 1881.

28 Even Johnston seemed to have known more about the terrain and conditions of the battlefield near Pittsburg Landing than General Grant. The area along the River Road, behind Pittsburg Landing, was described by soldiers as being "belly-deep to a horse," "mud, mire and backwater," "an almost bottomless morass." According to his aides, that was the road Grant wanted Wallace to use.

29 Force, Manning Ferguson. *From Fort Henry to Corinth.* 1881.

Both sides had scouted the ground around Pittsburg Landing. But the deep ravines, thick woods and tangled, impenetrable underbrush favored the defenders on that first day. The land and the deadly accuracy of rifled muskets made cavalry almost useless on both sides except to carry dispatches.

Many in the South blamed Beauregard for losing Shiloh. If he had attacked in line to hit the disorganized Union camps at once, they said, the whole Union Army might have been flanked and rolled up in a headlong retreat like the stragglers and deserters from General Prentiss's camps in the middle.[30]

But the gallant stand by Colonel Peabody, who bought time with his life, allowed Sherman and First Division commander Gen. John McClernand to fight a withering holding action on the Union right flank.

As the Confederate attack was blocked at the Hornet's Nest in the center, General Johnston moved to the right to seek a breakthrough. That Union left flank was held by Gen. Stephen Hurlbut's Fourth Division, just south of an old peach orchard. For an Illinois politician with a reputation for hard drinking and soft scruples, Hurlbut was giving the Confederates all they could handle.

The Confederate order of battle had disintegrated like the 6th Mississippi; brigades and regiments from various corps became mixed and confused.

Near 2:00, Johnston was informed by Gen. John Breckinridge of Kentucky, the former vice president of the United States under President James Buchanan, that the 45th Tennessee was refusing to advance. Johnston spurred his horse and found the men in a ravine that was protected from enemy fire. As he rode down the line, he tapped their bayonets with a tin cup he had picked up in a captured Union camp and told them to show the rest of the army what they could do with

---

30   From the US Army Staff Notes on Shiloh: "When attacking frontally, a commander had to choose between attacking on a broad front or a narrow front. Attacking on a broad front rarely succeeded except against weak and scattered defenders. Attacking on a narrow front promised greater success but required immediate reinforcement and continued attack to achieve decisive results."

their "toothpicks." When he said he would lead the charge, the men were shamed and rallied to their feet.

As Johnston rode at the front of the charge, bullets tore through his uniform, ripped the sole from one of his boots and grazed him in the shoulder. As the 45th Tennessee charged past him and pushed the Union soldiers back, he remarked to Gen. Breckinridge that he had nearly been killed.

A few minutes later, a courier rode up to Johnston and noticed he was very pale, slumping in the saddle. "General, are you wounded?" he asked.

"Yes, and I fear seriously."

As his staff gently lowered him from Fire Eater and laid him down in the shade of a nearby tree, they opened his tunic and shirt but could find no wound.

He had been struck by a bullet behind his right knee—a leg that was numbed by a dueling wound many years earlier. Unaware that the bullet had severed an artery, he quickly bled out, the blood filling his boot. He died at 2:15.

Death of General Albert Sidney Johnston. Sketch by Henry Mosler, 1862.

Tragically, he had a tourniquet in his pocket that could have saved his life. But Johnston had sent his surgeon to care for the wounded.

General Johnston would be noted in history as the highest-ranking officer killed in the Civil War. It was said that after the death of Johnston at Shiloh, "The South never smiled again."

"When Sidney Johnston fell, it was the turning point of our fate," said Confederate President Jefferson Davis, "for we had no other hand to take up his work in the West."

General Beauregard was leading the attack on the left side of the Confederate lines when Johnston was killed. He had to be notified that he was now in command. As Johnston's body was removed to be taken to Corinth, it was covered to avoid spreading panic in the lines. For an hour, the Confederate attack lost momentum.

Pittsburg Landing

Earlier, around 9:00 a.m., after his painful arrival at Pittsburg Landing, Grant told his aides to send orders to Gen. Lew Wallace to "come up" to the battle. General Prentiss was in retreat and had abandoned his camps in the middle of the Union Army's front. Sherman's Fifth Division on the right was falling back. It looked like the whole Union front was being thrown back into Grant's lap.

General Wallace was finally invited to join the battle that had been raging for four hours.

The orders were sent with Capt. Algernon Baxter, Grant's quartermaster, who boarded a steamboat for Crump's Landing at 9:30. Wallace, following Grant's orders to be ready to move in any direction, had moved west from Crump's Landing to Stoney Lonesome, at the northern end of the Shunpike Road.

The steamboat back to Crump's Landing, running with the strong spring-flood current, should have taken no more than a half hour. But it took Baxter two hours to deliver the orders, and then only after Wallace had sent a rider back to Crump's Landing to investigate the delay. Baxter was found at the landing and was rushed at a gallop to Wallace at Stoney Lonesome.

Gen. Lew Wallace.

Baxter gave the orders to Wallace at 11:30. By noon, Wallace and his Third Division of 5,800 men and artillery batteries were on the march to Shiloh that would change history, ignite a scandal that ruined his career and led to a blunder that caused thousands of avoidable casualties.

The long march to battle

Wallace mounted his horse, Old John, a magnificent stallion. His soldiers genuinely loved Old John as much as they admired Wallace and his skills as a horseman. In the mid-1800s, horsemanship was the measure of a gentleman and a man, and few in the army compared to Wallace for his perfect posture, almost effortless ease and agility in the saddle. As with nearly everything he did, he was self-taught.

He wore his uniform neatly and proudly. He was not a big man, but fit, strong and handsome, with piercing blue eyes behind a bushy mustache and a goatee that had grown like an untended garden until it looked like a living thing attached to his face. Shaving was next to impossible with scarce soap and dull razors, so beards became common among soldiers and officers. In their photos, many men on both sides of the War look like group pictures of Moses, Noah and the Prophets.

"I was hungry for war," Wallace wrote later in his autobiography. "Had I not been reading about it all my life? And had not all I had read about it wrought in me that battle was the climax of the sublime and terrible, and that without at least one experience of the kind no life could be perfect?"

He wrote to Susan after surviving combat at Fort Donelson, "I find my interest in battles rather increased than otherwise—in fact, I like the excitement and in very truth, I have never heard music as fascinating and grand as that of battle."

Lew Wallace was not only an innovative and fearless warrior and an excellent horseman, he was also a skilled, self-taught artist and a talented and colorful writer. After the war, he would become America's first worldwide best-selling author, with a book that became a classic and outsold everything but the Bible: *Ben-Hur, A Tale of the Christ.*

He wrote several books, but there is no account of Shiloh more vivid, poetic, detailed and thrilling than his own description in his two-volume *Lew Wallace: An Autobiography,* published after his death in 1905.

From Volume I:

> April 6, 1862! The gray light was still in the eastern sky, trembling between vanishing night and opening day, when a sentinel put his head in my tent door and woke me. "I hear guns up the river," he said. I had only to put on my boots and slip into my coat. In a few seconds I was out listening. Sure enough, there were outbreaks of musketry, with cannonading at short intervals. My staff-officers joined me, and there was no disagreement. "It's a battle." A steamboat, an adjunct to my headquarters, lay tied up at the landing. Thinking the ominous sounds might be better heard on the water, in company with Whitelaw Reid[31], who was sharing my tent as

---

31 War Correspondent for the *Cincinnati Gazette.* Reid left Wallace to climb aboard the *Tigress* and follow Grant, making his stories the earliest first-hand accounts of the battle.

guest, I went down to the boat. A number of officers and visiting citizens were on the hurricane-deck exercising their ears. There, too, the opinion was unanimous— "It's a battle." It was then six o'clock. I did not hesitate longer.

Wallace immediately sent orders for his troops to get ready to march in any direction: southwest, to join up with Sherman; southeast to Pittsburg Landing; or west to defend the rear and flanks of Grant's army in case the Confederates came from the railroad stop at Bethel Station to the west.

About half after eight o'clock the *Tigress* came up and veered over to the side of my boat. General Grant stood on the second deck by the railing (and) spoke to me. ... The conversation is given almost word for word. He asked, "Have you heard the firing?" And I answered, "Yes, sir, since daybreak." "What do you think of it?" "It's undoubtedly a general engagement." This was the moment for the order. I leaned forward to catch it, and had instead: "Well, hold yourself in readiness to march upon orders received." I was disappointed, and returned: "But, general, I ordered (readiness) about six o'clock. The division must be at Stoney Lonesome. I am ready now." He hesitated, evidently turning an uncertainty over in his mind, and then said: "Very well. Hold the division ready to march in any direction."

Disappointed, frustrated and in disbelief, Wallace waited. Known for interpreting orders creatively or ignoring them altogether, he chose *that* day to strictly follow orders. It would be his undoing and prolong the battle for another bloody day of desperate fighting.

So Wallace and his Third Division waited.

Ten o'clock came. No orders from Grant.

Ten-thirty. Then eleven.

"Still the pounding of the guns and the ruffling of musketry in the south, but no order."

Finally, near 11:30, he spotted his courier pounding up the road, with Captain Baxter in tow.

"I have an order for you," he said to me. "Here it is." At this, those surrounding closed in, while Captain Baxter put a piece of paper in my hand. I read what was on it twice over. Now memory does not fail me. I see that paper yet, a half-sheet of common foolscap, ruled. I see the tobacco stains on it, and the further defacement of bootheels. I see a hurried scrawl in pencil, not ink, without address or date—unenveloped and unsigned. Here it is, almost, if not quite, verbatim:

"You will leave a sufficient force at Crump's Landing to guard the public property there; with the rest of the division march and form junction with the right of the army. Form line of battle at right angle with the river, and be governed by circumstances." [32]

Wallace looked up and demanded, "Whose order is this?"

"General Grant's," Baxter replied.

"Why is it not signed by somebody?"

"General Grant gave me that order on the field verbally. Fearing to make a mistake in the delivery, I put the order in writing, as you see it, coming down the river. For that purpose I picked the paper from the floor in the ladies' cabin; and, not having ink, I used a pencil."

Wallace replied, "Very well, captain, I accept the order, and you may so report to General Grant. Now, how is the battle going?"

"We are repulsing the enemy," he said.

That battle report from Baxter could not have been more wrong. By that time of day the Union front was being rolled up like a rug, back to Pittsburg Landing.

Wallace calculated that taking the River Road would be nearly three miles longer than using the Shunpike to reach Sherman's right flank. "So, to save the two and three-quarter miles, and because it was nearer the right and in better condition, I decided to go by the Shunpike," he wrote.

After two hours on the march, the Third Division had covered five miles and had just crossed a bridge over Clear Creek, less than two miles from Sherman's camp, when a rider arrived with yet another order

---

32 *Lew Wallace; An Autobiography. Vol. II - Scholar's Choice Edition.* 2015.

from Grant. It was Captain William Rowley of Grant's staff, agitated, sweating and rattled.

He was greatly excited. "I've had a devil of a time in finding you," he began. I checked my horse. "What's the matter?"

"I've been sent to hurry you up ... Where are you going, anyhow?"

"To join Sherman."

"Sherman!"

"Yes."

He plucked my sleeve. "Come with me aside here." At the edge of the road, out of hearing, the captain broke out: "Great God! Don't you know Sherman has been driven back? Why, the whole army is within half a mile of the river, and it's a question if we are not all going to be driven into it."

Wallace was speechless. "Beaten—that army! Incredible! The idea struck me dumb—too dumb for question."

But as soon as he gathered his wits, the spark of an audacious idea lit the young general's face. Realizing he was now in the rear of the Confederate Army of The Mississippi as it attacked Grant at Pittsburg Landing, he saw opportunity.

"The advantage of an attack in the rear would be mine; and, though more might not have been in my power, I could at least have distracted the enemy and compelled him to notice me."

That would give Grant a breathing spell. It could trap the Confederates between Grant's rock at Pittsburg Landing and the sledge-hammer of Wallace's fresh Third Division in their rear. It could have brought a complete victory and routed the exhausted Confederates by the end of the day, sending them running back to Corinth, whipped.

Wallace wrote: "And I would have tried it had I been left to myself. Unfortunately, in that moment of suspense I received from General Grant his third order to me since morning."

Captain Rowley said, "He wants you at Pittsburg Landing—and he wants you there like hell."

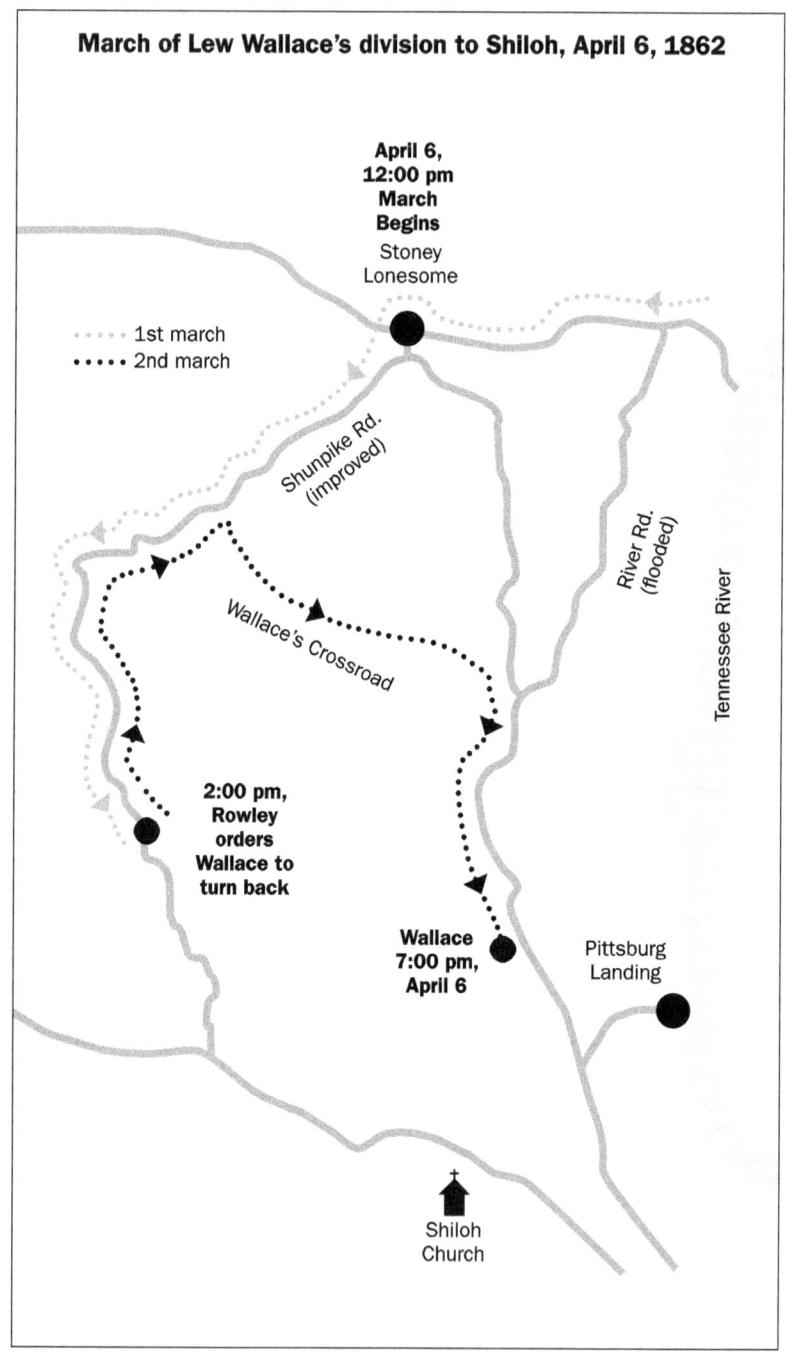

March of Lew Wallace's division to Shiloh, April 6, 1862

April 6,
12:00 pm
**March
Begins**
Stoney
Lonesome

· · · · · 1st march
•••• 2nd march

Shunpike Rd.
(improved)

River Rd.
(flooded)

Tennessee River

Wallace's Crossroad

**2:00 pm,
Rowley
orders
Wallace to
turn back**

**Wallace
7:00 pm,
April 6**

Pittsburg
Landing

Shiloh
Church

Map 2

Wallace was on the doorstep of an ambush victory, similar to his previous battlefield victories. But Rowley insisted Wallace had to double back and find a crossroad to the River Road and Pittsburg Landing because that was what Grant "ordered." So Wallace sent scouts to find a local guide, while Union troops just a few miles away were hanging on by sheer willpower and grit, desperate for reinforcements.

A local farmer said there was a crossroad that was not on the map, but it was in poor shape. That proved to be an understatement. Flooding from the surrounding creeks had turned the road into "a sheet of yellow liquid broken occasionally by tussocks of black mud," Wallace found.

As his infantry and heavy guns slogged through the bog, "the sheet covering the roadway turned into a thick mortar of the color of dirty chocolate."

Horses, cannons and wagons sank, so foot soldiers slogged back through mud up to their knees and heaved them out of the clinging clay… where they sank into the next sinkhole. On and on it went through the afternoon.

"A fire of impatience burned the soul within me, and I kept my eyes on the sun, which seemed to go down with the leap of a diver."

As they finally reached high ground, the gray skies dumped buckets of rain and the Third Division was greeted by clots of bedraggled deserters:

"Unarmed, hatless, wild-eyed, covered with mud, many of them dripping with the chocolate water of the creek, and all shouting: 'We're cut to pieces! Go back while you can!'"

For all he knew, Wallace was driving his division straight into an ambush by Confederates who had forced Grant's surrender at Pittsburg Landing.

Finally, stragglers informed him that he was on the east bank of Tilghman's Creek, just 400 yards from Confederate artillery on the opposite bank.

By then, it was past 7:00. The fighting was over. What could have been a three- or four-hour march to surprise the Rebs from behind, had turned into more than seven hours of misery, frustration and pointless confusion.

Wallace, whose favorite tactic was attack, had chosen the worst day of his life to follow orders that were as muddied as his men who emerged from the bog.

It would haunt him for the rest of his life.

Long after the widows had grieved; after the armless and legless men returned to their farms and cities on crude wooden crutches; after the survivors of pure hell at Shiloh had rejoined the sane world of children, wives, families and friends, only to find it would never be quite the same again—long after all that, the jousting generals fought on, waging a war of words on paper, re-fighting their battles, accusing each other of incompetence, failure and cowardice, condemning mistakes, garbled orders and missed chances, forever asking themselves "What if?"

And no battle was more controversial than Shiloh.

Grant said, "Shiloh has been perhaps less understood, or, to state the case more accurately, more persistently misunderstood, than any other engagement ... during the entire rebellion."

He was probably thinking of his 30-year dispute with Wallace.

Last stand at the Hornet's Nest

As Gillespie and the rest of the men in the Sixth Division under General Prentiss caught their breath and regrouped, bracing for another sledgehammer blow of infantry and artillery, their spirits were lifted by the sight of fresh troops from the 15th Michigan Infantry, who had just arrived the day before. But then they were stunned to learn that the raw recruits from Ypsilanti and Detroit had been sent into battle with no ammunition, nothing but their 18-inch bayonets, which had become increasingly useless against rifled muskets and canister artillery.

Some of the new men were shaken, with wide eyes; they talked about a nearby pond where the wounded crawled like animals, desperate for a last drink of water. The water was stained crimson red by blood.

Gillespie was lying flat on the lip of the sunken road at the edge of the Hornet's Nest. Empty ammunition boxes scattered behind them testified that they had fired more than 100 rounds each. The road behind them was littered thick with the torn remains of paper cartridges like dirty gray snow.

And then at 10, the Rebel charges began again... wave after relentless wave.

Not far away, the 6th Iowa and the 46th Ohio waged a furious firefight in an overgrown ravine that soon became paved with corpses. The Iowa boys lost 51 killed and 120 wounded. Their brothers from Ohio lost 34 killed, 150 wounded and 52 taken prisoner. Like the 6th Mississippi at Sherman's camps earlier in the day, the 46th Ohio was so shattered it took no part in the rest of the battle.

At the Hornet's Nest, Gillespie fired until his motions were automatic, thoughtless. He could hear the Rebel yells and screeches, rising high above the moans and gasps of the wounded—then on they came again, mowed down like grass before a thresher. He lost track of the time again. His ears were ringing like alarm bells and he could scarcely hear anything but the roar of cannons and his own rifle. Choking smoke made his red, bloodshot eyes water. At first, he had felt betrayed, angry. This was not glory. How could the Lord allow such murder and dismemberment of good, God-fearing men; friends, fathers, husbands, sons.

A bullet or a piece of shrapnel singed his thigh like a branding iron, but then another wave of gray infantry with smoke-blackened faces emerged from the battlefield fog and he forgot about that and everything else and stopped thinking. He fired and loaded, fired and loaded and fired again. The enemy charge was torn apart, stalled and fell back, leaving the writhing wounded and motionless dead where they fell.

He gulped air. Grabbed a quick sip from his canteen. Trickled water down the barrel of his musket to clean out the residue. Checked his ammunition pouch. It was getting low. He was about to call out for resupply... and then they came back, another charge by those rabid, howling Rebs.

Sometime after noon, Gillespie heard it passed around that General Grant had ridden up to General Prentiss and told him to hold his position "at all hazards." Gillespie didn't know what that meant. Hold to the death? Plenty of men around him had already done that. Others who were wounded crawled on their bellies away from the line, in the direction of that bloody pond. Some of the wounds made him want to gag but his mouth was too dry. He wondered: *What more 'hazards' could there possibly be?*

He was about to find out.

Thunder of doom

At 3:30, General Hurlbut and his men began to fall back, past the Bloody Pond, leaving the left flank of the Sixth Division exposed, where Gillespie and the 12th Michigan fought on. At 4:00, as the Confederates moved in to exploit the opening and flank the Union troops, Prentiss issued orders to refuse the line, bending it like a hinged gate until it swung back at a right angle to itself.

Across the open field strewn with maimed and dying men, the Confederate commanders had finally been forced to admit that infantry could not dislodge the stubborn Union soldiers. They began amassing artillery.

By 4:30, Brig. Gen. Daniel Ruggles of the Confederate Third Army Corps had lined up about 60 canons—the largest assembly of artillery ever seen in America. It became known as Ruggles' Line.

As the Confederate guns barked and roared, leaping back with each shot as crews rushed to load round shot, case shot, explosive shells, even lengths of chain, they rained destruction on the Hornet's Nest that sounded like the end of the world. General Prentiss ordered Hickenlooper and other batteries of artillery to retreat to Pittsburg Landing.

The infantry hunkered down, but with no artillery to protect them, they could not last long against another charge. The Confederates who pursued General Hurlbut's retreat would soon be in their rear and they would be surrounded.

Gillespie, curled up behind a fallen tree, felt someone grab his shoulder. It was Sergeant Cross, miraculously still alive, but with streaks of dried and fresh blood leaking down his face from a bandage around his hatless head. Gillespie was surprised to notice that above his bushy black beard, Cross was almost bald. He had never seen him without a hat before. Between the black powder stains, dried blood and his wide, bloodshot eyes, he looked like a demented ghoul.

"Private, I've seen you ride. And right now we need a good rider to get a report to headquarters. Are you able?" he shouted above the din or exploding shells and raining branches.

"This?" Gillespie looked down as if suddenly reminded of the dark-red wound on his thigh. "Yes sir, I can ride."

'A pretty lively corpse'

Capt. C.P. Searle of the 8th Iowa Infantry was at the right end of the collapsing Union line when the Rebs attacked again. By then, 14 of the 16 Confederate brigades on the field were moving to surround the remainder of the Sixth Division and the Hornet's Nest.

Captain Searle described what happened while Gillespie carried General Prentiss's urgent plea for reinforcements.

The enemy, being encouraged by additional forces, made another frightful assault from three directions—front and flanks—pouring shot and shell into our ranks with fearful effect. Finally, with two hundred or more dead and wounded, and after ten hours of hard fighting, with very little cessation, seeing that we were surrounded, the order came to retire, but too late. We started from the high ground on which we had been fighting down a ravine, on the retreat, hoping to be able to cut through the Rebel lines, which were at our rear and had been for two hours. We started back under a most galling fire of grape and canister, seeming to come from every direction. An incident here may not be uninteresting. Retreating on the double quick, with leaden and iron hail flying thick around us, a soldier a pace in front of me fell, and I was so close that I fell over him. At the same time a spent ball struck my left arm and another went through my canteen. My arm tingled with pain, and the little water left in my canteen was warm and running over me as I fell to the ground. I thought it was my lifeblood. In fact, I was sure I was killed, but spying a Reb close by, coming with all speed, for they had us on the run, I made one grand, desperate effort to gain my feet and, much to my surprise, succeeded without trouble. I assure you I was a pretty lively corpse, for I left old 'Butternut' far in the rear, and did not even say "Good day." The poor fellow that I stumbled over was not so fortunate. He had received his final discharge.[33]

At 5:00, General Prentiss ordered a retreat. It was too late. By 5:30, Union troops began to surrender. Many were shot anyway.

As Brig. Gen. William H. Wallace of Illinois tried to rally what was left of his 2nd Division and find a way to escape, he was shot from his horse by a ball that went through the back of his head and exited through his right eye.

Wallace was left for dead, but was found on the battlefield the next day. He died several days later in the arms of his wife, who had come to Savannah, Tennessee, to surprise him.

Before he died, the general gave his horse to Capt. John Wesley Powell so that Powell could get medical aid. Powell had been shot in the right arm while directing his battery of cannons. He lost most of the arm in a field hospital but returned to duty after the battle and fought at Vicksburg and Atlanta, among others. After the war he became one of the first to explore the Grand Canyon and much of the wild and rugged American West.[34]

General Prentiss tried to escape but was captured with others in a ravine that became known as Hell's Hollow. About 2,200 Union troops were taken prisoner.[35] Among them was Captain Searle, the "lively corpse" who did not run far enough.

My time had come to receive personal attention. A big, burly Rebel captain stepped up to me and said, "You d——d Yankee, give me

---

33 US Army Staff Ride notes for The Battle of Shiloh.

34 Powell's 1869 Grand Canyon expedition was described in *Down the Great Unknown*. Six of the 10 men survived.

35 While high-ranking officers could be exchanged, most Union prisoners taken at Shiloh were shipped to Camp Oglethorpe in Macon, Georgia, where locals complained that they could barely feed themselves, much less enemy soldiers. As the war dragged on, mistreatment of prisoners became horrific, especially at Andersonville Prison in Georgia.

your sword!" Oh, how I did want to give it to him point first. But discretion prevailed, and I gave it to him hilt first, which probably saved the burial squad two interments.

As nearly all of the Confederate regiments converged on the Sixth Division like wolves circling a wounded stag, Grant was able to organize a last stand of defense. His army, once spread out over three miles of farms to the south, now was curled in a defensive crouch just a half-mile from Pittsburg Landing.

But as his lines were crushed together, they got stronger.

Grant formed his own "Ruggle's Line" of cannons on the high ground he held, including big siege guns and the huge Navy guns aboard two gunboat steamers, the *Lexington* and the *Tyler*, wooden-clad gunboats built in Cincinnati, with massive 32-pounders and six 8-inch guns.

By 5:00, the Union artillery line had assembled 52 cannons, not including the gunboats.

Confederate Gen. Braxton Bragg believed one more hard push would force Grant to unconditionally surrender. Confederate Major General Leonidas Polk[36] later said his brigades were within 150 to 400

Gunboats Lexington and Tyler, built in Cincinnati, fire on the Confederate troops at Shiloh. *Harper's Weekly*, 1862.

36 Known to his men as The Fighting Bishop, Polk was the founder of the Protestant Episcopal Church in Tennessee. He was a cousin of President James A. Polk. He was killed in combat in 1864. He and General Bragg despised each other and tried to get each other demoted or fired.

yards of the enemy line. "Nothing seemed wanting to complete the most brilliant victory of the war but to press forward and make a vigorous assault on the demoralized remnant of his forces."

But as they advanced across a ravine, 52 Union cannons roared their defiance and the giant naval guns opened up from the river on the Confederate flank. The earth-shaking barrage was demoralizing, a murderous fire from cannons and rifles. Three times they tried to cross the "valley of death" and failed.

They would not advance a step farther. The Confederacy had reached its highwater mark at Shiloh.

"The shelling from the gunboats was unbearable," one Confederate commander said.

At about 5:30, believing Buell's Union reinforcements were still safely days away, General Beauregard called a halt to the battle. He spent the night in Sherman's abandoned tent near Shiloh Church. His dispatch to Richmond promised that the next day would bring complete victory. Ironically, he was in for a surprise just as big as the one he had sprung at Fraley Field so many lifetimes ago when the sun rose.

Night of horrors, dawn of decision

Grant's finest hours at Shiloh began with a courageous horseback ride along his front lines in the afternoon of the first day—so reckless that his staff implored him to be more careful. As Grant lingered in the storm of flying bullets and artillery, one of his scouts was decapitated by a shattered cannon ball that bounced off a tree, took off the man's head, then severed the legs of a soldier nearby.

Spattered with gore, Grant rode on.

A little while later, Grant visited Sherman during some of his hottest fighting of the day. A canister round smashed and twisted his sword scabbard at his hip, narrowly missing the kind of injury that killed Confederate General Johnston.

Wallace recalled, "In further illustration of the man under fire, a bullet cut his cigar off close to his lips. 'Here,' he shouted, 'one of you fellows bring me a match.' The match was brought, and, lighting a fresh cigar, he spurred on."

Grant narrowly missed by cannon shell. Albert D. Richardson, 1868.

General Sherman, known as "Uncle Billy" to his troops, was just as reckless. After being wounded in the hand, he still led his men into battle from the front and had three horses shot out from under him. Four days after the battle, he wrote to his wife:

> The scene on this field would have cured anybody of war. Mangled bodies, dead, dying, in every conceivable shape, without heads, legs... and the horses! I think we have buried 2,000 since this fight, our own and the enemy's. The wounded fill houses, tents, steamboats and every conceivable place. I still feel the horrid nature of this war, and the piles of dead gentlemen and wounded and maimed makes me more anxious than ever for some hope of an end, but I know such a thing cannot be for a long, long time. Indeed, I never expect it or to survive it.

By evening, both sides were exhausted.

"The sun went down in a red halo, as if the very heavens blushed and prepared to weep at the enormity of man's violence," wrote one Shiloh veteran. Soon it began to rain buckets and the skies thundered to mock the cannons that had raged all day.

Grant wandered into a field hospital in a cabin, hoping to dry off—and nearly threw up as he saw the butchery of bone saws and knives, and heard the shrieks of amputations and surgeries without adequate anesthetic. He returned to a spreading oak tree where he sat in the drenching downpour, thinking about his next move.

Gen. Don Carlos Buell and his Army of The Ohio had just arrived with four fresh divisions, adding 20,000 men to Grant's original 42,000. Buell expected Grant to order a retreat across the river.

General Hurlbut, driven back to Pittsburg Landing, miles from his original camp near the blooming Peach Orchard, was disgusted by Grant's lack of leadership that left every unit on its own to fight for its life.

Capt. Andrew Hickenlooper of Cincinnati, whose 5th Ohio Light Artillery had fought valiantly at the Hornet's Nest all day long, would say Grant's failure to build adequate defenses was "lame" and "unjustifiable."[37] He scorched Grant's absence from the battlefield.

"There was no common directing head or superior officer beyond the rank of division commander placed on the firing line whom all recognized and promptly obeyed ... There was no battle plan, no strategy, no tactical maneuvers and but few commands—certainly none that had any important bearing on the final results," Hickenlooper said.

Another Cincinnatian, Gen. Manning Force of the 20th Ohio, would put it less harshly. "The open way to Corinth was also an open way *from* Corinth to the Landing. This accessible front could easily have been turned into a strong defense, by taking advantage of the rolling ground, felling timber and throwing up slight earthworks. But the army had many things yet to learn, and the use of field fortification was one of them."[38]

Another soldier who had endured the worst, Joseph Rich of the 12th Iowa, said Grant and his army had sleepwalked into a battle after being "in a state of suspended animation for three weeks."

Even Sherman wondered if Grant would accept defeat and retreat.

---

37 Beemer, Charles G. *My Greatest Quarrel with Fortune.* 2015.

38 Force, Manning Ferguson. *From Fort Henry to Corinth.* 1881.

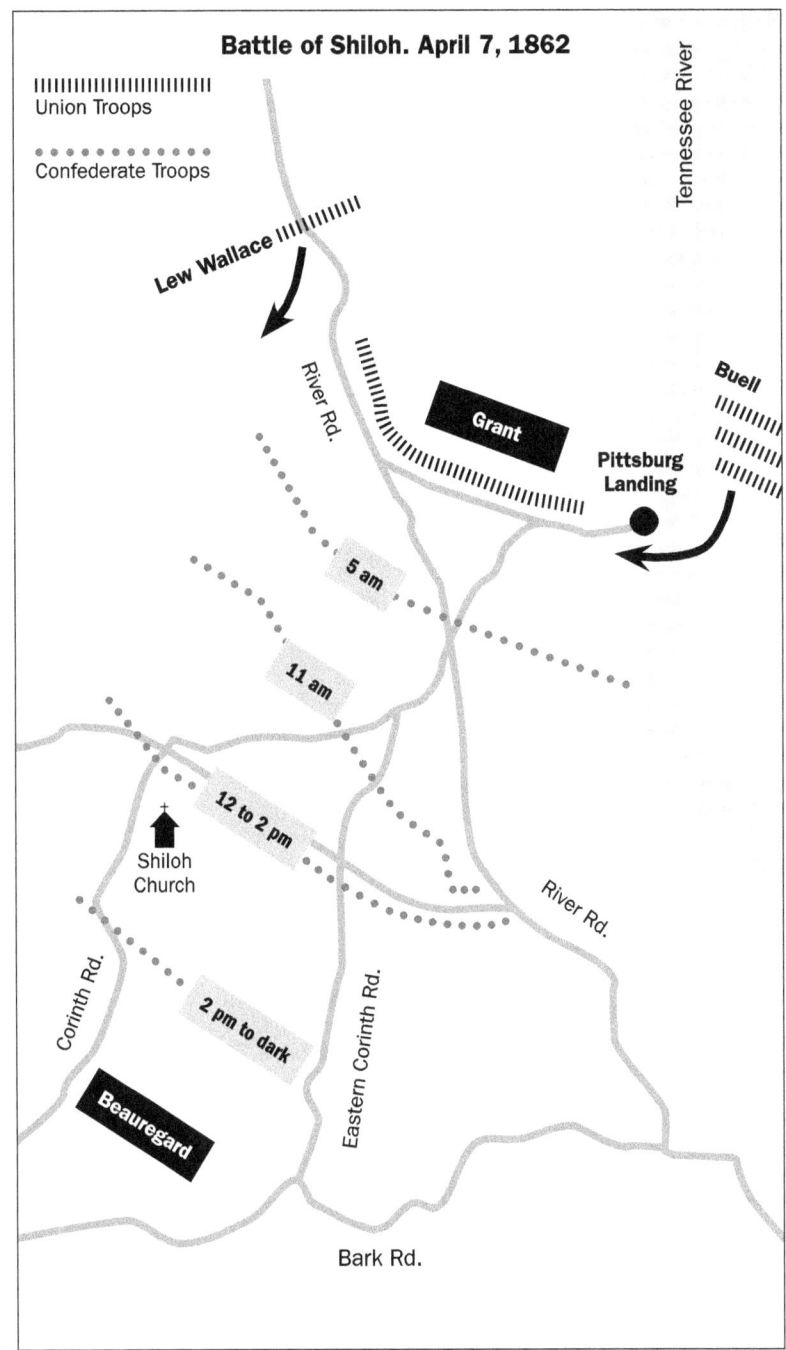

Map 3

As he stood with Grant under the dripping tree, he tried to console his old friend. "Well, Grant, we've had the devil's own day, haven't we?"

Sherman was surprised by Grant's terse reply: "Yes. Lick 'em tomorrow, though."

Grant was now fully awake.

Maybe it was the blood-soaked field hospital; maybe the scout whose headless body toppled to the ground; maybe just the smell and sound of battle that finally brought Grant back to being Grant. He shook off the infection of fear and caution spread by Halleck and resolved: Tomorrow his "defeated" army would counterattack and win.

He would say later, "Victory was assured when Wallace arrived."

Finally, in spite of Grant's carelessness and Wallace's frustration, the Army of The Tennessee was united under one fierce, angry commander. As General Beauregard was about to discover, that was a terrifying thing to behold.

SHILOH DAY 2
'Move out that way'

Gillespie woke before dawn on the second day, cold, wet, hungry, miserable and aching in every fiber and bone of his body. His wounded thigh had stopped bleeding but throbbed with every heartbeat and hurt worse now than when he was hit. His leg had stiffened like the blood-soaked blanket that he borrowed from a dead man outside a field hospital. He could recall no pleasant dreams of home. Only horrific nightmares that made him whimper like a dog and cry out in his sleep until he prayed he would never fall asleep again.

That was made easy by the constant booms of the gunboats that fired every 15 minutes all night to harass the Confederate Army and keep them on edge, wondering where the next enormous shell would shake the earth. Unfortunately, it worked as well on the Union soldiers, who agreed that the only lucky ones who slept were the dead. And those were everywhere.

They were stacked like firewood outside the surgeons' tents, not too far from the horrifying pile of arms and legs they had lost. The dead were mingled among the recovering, moaning and delirious victims of the knives and saws; they were scattered just outside the Union line, strewn across farm fields, in the underbrush and woods for miles, like fallen, rotting fruit from a monstrous tree of evil.

The torrential rain and constant cannon fire all night had discouraged rescue of the wounded. Their agonies made a hell's chorus of heart-rending pleas for mercy, help, mother, wife and children. The calls for "father" were mostly to the Lord, ending with pleading prayers to be shot and put out of their misery.

Gillespie's night was spent on the muddy ground, under that ragged, blood-soaked blanket. The steady rain had washed it clean, at least on the outside, but it could never wash away his memories of the day before and his jagged nerves. He had finally dozed off to the sound of young men from Sherman's division nearby, singing hymns that made him yearn for love, peace and mercy. One man read from his Bible from Psalm 78:

> "When God heard this, he was wroth, and greatly abhorred Israel so that he forsook the tabernacle of Shiloh. He gave his people over also unto the sword; and was wroth with his inheritance. The fire continued to consume the young men..."

Tears flowed like the steady raindrops, gradually rinsing away the blackened lips that distinguished men who had been in the hardest fights, whose tongues were still tarred from biting black-powder cartridges.

Their innocence was shattered, blown to pieces with their friends on the battlefield. Life as they had known it would never again be what it was. That world seemed impossibly far away. The carefree adventurers of yesterday's boyhood morning were now husks, hollowed out by grief, fear, shock and the terrible things they had seen and done. They had tasted the fruit from the tree of knowledge of good and evil. They had seen shining acts of heroic courage and self-sacrifice; and they had looked into the darkest corner of hell on earth that swallowed young lives with an insatiable appetite for blood.

He thought, "Thank you, Lord, for the rain. At least we can't smell it as much anymore." But that would not last long. Word came that they would advance again today to cross those fields of death again and whip the Butternuts. Back into the Valley of Death, where the stench of mangled human remains would make the strongest soldiers retch and gag, and make wild-eyed horses spook and rear.

Gillespie had ended the first day of battle on the right of the Union defensive line that curved around Pittsburg Landing like a protective hand. His fourth dispatch on his second horse had taken him to Gen. Lew Wallace, who had arrived sometime around 7:00 p.m. The orders he carried from headquarters sent Wallace to the farthest right flank, beyond which were only swamps that had sucked the energy from his men all day.

Wallace was weary and angry, still itching for a fight. But he was gracious and kind and offered Gillespie some coffee and biscuits in a tent lit by dim candlelight. So Gillespie stayed with the Indiana general and his Third Division. He felt comforted by the cool, professional attitude of the veteran Zouaves. They had not fought at Shiloh yet, but they had been tested before and seemed unfazed, ready for whatever tomorrow would bring.

He had heard that General Wallace appreciated a good horseman, and was proud that he was asked to stay nearby, if he was able, to carry messages as a dispatch rider for the Third Division. Gillespie agreed. He had no place else to go. His Sixth Division had ceased to exist. He had no idea where the 12th Michigan was after the Hornet's Nest. He gulped coffee, ate as many biscuits as he could stomach, and wandered off to find a place to sleep. Wallace's Third Division had no tents. They were back at Crump's Landing. So he joined the men on the wet ground. They were not allowed to have campfires in case the Confederates attacked or used the fires for artillery targets.

As the first hint of sunlight lit the gray skies, he painfully climbed into the saddle on a fresh horse provided by the Third Division, pushed his stiff leg into the stirrup and followed Wallace and his staff to the front lines, where a battery of Confederate cannons sat on a ridge just a half-mile away, black snouts raised in the air in arrogant defiance.

At 5:30, the Union cannons, including Wallace's batteries, cleared their throats and fired the first shots to open the second day of battle. It was then that Gillespie caught his first glimpse of General Grant, who rode up to give Wallace orders.

Grant's leg had been injured the evening before when his horse had fallen on him. On top of his twisted ankle, it made him so lame he had to be lifted into the saddle. Crutches were strapped behind him. But if he had to describe the general, Gillespie would have called him "quietly confident, almost cheerful."

The orders Grant gave to Wallace were very brief, simple, spoken softly and without a hint of drama, as if he were asking Wallace to pick up some fresh cigars and giving directions to the sutler's store. He gestured to the field in front of Wallace on the other side of a steep ravine made by the swollen Tilghman's Creek, and said, "Move out that way."

Wallace asked Grant what divisions would be on his left in support. Grant replied, "I will take care of that."

As Grant started to ride away, Wallace spurred Old John to catch up and asked, "Excuse me, General, is there any particular order of attack you would have me take.""

"No," Grant replied. "I leave that to your discretion."

Gillespie would wonder later why Grant never mentioned that Buell's Army of the Ohio had arrived and was taking the left flank with almost 20,000 fresh men, bringing Grant's forced to almost 57,000, even with the loss of almost 10,000 the day before. Posted all night on the right flank, Wallace had no way to know it.

But as dawn broke that morning on April 7, it was enough to know that the Rebs were in front of them. As he looked at Wallace on horseback, lit by the morning sun, his back straight, waving his hat to lead his men, it almost took his breath away. In spite of himself, he felt those old goose bumps of glory.

Perry Field, 6:30 a.m.

After an hour of cannon duels between the two lines, the Union Army began its infantry assault. Buell would attack south on the left flank, closest to the Tennessee River; to his right were the remains of General Hurlbut's battle-torn Fourth Division that had fought so hard at the Peach Orchard. Next was General McClernand's First Division, then General Sherman's Fifth Division, then General Wallace on the extreme right flank. Two divisions—the Second led by Gen. W. H. Wallace, and the Sixth led by Gen. Benjamin Prentiss—were wiped out. W.H. Wallace was presumed dead near the Hornet's Nest and Prentiss had been captured. What was left of the men who survived the Hornet's Nest were mingled with other divisions.

Col. John Thayer, commanding the First Nebraska regiment in Lew Wallace's Third Division, described the advance:

I shall never forget the picture the man and scene presented. The sun was barely rising of a cold, frosty morning. General Wallace was a princely figure, particularly in the saddle and he rode a handsome blooded roan stallion, a single-stepper that was the pride of the division. As he came riding up, his military accoutrements flashing in the red light of the rising sun, and the charger moving as though to the sound of music, he presented a sight that is not seen more than once in a lifetime.

Wallace rode out in front of his men, stood in his stirrups and waved his hat while his troops cheered and tipped their hats to him as they passed. None of them had any idea what to expect on the other side of the ridge they faced. But first, they had to cross Tilghman Creek, scrambling down the steep banks of a ravine, through the creek, and up the opposite bank, just as steep. At the bottom in the swollen creek, many men got mired up to their waists in the mud, but they were pulled out and the line marched on.

In his autobiography many years later, Wallace called it "an exciting and beautiful performance all through, from flank to flank, arms at right shoulder shift, no man hanging back, and the colors imparting warmth and splendor to the misty gray of the morning."

Across the creek and over the ridge, facing north was the Confederate Army's Third Brigade led by Colonel Preston Pond, with the Alabama Battery of Captain William H. Ketchum. They poured fire on the Union cannons behind the advancing Third Division until Pond realized he was cut off from his Confederate army, more than a mile out in front, with no support. He began to withdraw, leaving behind a regiment of Texas Rangers to support Ketchum's cannons.

The Confederates were soon just as confused and disorganized as the Union troops were the morning before. Colonel Pond wrote:

I was ordered ... to form on the extreme left and rest my left on Owl Creek. While proceeding to execute this order, I was ordered to move by the rear of the main line to support the extreme right of General Hardee's line. Having taken my position to occupy the crest of a ridge on the edge of an old field. My line was just formed in this position when General Polk ordered me forward to support his line. While moving to the support of General Polk, an order reached me from General Beauregard to report to him with my command at his headquarters.

Four conflicting orders had his troops marching in circles when they could have been holding a line. But their confusion was no comfort to Wallace's troops as they charged into Ketchum's artillery and the 8th Texas Cavalry Regiment known as Terry's Texas Rangers, who had been ordered to defend the cannons as a rearguard. The Rangers were veterans of the Indian wars in Texas and had exceptional skills at riding and shooting on the gallop. They were often used as shock troops. At Shiloh, they were under the command of Col. John Wharton.

As they crested the hill past the creek, Wallace and his men found the Confederates and their artillery had pulled back to a line of woods across an open field, near Sherman's camps from the day before. Ketchum and the Texans made a determined stand. Wallace saw that strictly following Grant's vague orders to "Move out that way" (west), would take him too far right, so he wheeled his line to the left. As they crossed the field, the cannon and musket fire was withering.

He called a halt to bring up his own batteries of cannons just before 10:00. Wallace and his men took advantage of the uneven ground to take cover and save hundreds of lives. The infantry was ordered to lay down behind mounds and hillocks; officers were ordered to dismount, to spare their lives.[39]

Gillespie was grateful. He had hugged the ground as desperately as anyone else the day before, and fired from a prone position at the edge of the Sunken Road. But Wallace had refined self-preservation into a life-saving tactic.

"Down we lay Zouave style, and let the shot, shell, grape and shrapnel pass over us," one of his soldiers wrote later. "The iron hail did us

---

39   Although engaged in some of the hottest fighting, Wallace's regiments suffered fewer loses thanks to his Zouave tactics. Other Divisions had as many as nine times as many casualties.

but little damage. There we lay, just beneath the brow of a little hillock upon which stood … (our cannons) continually pouring death and destruction into the (enemy) ranks."

General Wallace heard a sound behind him "as if someone were pounding a sandpile with a maul." He looked back and saw "an arm, torn from the shoulder of a soldier and stiffened like a stick, it's fingers all outspread, revolving end over end through the air." That arm was nearly his own. His mouth became dry as dust until he could hardly swallow. His commands came out in a croak. His eyes stung and his throat was raw from the thick clouds of gun smoke and storm of raining earth.

As cannons fired across the open battlefield, Wallace saw a horse emerge from the smoke. "The whole lower jaw had been shot off and hung dangling by a stringlike piece of skin. I had never in my life had an appeal for help from a brute so distinct and touching as then. Even yet I sicken at the recollection."

One of his men put the animal out of its misery with a pistol.

"At Shiloh there was nothing on either side to relieve the butchery but heroism," he wrote years later. "It was an unmitigated hell to the memories of all who happily came out of it alive."

The firing in front of the woods went on and on. Two of his regiments ran out of ammunition, but the support troops filled the gaps so fast "there was no observable cessation of the fire."

The Confederates sent a valiant cavalry charge into the Third Division's guns. It was doomed by the deadly accuracy of rifled muskets. Men and horses were shot down until they littered the plowed field like a strange crop awaiting the harvest, or sank into the muddy ground as if the dead and wounded were burying themselves.

One of Wallace's batteries of artillery ran out of ammunition and another rode in through a cloud of dust, a flurry of action and shouted orders. The cannons were unlimbered so fast the firing resumed almost immediately where the other battery left off.

In an artillery duel at Jones Field that lasted until noon, a battery of the 9th Indiana fired nearly 1,200 rounds.

Sherman and Buell attack

The Third Division under Wallace had been fighting for hours on the right flank before General Sherman finally moved out his Fifth Division at 10:00. Backed up by General McClernand's First Division in the middle of the Union attack, he was waiting for General Buell and the Army of the Ohio to move up and support his left flank along the river.

Buell and Grant did not coordinate their attacks. Buell was a reserved, aloof man, stiff and hard to read. Wallace once said of him, "In the atmosphere of that cold nature, humor could not live and wit was a plant too weak to flower."

Buell was also close to Grant's equal in rank, so Grant did not give him specific orders for the day. Perhaps that was because Grant had no apparent battle plan except to attack. But when Buell finally joined the battle, he quickly discovered the "unmitigated hell" that was Shiloh.

Ambrose Bierce of Ohio, a newsman who became a famous author and wrote [40]*The Devil's Dictionary*, was a soldier in the 9th Indiana Infantry, part of Buell's Fourth Division led by Brig. Gen. William "Bull" Nelson, a pugnacious 300-pound brawler.

In his essay *What I saw at Shiloh,* Bierce described what it was like when the fresh troops arrived late in the evening on the first day of battle:

> Hidden in hollows behind clumps of rank brambles were large tents, dimly lighted with candles, but looking comfortable. ... These tents were constantly receiving the wounded, yet were never full; they were continually ejecting the dead, yet were never empty. It was as if the helpless had been carried in and murdered, that they might not hamper those whose business it was to fall tomorrow.

As they marched into battle the following morning before dawn, they stumbled over dead bodies and "more frequently those who still

---

40 Bierce's 1881 dictionary blended wit with the cynicism of a combat veteran. Such as: "Love: A temporary insanity curable by marriage." "Cannon: An instrument employed in the rectification of national boundaries." "Accuracy: A certain uninteresting quality carefully excluded from human statements." "Conservative: A statesman who is enamored of existing evils, as distinguished from the Liberal, who wishes to replace them with others." "Telephone: An invention of the devil which abrogates some of the advantages of making a disagreeable person keep his distance."

had enough spirit to resent it with a moan."

There were deep, shaking explosions and smart shocks; the whisper of stray bullets and the hurtle of conical shells; the rush of round shot. There were faint, desultory cheers, such as announced a momentary or partial triumph. Occasionally, against the glare behind the trees, could be seen moving black figures, singularly distinct but apparently no longer than a thumb. They seemed to be ludicrously like the figures of demons in old allegorical prints of hell. ... Those of us who had the good fortune to arrive later could then have eaten our teeth in important rage.

The men thrust forward their heads, expanded their eyes and clenched their teeth. They breathed hard, as if throttled by tugging at the leash. If you had laid your hand in the beard or hair of one of these men it would have crackled and shot sparks.

Bierce and his 9th Indiana were in some of the hardest fighting as part of Col. William Hazen's 19th Brigade. Hit by a vicious Confederate counterattack, Hazen's troops suffered some of the worst casualties of the battle. One unit, the 41st Ohio, lost 140 killed or wounded out of 371 men as they fought for Sherman's camp near Shiloh Church. "The shattered regiments steamed back in confusion, leaving a gap in the division line," wrote Col. Manning Force of the 20th Ohio.

Bierce described it:

Then—I can't describe it—the forest seemed all at once to flame up and disappear with a crash like that of a great wave upon the beach—a crash that expired in the hot hissings , and the sickening "spat" of lead against flesh. ... What we had found was a line of battle, cooly holding its fire until it could count our teeth.

He described a ravine where the forest floor had caught fire and roasted wounded men who "perished in slow torture." The corpses had "hideous grins," some "swollen to double girth, others shriveled to manikins."

Bierce, in command of a platoon, saw the Union line break.

Then the storm burst. A great gray cloud seemed to spring out of the forest into the faces of the waiting battalions, It was received with a crash that made the very trees turn up their leaves. For an instant, the assailants paused above their dead, then struggled forward, their bayonets glittering in the eyes that shone behind the smoke....[41]

The line of blue staggered and gave way.

General Nelson's Fourth Division was the first of Buell's army to reach Pittsburg Landing the day before. But on the second day, it went into battle without any artillery. Grant's poor preparation haunted the soldiers again: their cannons had been left behind at Savannah.

As Buell's front fell back, as if recoiling in horror, Sherman's troops followed, leaving a gap on the left of Wallace's Third Division as they fought relentlessly just north of the Shiloh Church—ironically, in the same place where Wallace would have emerged the day before if he had not been ordered to backtrack.

Confederate General Beauregard was on the brink of achieving what General Sidney Johnston had planned before his death: seize Pittsburg Landing and drive the Union into the swamps.

By 2:00 p.m., the Confederates were holding a line along the Hamburg-Purdy road—matching the battlelines of the previous day around the Peach Orchard and the Hornet's Nest.

Col. Manning Force, leading the 20th Ohio, recalled that the fight there raged "with a fury surpassing any portion of the battle of Sunday." Ammunition was running low.

"Wallace's left flank was exposed," Force continued. "The 1st Nebraska, having fired its last cartridge, the 76th Ohio leaped into its place."

Force and his 20th Ohio were hit by an artillery battery at close range, but "dashed through a fringe of bushes and drove a battery from the field beyond."

Amid all the screams, deafening roar of cannons, thick smoke from muskets and exploding shells, soldiers watched an almost mythical

---

41   Bierce, Ambrose, *What I Saw of Shiloh*, 1881.

scene take place that was told and retold by Shiloh veterans for decades to come.

The dangerous gap on the left that would allow Beauregard's counterattack to break the Union front was suddenly filled by the arrival of a former Prussian general, Col. August Willich,[42] and his all-German 32nd Indiana Regiment. Colonel Force described it:

> Col. Willich ... passed around to the left and ... charged upon the enemy in that quarter, drove him into the timber, then deploying in line opened fire. Willich became subject to so hot a fire ... that he was compelled to withdraw. Dressing his lines, he charged again. Observing undue excitement in his men, he halted his regiment, and in the midst of the battle, exercised the men in the manual of arms.

As his men stood at attention under continuous Confederate fire, Colonel Willich's commands rang out in his heavy German accent:

"Shoulder arms!"

"Present arms!"

"Fix bayonets!"

As the rest of the men in blue watched in astonishment, the Indiana troops went through the elaborate 10-step parade ground ritual. As men fell, others closed up the ranks and continued the precise drill as if they were lined up for inspection.

"Having thus steadied them, he resumed the charge and again drove the enemy into the timber," Force wrote.

The Union lines cheered the Indiana soldiers and rallied to the attack. For the Confederates, it was demoralizing. They had thrown everything they had at the enemy only to watch the Yanks conduct a manual of arms as if the Confederate cannons and muskets did not even exist.

When Wallace found out that Willich's regiment was part of Buell's Army of The Tennessee, he realized for the first time that Grant's army was reinforced by Buell. By then it was past 1:00 p.m.

---

42   August Willich was the editor of the local *German Republican* newspaper in Cincinnati and was credited with sending local Germans to the polls to elect Lincoln. The former Prussian officer was a member of the Communist League in Germany. One of his officers was Fredrich Engels. He once challenged Karl Marx to a duel, but Marx refused to fight.

Gen. Pierre T. Beauregard

By attacking the left flank of the Confederates, Wallace had broken their counterattack toward Pittsburg Landing and saved the day for Grant and Sherman again.

Wallace recalled: "Two o'clock came, then three o'clock—and in all that time the woods smoked and flamed without intermission; and, listening to the sounds, it did not seem possible that a man could come out of the infernal contact alive to tell of it."

As I was in my thirty-fifth year, the youngest of the grade in the service, I now often look back wondering where I got the confidence that possessed me; and sometimes there steals into the reflection a vague suspicion that the thing called courage, if a quality at all, is chiefly compounded of inexperience and ignorance."

Disorderly retreat

At about 3:00, Grant rallied two regiments just as Gen. Sidney Johnston had done before he was killed the day before, and led a charge that broke the Confederates near Shiloh Church. "Endurance has its limits," Colonel Force wrote. "The intense strain of two days was telling. Beauregard saw his men were beginning to flag; exhausted regiments were dropping out of line."

Col. Charles Whittlesey, commanding the 3rd Brigade of Wallace's

Third Division, described the collapse of the Confederate lines.

"There being signs of a retreat farther to the south, Lieutenant Thurber was directed to sweep the ground in front, which he did with his two howitzers and three smoothbores in fine style. Two prisoners captured near there, one of them an officer in the Creole Guard, stated that General Beauregard was endeavoring to form a line for a final and desperate charge on our right when Lieutenant Thurber opened upon him, and the result was disorderly retreat."

The Confederate tide that crested at the doorstep of Pittsburg Landing on Sunday now receded back to Corinth. At 3:00, Gen. Beauregard gave orders to retreat.

Wallace attempted to pursue and almost lost his horse Old John in a reeking mud-bog that stank of blood, death and decay. One of Wallace's regiments skirmished with the retreating Confederates but was driven back by cavalry.

The Yankee hounds were called off. Grant chose not to pursue the defeated, exhausted Army of The Mississippi, although Wallace's Third Division and Buell's Army were still fresh and willing. It was a relapse into the Halleck brain-fog anxiety that would teach a hard lesson to Grant in the new School of War. Failing to pursue and annihilate the

CAVALRY CHARGE AT SHILOH.

Gen. William Tecumseh Sherman at Shiloh. 1891.

ragtag, broken Confederate army would be enormously costly. It would prolong the war, costing thousands more lives. That butcher's bill would be paid in blood in another terrible battle at Corinth in October. And it would eventually turn Grant into the relentless attacker and merciless pursuer who crushed Gen. Robert E. Lee at the end of the war.

There was a skirmish by Sherman against the cavalry of Confederate Gen. Nathan Bedford Forrest the following day at Fallen Timbers, on the way to Corinth. But Shiloh was over.

The war would drag on for years. The most terrible and decisive battle was still to come at Gettysburg in July the following year, 1863. But for North and South, Shiloh shocked the nation to its knees—in prayer and grief.

Both sides claimed victory. Yet newspapers in North and South were filled like cemeteries with the names of the dead. Mixed among the missing and the dead were scraps of letters from the survivors of the battle.

Both sides claimed victory. W.E. Minor of the Confederate 6th Kentucky Regiment of Volunteers wrote:

> The battle of Shiloh sends a thrill of electric fire through the entire South. Her sons, from every sunny field, will desperately rally around the pillar of her rising hope, until our banner of stars and bars shall be recognized by the civilized world as the Aegis of Civil Liberty and a terror to those who may presume to invade the sacred precincts of domestic peace. The North don't understand our spirit. They mistake for what we are fighting. They had as well try to quench the fire of eternal life as to try to subjugate those who are satisfied they are fighting for their mothers, fathers, sisters, kindred, and the tender ones of their hearts... Let the North pay tribute to their Caesar and let the South to theirs, for peace can never exist with them as one Nation.[43]

In spite of the editorials and saber-rattling news stories, the South had lost the battle and its most promising military leader, General

---

43 *The Natchez Weekly Courier*, April 30, 1862, Page 1. via Newspapers.com

Johnston. With Johnston leading, the South might have won Shiloh and taken its campaign north through the Ohio Valley and Kentucky, which was his plan to break the back of the Union.

The North won the battle but lost confidence in Grant, who was publicly blamed for the shocking slaughter. Halleck made sure it was Grant, not himself, who took the arrows of criticism. Most of the press that mattered clustered in the East, around New York, Boston and Washington, DC. They were easily manipulated by Halleck, with hand-fed rumors of Grant's drunkenness and incompetence. He used Shiloh as an excuse to demote Grant again and take over command of the next battle at Corinth.

Both sides lost hope that the war would end quickly. Just as soldiers lost their innocence, their families lost their illusions of flag-waving glory and swift victory parades. The casualties at Shiloh outnumbered the American Revolution, the War of 1812 and the Mexican War combined. North and South alike abandoned their bright patriotic colors for mourning black. The divided nation shared a common bond of grief, as the nation wept for sons, brothers, fathers, husbands.

Even the White House was not spared. First Lady Mary Todd Lincoln lost her brother, Samuel Brown Todd, who was killed at Shiloh as he served with the Crescent Regiment of Louisiana Infantry, fighting with the Confederates against his brother-in-law, the President.[44]

Over two days, the battle claimed almost 24,000 casualties. The total population of the nation at that time was fewer than 32 million. By the end of the war, 750,000 would be killed. Nearly one in five young men of military age would be lost. Hardly a town, village, farm or family would be unscathed by the Grim Reaper's scythe.

Newspapers exaggerated enemy losses and minimized their own. But losses on both sides at Shiloh were about equal: According to battlefield

---

44   The First Lady had four brothers fighting for the South. Three served at Shiloh; two were killed in the war; one served as commandant of the notorious Libby Prison, but was removed by Confederate President Jefferson Davis because of his extreme cruelty to Union prisoners. Her brother-in-law, Charles H. Kellogg of Cincinnati, sought patronage favors from President Lincoln, then betrayed the Union on a secret mission to the South to aid the Confederacy. He assisted in a field hospital at the Battle of Shiloh.

reports after April 7, 1862, the Confederates lost 10,917 killed, wounded and missing: the Union lost 12,217, including 3,022 who were taken prisoner, mostly from the surrender of Gen. Prentiss at the Hornet's Nest.[45]

Shiloh was the first taste of the bitter tears that would fall like rain for decades to come.

General Beauregard was blamed for the Confederates' defeat because he stopped his attack too soon, when victory was within his grasp. Others blamed him for not sticking to General Johnston's plan to take Pittsburg Landing, where the Confederates could have blocked reinforcements by Buell's army that sealed their doom.

General Grant was blamed for his failure to pursue the broken Confederates to Corinth, allowing them to regroup and reinforce for the Battle of Corinth that followed. He was criticized as an incompetent, unprepared drunk. But when President Lincoln was urged to remove him, Lincoln replied, "I can't spare that man. He fights."

Eventually, Grant allowed his staff to deflect blame to an easy target. The most persistent controversy that emerged from the smoke, dust and stench of the Shiloh battlefield was hung like an albatross around the neck of the Union's youngest general: Lew Wallace.

---

45 Theodore Ayrault Dodge, *A Bird's Eye View of Our Civil War,* James R. Osgood & Co., Boston and New York, 1883.

BATTLE FATIGUE
'Somebody in the dark gave me a push'

In 1866, four years after the Battle of Shiloh, the dead rose again.

Disposing of more than 5,000 corpses and thousands more dead horses, not to mention cartloads of amputated limbs and pieces of bodies strewn all over several miles of dense, swampy ravines and plowed, muddy farm fields, was no easy task.

Many of the Confederates were hastily dumped in a half-dozen unmarked mass graves. Teams of soldiers were assigned to clean up battlefields where bodies were so thick they could walk across the dead without touching the ground. They gathered the bodies, stacked them in wagons, then hauled them to shallow trenches fifty-feet long and dumped in as many as 600 beloved sons of the South.

Union soldiers were buried with more dignity, in marked graves when identification was possible. Some were later exhumed and taken home by their families.

"The dead are numberless; the roadsides beyond the battleground are strewn with dead Rebels who fought like tigers," Wallace wrote to his wife, Susan. "This soldiering business sadly deadens that very good thing so carefully cultivated by Christians—humanity."

Manning Force described missions of mercy that descended on Pittsburg Landing before the Red Cross was born from Civil War battlefield experiences in 1881:

> When news of the two days of fighting was received at the North, the people of the Ohio Valley and St. Louis were stirred to active sympathy. Steamboats bearing physicians, nurses, sisters of charity, and freighted with hospital supplies were at once dispatched and soon crowded the shore of Pittsburg Landing. There was need for all that was brought. Besides the thousands of wounded were other

thousands of sick. The springs of surface water used in the camps, always unwholesome, were now poisonous. The well lost their strength; of the sick, many died every day. Hospital camps spread over the hills about the landing and the little town of Savannah was turned into a hospital. Fleets descended the river bearing invalids to purer air and water.[46]

The wounded were gathered in farmhouses, barns, sheds, wherever shelter could be found for scarce surgeons to do their grim business. But there was not enough room. Suffering men were left outdoors on the cold ground, in the rain and mud. If they survived, they were taken aboard steamers by a small army of civilians who arrived to give them aid, and sent north to hospitals, including Camp Dennison,[47] an induction boot camp in Indian Hill, near Cincinnati.[48] As those wounded men waited for days at Pittsburg Landing, lying in cold mud under drizzling rain, a strange "angel's glow" arose from their bodies.

It was described as an eerie blue-green radiance that became visible as the sun went down. Doctors noticed that wounds that glowed healed faster. With no other explanation, it was believed to be a divine miracle.

The mystery was solved in 2001: It was bioluminescent bacteria, Photorhabadus luminescens, that destroyed pathogens and prevented gangrene. The bacteria were carried by a type of flatworm common to that part of Tennessee. As the men became hypothermic, their dropping body temperature allowed the bacteria to multiply and clean their wounds. For those who had the angel's glow and lived, it was indeed a divine miracle.

In that landscape haunted by glowing wounded and rotting dead, the

---

46 Force, Manning Ferguson. *From Fort Henry to Corinth*. 1881. Many of the doctors and nurses were sent by the Cincinnati Sanitary Commission.

47 As many as 50,000 soldiers went through Camp Dennison during the war, with up to 12,000 there at one time. It was named after Ohio Gov. William Dennison. The camp covered 700 aces, leased to the US government by local landowners Nimrod Price and Alfred Buckingham. After the war, the camp was closed and the barracks were dismantled, providing construction materials for nearby homes.

48 A doctor who served with the Army at Camp Dennison, John H. Salsibury, has been credited with the invention of Salsibury Steak there during the Civil War, to help patients who were unable to chew and digest tough cuts of beef. He also created the Salsibury Diet.

burial parties did their grisly work. But not with enthusiasm. The corpses they buried under a few spades of mud kept popping to the surface for years, according to Lt. Col. Wills DeHaas of Marietta Ohio, a Shiloh veteran with the 53rd Ohio Infantry that fought at Sherman's camp.

"After the battle of Shiloh, General Grant ordered the dead of both armies to be buried," he wrote after the war had ended. "The inhumation, however, consisted of little more than a thin covering of earth, which the heavy rains have long since washed off, and the remains of brave men who periled all for their country's sake lie exposed to the elements. This fact is disgraceful to the government and the people, and should be remedied with the least possible delay. Instead of squandering means over idle parades, it should be our duty and pleasure to give the bleaching bones of our gallant dead the rites of decent burial."

Eventually, his protests helped to create the National Cemetery at Shiloh. But not before vandals and vultures descended while the bodies were still unburied. Wallace wrote, "I have seen them cut down trees to secure bits of shells, cut off horse tails, pick up the shoes of dead soldiers."

Even the bloodstained floorboards of the humble Shiloh Church, which had been used as a hospital, were carried away by souvenir hunters. The church was "utterly demolished," DeHaas said. [49]

The dead who refused to stay buried.

The house of worship stained with blood and demolished for ghoulish curiosity.

Both were metaphors for the other battle that continued long after the war.

It was a battle of ink, not infantry, and pens that slashed like swords. From a soldier's point of view, Shiloh veteran Ambrose Bierce's sardonic definition of an "egotist" fit the Civil War generals like a boot in a stirrup: "A person of low tastes, more interested in himself than in me."

The generals refought their battles in books, essays, speeches and

---

49 On June 16, 1862, just two months after the battle, an item in *The Cincinnati Enquirer* announced a local exhibition of "portions of Shiloh Church from Pittsburg Landing." The congregation worshipped in the woods until a new church was built in 1875. The replica now preserved by the US Parks Service was built in 1952.

reams of official reports. They passed blame for defeat like a contagious disease and took credit for victory the way a hypochondriac pops pills.

For some, it was not just a matter of reputation, but political advantage. By the end of the war, many generals ran for Congress and the Senate. US Grant had gone from Shiloh bungler to Appomattox hero, and was lifted on the shoulders of the Republican Party as a candidate for President in 1868.[50] The man from Point Pleasant and Georgetown became the second US president from Ohio.[51]

He was among the most unpretentious and ordinary generals. His shabby, unkempt clothes, trademark cigar and slouch hat made him appear to be the least likely suspect chosen from a lineup as a perpetrator of politics. But Grant reluctantly agreed to run to reunite the nation. And once he threw his battered hat in the ring, it would have been beyond inconvenient for the dead controversies of Shiloh to rise again from their shallow graves.

So his staff massaged the record. Maybe it was jealousy. Wallace had risen from colonel to major general in just six months. Spite, loyalty, self-protection, or the military version of bureaucratic mendacity— whatever the reason, Grant's top aides used their initial reports to hang the blame on Lew Wallace for nearly losing Shiloh. And just as Halleck cultivated rumors that damaged Grant, Grant allowed the sabotage of Wallace with his silent consent.

Hang it on Wallace

John A. Rawlins was a friend and neighbor of Grant from Galena, Illinois. Before the war he was a lawyer, known for his imaginative cursing and quick temper. He became Grant's right hand of protection as his chief of staff. It was Rawlins who stopped Grant's hand when it reached for one drink too many. And it was Rawlins who sent Grant's

---

50 Grant and the Republicans supported enfranchisement for blacks. He defeated New York Governor Horatio Seymour, whose Democratic Party platform opposed voting rights for African Americans. Grant appointed his longtime friend and aide John Rawlins Secretary of War.

51 The first was William Henry Harrison, who was president for one month before he died in office on April 4, 1841.

military secretary Lt. Col. William Rowley to find Wallace on the first day at Shiloh and urge him to turn around his Third Division just as it approached the battlefield in the enemy's rear.

"I hold Rowley's coming my greatest quarrel with fortune," Wallace said years later. "Oh, if he had remained lost in the woods an hour longer."

According to a damaging report by Rawlins that Grant approved, Wallace got lost and was in no hurry to reach the battle. "His presence then would have turned the tide of battle, which was raging with great fury; saved lives of many brave men, and ere the setting of that crimson spring day's sun secured to us certain victory," Rawlins wrote.

He also insisted that Grant had ordered Wallace "to Pittsburg Landing, on the road nearest to and parallel with the river, and form in line at right angles with the river." According to Wallace and other witnesses, that was a lie. Rawlins also knew it was untrue, because he had dictated the original, vague order.

That official report conveniently ignored Grant's careless lack of preparation and unsigned, incomplete orders to Wallace to join Sherman's position on the right. It never mentioned that Wallace told Grant that his men had improved the Shunpike Road to get to Sherman faster and avoid the swampy River Road. And it conveniently buried Rowley's mistake that added hours to Wallace's march with "orders" to turn around and head east to the River Road across an unmapped bog. Rowley told Wallace that order to backtrack came directly from Grant.

Had Wallace been left alone to join the battle, his Third Division would have marched six miles, not 15, and could have arrived in time to outflank and possibly rout an exhausted Confederate attack.

A year after the Battle of Shiloh, Grant escalated the slander of Wallace in a report to Halleck and the War Department. He wrote that he wished he had replaced Wallace before the battle. "I do not doubt but the (Third) division would have been on the field of battle and in the engagement before 10:00."

That was impossible. Grant's orders didn't get to Wallace until 11:30.

Maj. Gen. Henry Halleck

For years, Wallace was unable to respond to the insinuations that he had been a coward and shirked his duty. The report was passed up the chain of command to General Halleck, who hid it from Wallace and the public. In March 1863, Wallace implored Halleck to explain why he had been relieved of command, begging for a chance to correct "prejudices against me." He got no reply.

He appealed to his friend Gen. William Tecumseh Sherman for advice and support. Sherman knew Wallace had not been lost and did not take the wrong road. But Sherman was loyal to Grant and kept his silence for 30 years while Wallace was made the scapegoat.

Lew Wallace's romantic ideals of glory and honor were vandalized and demolished like the Shiloh Church.

But the truth would not stay buried.

For years after the war, Wallace's men defended him and called out Rawlins and Grant's staff as liars. Col. Fred Knefler of the 79th Indiana Volunteers was Wallace's adjutant at Shiloh. He said, "The people are being educated to the lamentable fact that our highly educated West Point officers are an abominable humbug and nuisance to the country."

Grant knew his orders to Wallace were muddled, and also knew that Rawlins and Rowley had made things worse. But Halleck, Grant and Grant's staff—Rawlins and Rowley—controlled the official record, and that record shaped stories reported by the press. Newsprint history made "lost" Wallace the cause of Grant's near defeat at Shiloh.

When Wallace was about to be sent to Grant at Corinth, Grant said he wouldn't take him unless his rank was reduced. Wallace's ego, dignity and pride made him an easy target for what he called "the West Point clique." But considering how his initiative and leadership on the second day at Shiloh helped seal the victory for Grant, it was a low blow. Wallace was left in the dark again about the "awful mystery" of why he was put on the shelf as decisive battles continued.

Halleck's slow-motion march

On April 11, as the wounded and dead still littered the ground, Halleck arrived at Pittsburg Landing, demoted Grant, and took over a reinforced army of more than 100,000 to capture Corinth.

He quickly proved beyond a doubt that he was unfit to take command.

He stalled for three weeks before he finally set out to face the enemy—at the pace of a crippled, comatose snail. "Old Brains" moved his huge army just one mile a day, so he could stop to build elaborate siege defenses every night. He took more than a month to cover the same 20 miles that the Confederates had marched in three days. Apparently, the West Point professor was afraid that a small, beaten army under Beauregard would attack an army three times bigger.

He was "leisurely," "deliberate," and definitely not "energetic," according to accounts written in 1883.[52]

At one point, as Yankee troops had a chance to overrun Corinth and take the city easily, Halleck called them back.

When he finally arrived in Corinth on May 28, Beauregard had cleverly slipped away. "Old Brains" was outsmarted. The Confederates

---

52   *A Bird's Eye View of Our Civil War*, Dodge, 1883.

left behind a band to make noise, drummer boys to keep campfires lit and an empty train that went back and forth over the same stretch of track to imitate the arrival of fresh troops, while Beauregard's army and artillery escaped along with most of the townspeople.

Beauregard's final evacuation orders said, "Whenever the railroad engine whistles during the night near the entrenchments, the troops in the vicinity will cheer repeatedly, as though reinforcements have been received."

Wallace said, "Corinth was not captured. It was abandoned."

When the Union soldiers marched in, they found dummy guns and scarecrow gunners. They found Confederate graves and a deserted town overflowing with sick and dying soldiers.

But Halleck told a different story in his report to Washington. He called it "A victory as brilliant and important as any in reported history." He claimed to have captured 10,000 prisoners and 15,000 stands of arms.

Wallace and Maj. Gen. John Pope, whose Army of The Mississippi reinforced the Union, said Halleck's claims were fantasy.

'Oh, the lies'

In July, Halleck was recalled to Washington. But not to be fired, reprimanded or demoted. In one of those patented idiocies that are a Washington specialty, he was *promoted* to command all Union armies. Halleck's lies and schemes worked; he had promoted myths of his own success until they became a Washington reality.

Wallace, romanticizing old virtues such as honor, was unable or unwilling to play that game.

Frustrated by Halleck's glacial march to Corinth, he had vented to some visitors from St. Louis who stopped at his tent for a drink. He told the men how disgusted he was by Halleck's order, "It is better to retreat than to fight," and explained how Corinth would have already been taken if he had been in command.

Then as they left he realized: "Good Heavens, those fellows are of Halleck's staff... They will go straight and tell him all that I have told them!"

Wallace knew his rash comments were like "a loaded car with broken brakes rushing on a downgrade." Sure enough, they were Halleck's men. "I had made an enemy, and he was in a high place and going higher."

Halleck quickly put Wallace at the top of his list of civilian "amateur" soldiers he detested. When Wallace returned to Indiana on leave that summer, he was left there. No reprimand. No public accusations. He was quietly relieved of command without explanation and his Third Division that was so effective was dissolved.

He found out about it in a meeting with Indiana Gov. Oliver Morton, when Morton asked him to do recruiting speeches.

Wallace tried to decline, but "the governor then brought out a telegram from Secretary (of War) Stanton ordering me to report to Governor Morton. It required no Solomon to tell that this was the very thing lying big in my fear—I stood actually relieved of my command. The division was no longer mine."

He said, "I did not ask for this, governor. Did you?"

"Yes."

"It was an unwarranted liberty with me, sir. I will make the speeches for you rather than do nothing, but you have laid me on the shelf."

"I can get you back again."

"You are influential, I know, but not where that power lies."

"Who is the man?"

"General Halleck."[53]

Looking back, Wallace wrote, "Every life has its ups and downs. There is a difference, however; some, once down, stay down. Now suddenly somebody in the dark gave me a push, and I fell, and fell so far that I could almost see bottom. Who did it? It took me a long time to find out."

Like Gen. George Patton 80 years later, Wallace was a brilliantly effective warrior whose sin was to be unconventional, outspoken and unwilling to play the petty political games of military advancement. He did not know how to "get along," or keep his mouth shut. And like Patton before Normandy, he was yanked from the game and put on the bench.

---

53 *Lew Wallace; An Autobiography. Vol. II - Scholar's Choice Edition.* 2015.

He continued to defend Grant and refuted rumors that Grant had been drunk at Shiloh. Later, as Grant ran for President, Wallace abstained from public comments about Grant's failures at Shiloh.

Then in 1868, the widow of General WHL Wallace of Illinois found papers that showed he was preparing to send his cavalry to meet Gen. Lew Wallace on the Shunpike Road, not the River Road, in case of an emergency. Clearly, both Wallaces knew what route he would take to the front.

Looking back, Lew Wallace wrote, "Oh, the lies, the lies that were told to make me the scapegoat to bear off the criminal mistakes of others in connection with that awful first day! It took General Grant about a quarter of a century to work himself up to an admission that I was blameless. But think, my brave comrade, think of what I suffered in the meantime! Think, too, that the slanders have gone into history, and may never be corrected."

BOOK II:
NEW MEXICO TERRITORY

1879

Palace of the Governors, New Mexico.

JORNADA DEL MUERTO

('JOURNEY OF DEATH')

'This here is Mr. William Bonney'

Duck was all sinewy gristle and bone, with sharp elbows and a sharp wit to match. But he had a calm and easygoing presence that belied a surprising animal strength for a slender man. Gillespie had once seen him walk up and grab a plunging, kicking mule by the ears and slam its head into the sideboards of a wagon so hard it sent wood splinters flying.

"Splinters from the wagon, not the mule's head," Gillespie would add when he told the story.

The effect on the mule was an immediate improvement in personality—but Duck's placid expression was unfazed. "There," he said to the mule, almost kindly, as if he had just fed it a fresh carrot.

Gillespie never asked where Duck got the nickname. It seemed impolite and perhaps imprudent, seeing as what happened to that mule. But the story he heard whispered behind a flattened hand was that Duck had escaped an ambush by Comanches, finally chased down and bridled a swaybacked runaway draft horse, then rode the broad-beamed mare sixty-some miles back to Santa Fe. By the time he arrived he was so sunburned and bowlegged, the Indian scouts gave him an unpronounceable name that meant something like "Burning-Face-Duck-Walking."

Shortened to Duck, or "El Pato" among the Mexicans.

Cavalry troopers who had been with Duck in a gunbattle had another version. They insisted the nickname originated in Duck's uncanny ability to avoid occupying the same space with flying arrows and bullets. He was a living and breathing illustration of the soldier's Psalm 91:7: "A thousand shall fall at thy side, and ten thousand at thy right hand; but it shall not come nigh thee."

Duck leaned forward and stirred the fire with a sun-scorched branch of mesquite, then poured himself some cowboy coffee, holding onto the hot tin coffeepot with the grimy rag of a neckerchief he wore. It had once been yellow but was so stained now it would be almost invisible lying against the parched brown desert soil.

"Second day at Gettysburg," Duck said in his soft drawl, swirling his cup to savor every last pinch of coffee grounds that had been dumped in the pot. He said it as if answering a question Gillespie hadn't asked. It was their evening ritual. As they relaxed after a long ride through the desolate New Mexico landscape, they would spill stories of their vivid experiences in the recent war. They were not things they could share with someone who had not "seen the elephant." But it made them feel better a little bit, like throwing up when you're room-spinning, knee-walking drunk. Anyone else might be offended or shocked by the grisly things they described. But other veterans, also under the influence of pain and nightmares, would take it in stride. Or even laugh. They understood.

"Let it all out," was their attitude, like patting a retching man on the back.

Gillespie waited. Duck continued. "That vainglorious fool Dan Sickles ignored his orders from General Meade and led our corps nearly a mile out in front of the rest of the army, hunting for headlines to boost

Gen. Dan Sickles. Mathew Brady, 1863.

his political career in New York. We should have been with Meade on the high ground up on Cemetery Ridge."

Duck stared at the fire and paused, as if still too angry to go on. The War Between the States had ended 14 years ago, but memories still bled like fresh wounds. They were camped on the outskirts of an abandoned cluster of sun-blackened adobe houses—low, mean buildings with short doors and stingy windows. They looked like jails for outlaw children. The dark interiors were occupied now by scorpions, snakes and poisonous spiders, so Gillespie and Duck kept their distance.

Gillespie said, "Didn't Sickles say Meade's orders were confusing?"

"He has said a lot of things, never the same alibi twice. Meade ordered him to extend our left in front of Little Round Top. If he had followed orders, there would have been no need for all those heroics there. Instead, he led a charge directly into one of the South's best generals, James Longstreet.

"We should have been on Cemetery Ridge, behind big boulders that made better cover than the walls of Fort Selden. But just as you might expect from a simpleminded state senator and stuffed-shirt congressman, he put the whole Union line in peril, leading us right into Longstreet's cannons and infantry with no support on either flank. It was the most lunatic thing I ever saw. There was no honor in it, just butchery, all for his pride and political career. After the war he even tried to claim that he saved Little Round Top."

"I heard he lost his leg to a cannonball that day," Gillespie said.

"And deserved it," Duck said, as hot as the glowing end of his fire stick. "Too bad they didn't take his head, for all the men he got killed. Four thousand died in the Peach Orchard and the Devil's Den so he could play hero."

"There must be something deadly about peach orchards," Gillespie said. "We had a terrible fight in one at Shiloh, too. I heard Sickles kept the leg."

"That's true. The man had some grit. They say he pickled the dang thing and gave it to a museum in Washington. He still goes to visit that leg. Who would do something like that? They should have used it to kick the New York hooey out of him. He got his headlines, though. And got elected. We used to sing a ditty about him while we were marching."

Duck recited:

"New York Senator Dan Sickles
"As a Gettysburg general was quite fickle.
"He killed four thousand men
"To get himself elected again,
"Now his leg's in a barrel of pickles."

Gillespie chuckled. "Wasn't he the same one who shot and killed his wife's lover before the war and got clean away with it by claiming he was insane?"

"That's the low-down dog. Being crazy was probably the only thing he ever claimed that was accidentally true." Duck looked up at Gillespie. "I never met a man so vain and stupid. How about you?"

"Well," Gillespie said after a while. "In Corinth, I saw men who drank gray, putrid water right off the top of shallow graves and half-buried, rotting horses." He shook his head as if to shoo off a fly. "That was fatally stupid. They soon died in a way I wouldn't wish on my worst enemy. But when we got there we were so thirsty, I have to confess it crossed my mind to take a sip of that gray rotgut myself."

"Nobody talks much about Corinth," Duck said.

"No, coming so soon after Shiloh, it was mostly overlooked. People forget that Corinth was the reason for Shiloh. It was our objective all along—the railroad crossroads of the South. Capture Corinth and cripple the Confederacy, they told us.

"And everyone back East was focused on the battles in their back-yard. Except for Shiloh and the way it shocked the people back home, things that happened here in the West were mostly ignored. Same as our escapade out here today in the *Jordano del Muerto*."

"Maybe better ignored," Duck said, spitting coffee grounds that stuck to his lips into the fire. "And please don't tell me how this godforsaken place got that cheerful 'Journey of Death' name. I'd druther not know about that... among other things we are doing here today." He gave Gillespie a sidelong look.

Gillespie nodded his acknowledgment with a smile, then continued. "Corinth couldn't compare to Shiloh for the harvest of dead. Now *there* was a journey of death if I ever saw one. But in a manner you can't measure with paper and ink, it was worse. What men went through during the siege of Corinth was terrible in some ways that combat couldn't match. The Rebs had pulled out by the time we took it. They left nothing behind but dying men and stinking graves. About 5,000 men too sick to raise a hand in surrender.

"That little crossroads town was overwhelmed. There was not enough water, and what they had was bad to start with. The town was surrounded by a stinking bog they called the Dismal Swamp. There was not enough food. The Rebs were eating rotted horsemeat crawling with maggots, and who knows what else. And the water... Well, when a man drinks from puddles that seep up from dead men, you can imagine how desperate he is."

Duck leaned back against his saddle, laced his hands behind his head and stretched his long, bowed legs out. "That's something I just can't never shake loose of, that aching thirst in battle. There was never enough water in my canteen. I felt like I could drink a lake and still be parched. But I pray to God I never get *that* thirsty."

"I heard the Rebs called it the 'Miracle Cure,'" Gillespie said. "It was guaranteed to put you out of your misery."

He took off his hat and wiped his brow with his shirtsleeve. The New Mexico sun was low, but still hot enough to raise blisters on the back of a shovel. "But as for stupid," Gillespie continued, "you have to go right to the top. I mean the generals. I was regularly amazed at how small those big men could be. The bigger they looked, the smaller they behaved. Your General Sickles was unfortunately common."

Duck grunted agreement. He said, "Like most soldiers, I guess, I always reckoned they were better men than the rest of us. Patriots. True believers in the cause. Wiser. Better trained. Men who get heartsick over the loss of life and limb just like the rest of us."

Gillespie nodded. "We thought they fought for us the way we fought for each other more than for blue or gray. But the more time I spent around generals and their bootlick lackies, the more I discovered they fought each other as hard as they fought the war. It was a surprise they won any battles at all when they were so busy looking backward to see who might be gaining on them in medals and headlines."

"Sickles all the way," Duck nodded.

Gillespie took a sip of his coffee. "It was like two wars. There was the one we fought. And there was another one going on behind the scenes—a war for promotions and glory and their prideful notions of honor."

Duck asked, "Such as?"

"Such as our boss the governor."

"I share most of your admiration for the man who made me an agent of the Territory of New Mexico," Duck said, "but the way I heard it he brought a lot of that scandal onto himself."

"That's fair enough. General Wallace was a genius in many ways. There was nobody I'd rather be with in a fight. If you saw him leading an assault on his charger Old John, you'd agree. But the rest of the time the man could not get out of his own way. He took to orders the way a wild horse takes to a bridle. He always figured he knew better, and usually he was right. But if there's one thing the military can't tolerate, it's being wrong."

"I heard he ignored Grant's orders at Fort Donelson," Duck said.

"Yep. And a good thing he did. He pulled Grant's bacon out of the fire more than once, and President Grant sat back mum while his staff made Wallace a scapegoat. What's that saying about lies from that book-writer you like, Twain?"

"The difference between a lie and a cat is that a cat has only nine lives," Duck quoted.

"That's good. But I'm thinking of the other one: Something about how a half-truth is the most cowardly lie."

"Andrew, you never did say how was it you enlisted in Michigan and wound up with Wallace in Tennessee and Mississippi?"

"Probably about the same as how a Kentucky boy like you ended up with Sickles at Gettysburg. Long story," Gillespie replied.

"I got nowhere to go and all day to get there. Tell on."

Gillespie dumped out the rest of his coffee, laid down the cup and continued.

"It was like this. On that first day at Shiloh in the Hornet's Nest, we were fighting for our lives, almost surrounded. Someone who had rank heard I could ride and next thing I know they pulled me off the line and sent me hell-bent back to Pittsburg Landing. I was ordered to report to Grant or anyone in charge and tell them we needed reinforcements the way a choking man needs air. Then on the second day, they put me on a fresh horse again, to carry orders to Wallace on the right flank. He must have liked me, because he kept me so busy I wore out two horses, sad to say, shot dead or blown. After that, I just stuck with him. There wasn't much left of my company."

"Something tells me there is a lot missing between that choking man and your friendship with Governor Wallace. But how is it you learned so much about the scrap between Wallace and Grant if you weren't with Wallace when the battle began?"

"Wallace himself. That man can talk. If you have an hour or two to spare, just say 'Shiloh' and stand back, it will all come bubbling out like an uncorked barrel of beer. After he told me some things, I made it my business to find out more. I lost a lot of friends on the first day, waiting for reinforcements that never came. I wanted to know why. I felt like I owed it to them."

"Look over there to the south," Duck interrupted. "That cloud of dust. Might be our new friend William."

"I'm pretty sure he does not favor that name."

"That's why I do," Duck chuckled. He reached back and drew his lever-action Henry rifle from its scabbard on the saddle he leaned against, worked the lever to seat a .44 caliber cartridge and then settled back with the Henry across his knees.

Gillespie watched the wispy dust cloud, thought briefly, then drew his .44 Colt single-action army pistol, also chambered in Henry .44

rounds. It saved confusion, which was a lesson both men had learned the hard way in the war. There was nothing so dispiriting as finding out in the middle of a hot battle that some drunk quartermaster's assistant or crooked contractor had sent .60 caliber balls to a regiment armed with .58 caliber rifles.

He hefted the heavy pistol, spun the chamber to check all six rounds, slid it back into his holster and then eased it back out just a touch to make sure it would draw freely.

Then they both sat back to wait, watching the heat-shimmered riders draw closer.

"I make it more than one," Gillespie said.

"Three," said Duck.

Gillespie nodded. Duck had sharper eyes.

"So, you were saying?" Duck asked.

"Seems to me Wallace might have been able to patch things up with Grant if not for General Halleck, who could make Dan Sickle out like a raw political amateur. Now there's a man who never let men's lives get in the way of his political ambitions. But the final straw for Governor Lew was letting himself be pulled into quicksand by those sidewinders in Washington."

He held a hand over his eyes and squinted. Indeed, it was three riders. Gillespie figured they had been watched and the extra man was no accident: three on two, if things came to that. But they were still a long way off, so he told Duck about how Wallace was invited to testify at the Congressional Joint Committee on the Conduct of the War in July, 1862, just three months after Shiloh.

"That committee was more interested in ruining Grant and Lincoln than it was in finding anything out about Shiloh," Gillespie said.

"I'm hardly surprised," Duck replied. "If not for prevarication there would be no such things as politicians. 'Take the truth out of him and he will shrink to the size of your hat. Take out the malice and he will disappear.'"

"Twain again?" Gillespie asked.

"Yep. I believe he had Sickle in mind."

Gillespie laughed. "I like the one where he said Dan Sickle loves his lost leg more than the one he kept."

Duck was an avid reader and often surprised Gillespie and others with his "book larnin'," as Duck put it. Most were even more surprised when they discovered he had been a lawyer in Lexington before the war. He chose the North. His older brother fought for the South. He survived. His brother died at Antietam. Kentucky, Missouri, Tennessee—a lot of border states sent brothers to opposite sides in the war. Some even met across the points of their bayonets.

Gillespie resumed and told Duck how Wallace had burned his last bridge. Led on by oily flattery and clever, leading questions from the congressmen, Wallace agreed that he was surprised when Grant gave no orders to pursue the routed Confederates on the second day at Shiloh. Then he answered yes, he was certain they could have been driven out of Corinth, making the siege of the city unnecessary and sparing thousands. Asked if his own initiative had saved victory at Fort Donelson, Wallace again replied, "Yes."

The implicit criticism of Grant made a splash in Washington and rocked the Union Army, sending ripples across the West Point pond.

"And then he pointed that finger right at Halleck," Gillespie recalled. "He said Grant didn't pursue because Halleck had ordered him not to, and Halleck was nowhere near the fighting. In a few sentences, he managed to paint Grant as Halleck's fool, and Halleck as a yellow rocking-chair general."

"I can see as how that might put chiggers in their drawers."

Gillespie chuckled and glanced up at the riders. Closer now. "Looking back, though, it worked out for the best. Without Lew's mistakes, he would never have wound up in Cincinnati. And if he wasn't there, Cincinnati could have been blasted to craters and rubble like Vicksburg. But that's another story."

Gillespie stood. As the three men on horseback approached, he could hear the creak of saddles and jingle of spurs. "I reckon we oughta get on our feet and greet our distinguished guests," he said, loud enough for the visitors to hear without catching the twinkle of humor in his eye that made Duck smile.

Gillespie was five foot eight. Duck was about four inches taller. Gillespie was thick and broad in the shoulders, with shaggy reddish-brown hair under a hat the color of dust. He had a square jaw and deep blue eyes that looked friendly and innocent most of the time. At other times they could look as hard and pitiless as glass marbles. He had a happy spirit that was wounded but not crushed by the war.

Duck was lamppost slender, lanky, with no hair under his brown sombrero. He claimed his hair all fell out while he was recuperating from typhus in a field hospital after Gettysburg. He said he'd rather be mistaken for a cattle-rustling vaquero in a sombrero than get a blistered, sunburned scalp again. His cynical sense of humor masked a hair-trigger intolerance for injustice and cruelty that no amount of battlefield brutality could extinguish.

McCarty, a.k.a. Bonney, a.k.a. Antrim, a.k.a. the Kid

The riders reigned their horses from a slow walk to a halt, three abreast, but did not dismount. They looked down at Duck and Gillespie, enjoying the superior perch to make a point that was largely lost on their hosts.

Billy the Kid

"I don't see no badges," said a small, raggedy man on the left who wore the threadbare, faded britches of a Confederate infantryman. Duck placed the accent in Arkansas.

"We have 'em. Don't wear 'em unless we have someone important to impress," Gillespie said.

That went clean over the small man's head, but Gillespie noted the hint of an amused smile around the lips of the man in the middle. That one was better dressed, wearing dusty dark-blue suit pants, a black vest and a shirt that had once been white, with a reddish string tie. The Kid had worn a dark derby in the wanted posters, but now sported a black sombrero, like Duck's. He did not wear bandoliers of cartridges shown on the posters. Just a simple gun belt with what looked like a Colt .45 in easy reach and an 1873 Winchester rifle in his bleached leather saddle scabbard.

"You must be William McCarty," Duck said, pretending to be amazed, as if he was finally meeting the hero of his favorite dime novels.

The man Duck addressed lost his smirk and scowled under his sparse beard. The look in his eyes almost made Gillespie take a step back, it was that glaring hot.

"No?" Duck said. "Then we must've showed up for a meeting with the wrong desperadoes."

"Wrong," the third man on the right said. He looked like a Mescalero Apache to Gillespie. He had a small head and a receding chin framed by long, greasy braids that drooped from his hat like snakes hanging from a tree. Knife wounds or ritual scars decorated his face and upper arms. When he opened his small mouth, the few teeth he had were shy and stayed hidden in the back of his mouth.

Unfortunately, his thoughts did not. His obsidian eyes had the empty look of casual cruelty.

"Ahm sure y'all know of whom you are talking to," the first man said. "This here is Mr. William *Bonney*. You may have heard of him as Billy the *Kid*. Our pardner over there is *Toad*." He said the names like a circus ringleader introducing death-defying trapeze artists and lion tamers.

As he said "Toad," the small Reb with wild, dirty-blond hair poking out of a derby tipped his head sideways toward the Apache on the right, whose upper body swelled up like the corpses Gillespie and Duck had seen and smelled at Shiloh and Gettysburg.

"As for me, those who live to tell of it call me *Cottonmouth*," the little man boasted with a lifted chin. He had a face that was permanently pinched, as if he smelled the hot breath of the law somewhere nearby. His small mouth seemed too crowded with all the crooked teeth that Toad was missing. He wore tall black boots over his pants, with tarnished silver inlays to match his silver spurs. His left hand was lacking a thumb and two fingers.

"Is that because you resemble a rattlesnake, or did you get that name from the way you talk like your words are smothered by a mouthful of cornbread?" Duck asked, sounding sincerely curious.

The Kid turned slowly and gave Cottonmouth a long look that contained a question in raised eyebrows: "You gonna just sit there and take that?"

Cottonmouth's face puckered and ticked, his eyes blinked rapidly, his twitchy good hand darted toward his sidearm—and then stopped, hanging in space. Duck said quietly, "I wouldn't." Duck's Henry rifle was aimed from the hip, squarely between Cottonmouth's narrow eyes.

"Three," Toad said in a voice that seemed to come from the bottom of a dark well. As he said it, he pointed at his friends. Then he pointed at Duck and Gillespie: "Two." His face betrayed nothing. No fear. No humor. It was as blank as a cloudless Western sky. But the eyes said murder as plain as a headline.

Gillespie gave that a beat, then replied mildly, as if describing seating arrangements for a wedding party: "Duck shoots the garter snake, I shoot the Kid, and you will be unable to hit anything on that bucking pony once the gunfire commences."

They were all silent, waiting.

"You could *try* that," said the Kid.

Gillespie nodded and said, "Yes, I could, but let's all just calm down a bit and get to our business before someone meets an untimely death like so many of Mr. Bonney's unfortunate acquaintances."

The Kid seemed to think it over, decided to take it as a compliment, sighed and began to dismount. "I will hear what these Pinkertons have to say, boys," he said. Gillespie caught the insult in the word, but heaved an inner, silent sigh of relief. This was supposed to be a truce mission, not a gunfight. His Shiloh thigh ached just thinking about getting shot again.

As the Kid dismounted, Gillespie noted that he was an average-sized man, not really a kid. The prominent front squirrel teeth gave him away if there was any doubt which one was the notorious Kid Antrim, a.k.a. Henry McCarty, a.k.a. William Bonney. And his voice explained the nickname. It sounded like a boy's voice before it breaks into manhood.

"Let's give 'em space, Duck," he said softly, backing away with his hand still resting on the walnut grip of his holstered pistol.

"Dang," Duck said, "I was hopin' to see that Toad croak."

Cottonmouth refused to dismount and stayed in the saddle, radiating menace, glaring at Duck, who smiled back. Toad dismounted to stretch his legs and stood by his horse, rummaged in his saddlebag and found some dark, boney thing to gnaw on, oblivious, looking into the distance but missing nothing. The Kid squatted near the fire and

Interior of the Tunstall Store in Lincoln, New Mexico, where
the Lincoln County War shootout took place.

accepted a cup of coffee from Duck with a polite thank you, beaming an engaging smile at Gillespie. "Play your hand," he said.

The Lincoln County War

Two days later they were back in Santa Fe, sitting in The Palace of the Governors, a sprawling, crumbling adobe mansion built by the Spanish in 1610, now inhabited by the latest territorial governor.

"So, nobody got hurt. Did you deliver the message?" Gov. Lew Wallace sat behind a dark wooden desk that was the color of pipe tobacco and the size of a fat man's coffin.

Gillespie was seated in one of two armless chairs with cloth-covered cushions, facing the desk. The chairs were brocaded in a faded floral pattern that looked out of place in the West, especially in contrast to the dusty, sun-blasted men who sat on them. "Well, I think Cottonmouth got a bad bruise on his pride, but otherwise, yes, we delivered your message."

"And?"

The shaded office behind thick adobe walls was like a drink of cool water for Duck and Gillespie. They were in no hurry to leave. Duck answered: "Well, by the look on their faces like a dog listening to a squeezebox, I don't think any of them quite understood the word 'amnesty' until Andrew explained it. But I think the Kid is ready to cooperate and keep his word that he won't kill anyone for a few weeks."

"More than willing," Gillespie nodded with a wry smile. "Unless provoked."

Lew Wallace had tried for various appointments. He was offered an ambassadorship to Bolivia but declined. Finally, in return for his campaign help, President Rutherford B. Hayes sent him to New Mexico, to stomp out a raging brushfire called the Lincoln County War. In his spare time, he was also expected to deal with raiding Apaches led by bloodthirsty war chiefs named Victorio and Geronimo. By comparison, Bolivia would have been as civilized as Paris.

"All three were Lincoln County Regulators, I suppose," Wallace said.

"They like to call themselves that when they aren't pretending to be ranch hands," Gillespie nodded, rotating his dusty hat in calloused, cracked hands. He tapped a boot toe and saw tiny puffs of dust rise from the Turkish carpet.

Duck added, "I figure the only thing they know about ranching is shooting up the whiskey bottles they empty behind a barn. They look like they are held together by dirt, mischief and meanness. That Apache made my trigger finger jumpy. I think I've seen that hombre somewhere before. He is bad medicine down to his toenails."

"What about the Kid, McCarty?" the governor asked. He sat behind a stack of strewn, handwritten pages he had been reading and scribbling on when they walked in.

"Billy the Kid, also known as Bonney, also known as McCarty, also known as Antrim, is definitely a Regulator," Gillespie replied. "He claims to have killed twenty-one men. I am skeptical, but I wouldn't bet my last peso against it. The other two are just ticks on the hound's back. They go where he goes."

"Sometimes I think it was easier duty at Crump's Landing," Wallace grumbled, running a weary hand through his long hair. He still wore his bushy veteran's beard like a badge of honor. "We knew who the enemy was. He was the soldier in butternut and gray who stood out in the open and shot at us like a man. But here...." He shook his head and lit a small cigar, leaving the box open and spinning it around on the desk toward Gillespie and Duck, who each helped themselves and did likewise. Gillespie pulled a stick match out of his vest pocket, lit it on his boot sole, and shared the flame with Duck.

Wallace continued through fresh clouds of blue smoke that swirled in shafts of morning sunlight. "I'm beginning to get the lay of the land, and I don't like it. We have this dry-goods merchant Dolan and his gang called 'The House,' with his mob of outlaws. Then there's John Chisum allied with Alexander McSween, who was partnered with John Tunstall until Tunstall was killed by Dolan. When was that?"

"Last February 18," Gillespie replied. "That's what really lit the fuse on this range war."

"That lit a fire under President Hayes, as well," the governor nodded.

"Tunstall was a British citizen, and that got their ambassador involved all the way to Queen Victoria. It may be hard to tell around here, but we are allegedly a civilized nation now. It won't do to have range wars and Apache raids in the Territory of New Mexico. So tell me more. You've been here a while longer than I have."

"Just a few months," Gillespie said. "When we got here to reconnoiter, as you officers like to say, Tunstall was already dead, killed by the Jesse Evans Gang, which was part of The House run by L.G. Murphy and James Dolan. The Irish had control of all the dry goods and government contracts to supply beeves to Fort Sumner and the reservations. They did it mainly by rustling—a specialty of the Evans Gang. And they liked to rustle from the biggest cattleman in the Territory, John Chisum."

"Which is why Chisum took sides with McSween and Tunstall?"

"Correct. You could say Chisum started it all by hiring about seventy outlaws to run homesteaders off their land. The sod-busters retaliated by rustling his cattle, of which he has more than enough to spare. The Evans Gang stole enough of Chisum's cattle to feed New York. Then Tunstall showed up—a proper Englishman with money, class and a pedigree—and upset Dolan's Irish monopoly by competing for dry goods sales and cattle contracts. Dolan sent Evans to kill Tunstall, thinking that would be the end of it. He didn't reckon on Tunstall's Lincoln County Regulators, including the Kid, who vowed to get even. First thing they did, the Regulators shot down Sheriff Bill Brady and Deputy George Hindman, both Dolan's men. They ambushed them from the corral behind the Tunstall store on the main street in Lincoln."

'I'd druther be shot'

Wallace frowned. "There's nothing I abhor more than bad lawmen," he said. "Are you sure this is local history and not the Old Testament? You have more actors than the works of Shakespeare."

"Just pretend you're back in Washington and it will seem as simple as a McGuffy's Reader," said Duck, sounding innocently helpful.

Wallace gave Duck a piercing look and waved his hand at Gillespie to continue the saga of the Lincoln County War.

Gillespie said, "I don't know about Shakespeare, but Lincoln County has a lot in common with Babylonian debt slaves in the Old Testament. The House owned everything. Murphy and Dolan would drive the homesteaders and farmers into debt, then take all their land and live-stock if they couldn't pay."

He explained the two camps: Murphy, Dolan, the Evans Gang and Sheriff Brady on one side. On the other, McSween, Tunstall, Chisum and their Regulators, including the Kid. "It comes down to Dolan's House and the Evans Gang against McSween and his Regulators."

Duck said, "After the Regulators killed Brady and his deputy, they say the Kid ran right up to the sheriff's body while lead was still thick in the air, to grab his new Winchester rifle that Brady had took when the Kid was in jail. One of Brady's deputies got off a shot that hit two men with one bullet, including the Kid."

"Serious?" the governor asked.

"Apparently not serious enough," Gillespie replied. "He's still alive."

"Tell him about that jail," Duck said.

"The 'carcel," as they call a jail here, was just a dark, stinking hole in the ground. That's where Brady put the Kid when he was arrested for stealing horses. Tunstall posted his bond, freed him and gave him a job, so he was plenty loyal to the Englishman."

"So he has at least one scruple," Wallace said. "I am beginning to apprehend why President Hayes said Lincoln has the most dangerous street in America. What happened next?"

"The Brady killing was followed by the Fritz Ranch Gunfight. Six killed over two days. The Regulators shot at US Cavalry troopers who were sent to restore order. Two Regulators who were taken prisoner were murdered. The newspapers named it the Blackwater Massacre, but they are prone to overstatement at times."

"At *all* times," Wallace agreed. He picked up a folded copy of the Santa Fe *Weekly New Mexican* and read aloud: "As this state of lawlessness and disorder dragged along and crime and fiendish atrocities became rife, the news spread further into the interior of that state of desperadoes." He looked up and added, "By 'state of desperadoes,' they mean Texas."

He continued reading: "And soon recruits flocked to the scene of violence and spoilation until the lawless mob numbered hundreds of as villainous characters as ever went untouched by justice."

"I'd say that's surprisingly close to the truth," said Duck. "But ain't that the same newspaper that called Governor Axtell 'a pure and upright man' *after* he was removed for corruption?"

Wallace smiled and asked Gillespie, "What else?"

Gillespie continued. "Well, then all hell broke loose last July at the Battle of Lincoln. It was a five-day shootout. They say the rifle fire was so hot two men jumped into the bottom of a privy for shelter."

"I'd druther be shot," Duck mumbled.

Gillespie continued: "McSween's house, where the Kid and others were holed up, was burned down. There were three women and five children in the house, but the sheriff and Dolan's men held their fire to let them escape."

"Chivalry is not dead," Wallace said. He had read the *New Mexican* reports on the battle published in Santa Fe on August 10, 1878:

> Night comes on and the sheriff's men rush the house in which McSween and his best men are stationed. They cling close to the walls under the portholes and take some of the windows. The house is fired; shots and shrieks, curses and yells, and the fierce flames make the night a horror.

Wallace asked, "And Colonel Dudley from Fort Stanton was involved, in violation of the recent Posse Comitatus Act that prohibits military participation in civilian law enforcement?"

"That's right. Both gangs had lawmen with warrants to serve. The bright line of the law is harder to find than the Mexican border out here. But yes, Dudley showed up with forty soldiers, a Gatling Gun and a twelve-pound howitzer. He pointed that cannon at the McSween gang's hideout. Those outlaws wisely vamoosed, so he dragged the big guns over to McSween's house, threatened to blow it up and then set it on fire."

Duck added, "Witnesses told us Colonel Dudley may have also been involved in the bushwhacking of that lawyer Huston Chapman."

"Why would Dudley care about Chapman?"

"Susan McSween hired Chapman to sue Dudley for arson of the McSween house. And Sheriff Brady was an officer at Fort Stanton with Dudley. So there's a connection between the House and the Fort that goes deeper than cattle contracts."

"I see," the governor said. Gillespie could see, too: The governor was angry. His blue eyes were cold and flinty—it was a look that made Gillespie grateful he was not the target, just the messenger.

"This is the same Colonel Dudley that Colonel Hatch tried to remove as unfit for duty because of drunkenness?" Wallace asked.

"Yes, that's your man," Duck said.

"Hatch is an honorable officer," Wallace said—a high compliment. "I would trust his word about Dudley."

Gillespie said, "You may recall Colonel Hatch at Corinth. He led the 2nd Iowa Cavalry."

"Yes. Those Iowa boys were hard fighters. I'm also eager to see Colonel Hatch's Buffalo Soldiers. They bring to mind what I implemented in Cincinnati when I formed the Black Brigade. Please continue, Sergeant Gillespie," Wallace said.

Gillespie reached over to help himself to another cheroot, lit it, dropped his smoking matchstick into an ashtray on a low table between his chair and Duck's, and resumed. "During the Lincoln shootout, the Dolan gang captured a few dozen Regulators, including twenty Mexicans. McSween was caught in his burning house and offered to surrender, then changed his mind and started shooting—so says the sheriff who is Dolan's man. A deputy named Bob Beckwith was killed. So was McSween. The Kid ran through the flames and escaped through the back of the house, shooting his way out."

Duck said, "Some are saying McSween hired all those Mexicans so as to get some killed and stir up another border war. Mexico flew its flag over all this Territory not thirty years ago."

Wallace sat forward with a concerned frown. "Lawlessness, political corruption, bribery, range war, arson, cattle rustling, Indian raids and now war with Mexico? I'm beginning to see why Governor Axtell was so resentful about being removed. Who would want to miss so much sheer *adventure*?" He spoke the last word sarcastically.

"Axtell was as crooked as a scorpion's tail, and just as poisonous," Duck said. "About what you could expect from a San Francisco lawyer and crony appointed by President Grant."

Wallace let that pass. He would not speak ill of his old commander, but he wouldn't argue about it, either. He turned back to Gillespie. "This town of Lincoln sounds lively."

Duck blew out a blue cloud of smoke and interrupted, "Ya know, Governor, maybe you should get a couple of those rangers like they have in Arizona Territory. Down in Tucson they like to say 'One riot, one ranger.'"

"I *have* rangers," Wallace snapped. "They are smoking my cigars right now."

He turned again to Gillespie. "This Kid of many names wants me to meet him in Lincoln? He wants to accept my offer of amnesty?"

"It's about two hundred miles south," Gillespie said. "Rough country down there between Capitan Peak and Fort Stanton, where they are trying to corral the renegade Apaches. Yes, he says he will testify. He can't qualify for amnesty. Too many wanted posters and warrants for murder. He wants a pardon."

"I've heard from Susan McSween. She said the lawyer Chapman was killed by Dolan. And she seems to like this Kid."

Duck observed, "I've noticed women seldom protest about injustice when homely outlaws are hanged."

Gillespie laughed and added, "He's likable. Women find him attractive. They say he can sing like a bluebird, speaks fluent Spanish and charms the senoritas out of their bloomers. Cardsharp, too. But I've seen his type before. Like the soldiers who enjoyed their killin' work too much. He has that look about him. And she's right about Dolan killing Chapman. But the way things work around here, Dolan has nothing to fear. He was acquitted for the murder of Tunstall. He's glove-tight with the Santa Fe Ring and their crooked courts."

Governor Wallace nodded. "I've had the misfortune to make the acquaintance of some of those dry-goods tycoons and cattle barons who rule the state. Hard to credit, but many are called lawmakers. Apparently there's nothing in that job description about keeping the laws they make."

He asked about the Apache problems. Duck offered his theory that the range war over cattle contracts was connected to the Apaches. "Dolan and Tunstall are mainly fighting over contracts to starve the Indians on bad beef and pocket the profits," he said. "Victorio is not stupid. He's been on the warpath ever since his people were sent to San Carlos in Arizona Territory. We keep runnin' out of land nobody wants, and they don't want it either."

Wallace paused, looked out the window at the sunbaked plaza, and came to a decision: "I feel like taking a long ride to get a look at this Territory I am supposed to pacify. Let's pay a visit to Fort Stanton. And Lincoln."

A week later, they rode for southern New Mexico: Wallace and Gillespie on horseback, Duck driving a wagon with supplies and tents for what he liked to call their "Jornada del Muerto."

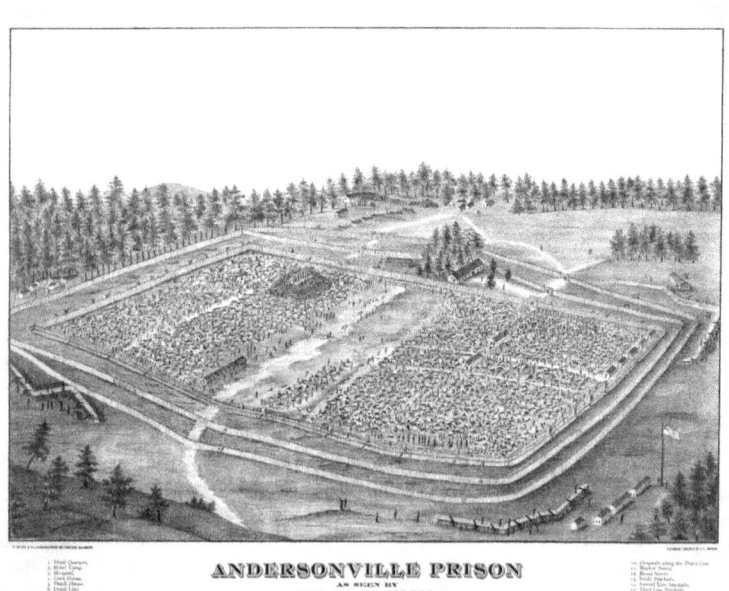

ANDERSONVILLE PRISON
AS SEEN BY
JOHN L. RANSOM,
AUTHOR AND PUBLISHER OF "ANDERSONVILLE DIARY, ESCAPE AND LIST OF THE DEAD."
WASHINGTON, D. C.

From Corinth to Andersonville

At the end of their second day's ride, after a meal of tortillas, beefsteak and pinto beans, their evening discussion turned to Apaches, outlaws and, as always, the recent war.

Wallace was especially interested in Corinth. "I had hoped to return after a brief leave home in Indiana," he told Gillespie and Duck, "but I found out later General Grant would not have me there. The reason for that remains unclear."

"Just as well," Gillespie said. "It was a lot easier taking Corinth than leaving it. Mississippi in the summer is hotter than Hell's bakery. I figured the Rebs were smart to let us cook there all summer and come back in October. We had it for 16 weeks before Gen. Earl Van Dorn came back with fresh reinforcements on October 3. By then I would have gladly paid them to take it. One of the Confederate officers called it 'A sickly, malarial spot, fit only for alligators and snakes.' He had it right."[54]

"Bad groundwater to begin with," Wallace nodded. "It was filtered through layers of decaying limestone and magnesium oxide. Hardly fit to water weeds. Beauregard reported later that he lost as many men to sickness at Corinth as they lost in combat at Shiloh." He returned to the battle. "I heard that Van Dorn's infantry fought their way as far as the steps of the Tishomingo Hotel at the railroad crossroads before being driven back in defeat."

"You heard true. The fighting was house to house in the heart of town. We fought all day the first day. They attacked at ten that morning, and Van Dorn finally called a cease fire at six o'clock, after driving us back two miles until we were backed up to the outskirts of Corinth. Like Beauregard at Shiloh, he was that sure of victory the next day."

"And the following day was worse?"

Gillespie nodded and described the extreme slaughter at a fortified artillery emplacement, Battery Robinette, which was taken by the Confederates, then retaken by the Union soldiers. At one point,

---

54   Cozzens, Peter. *The Darkest Days of the War: The Battles of Iuka & Corinth*, 1997, University of North Carolina Press.

canister, grape and shells hit the Confederate attackers so hard, the ground was a solid mass of writhing bodies. "It was bayonets, swords, knives, muskets for clubs, bare hands...."

Gillespie had to stop, unable to continue.

After a polite silence while Wallace and Duck looked at anything but Gillespie, Duck changed the subject. He asked Wallace about his experience as a jurist in two historic trials: the assassins of President Lincoln and the war criminals who ran the Andersonville Prison where so many soldiers were starved, beaten and shot.

Wallace got up, went to his trunk in the wagon, and came back with a black portfolio. "Being a brother of the bar, you would know how tedious and boresome court can be," he told Duck, handing him the book. "These are the sketches I made while we listened to testimony, testimony and more testimony."

As Duck paged through, he marveled at the lifelike inked drawings of defendants and witnesses who had testified about the notorious commandant of Andersonville Prison, who caused the death of so many Union prisoners from starvation, contaminated water, disease, beatings, torture and shootings. There were sketches of prisoners who looked like barely human skeletons, their eyes somehow expressing the hopeless agony.

A few pages away were the conspirators in the assassination of President Lincoln: David Herold and Lewis Powell, who attempted to assassinate Secretary of State William Seward while John Wilkes Booth shot Lincoln; huge George Atzerodt, who was sent to kill Vice President Andrew Johnson, but got drunk; and ringleader Mary Surratt, wearing a veil. All were hanged.

Duck was moved. "They aimed to kill Grant too?"

"Yes," Wallace said. "Seward was badly cut about the face with a knife, but survived. The actor Booth was hunted down, trapped and was shot in the neck in a burning barn."

Gillespie said, "I heard the assassins were buried next to the gallows where they were hanged."

"Correct," Wallace said. "We wanted no attention drawn, no

Painting by Lew Wallace of the conspirators in the assassination of President Lincoln. Booth was already dead during the trial. Wallace painted him with the green pallor of a corpse. Courtesy of the General Lew Wallace Study & Museum, Crawfordsville, Indiana.

opportunity for Southern sympathizers and Northern Copperheads to martyr them. President Johnson released the bodies to their families about four years later. There were others involved and sent to prison. Better they are all erased from history."

Gillespie said to Duck, "General Wallace knew Lincoln."

"I met him a few times," Wallace said. "Knew him? I don't know if anyone really knew the man. He was as deep as a river. A man of great faith and humility."

"So he would not have punished the South as President Johnson and others have done?" Duck asked.

"I believe you're correct," Wallace said. "His goal was to unite the nation, not rub turpentine into the wounds. He said as much at Gettysburg."

'The Dead Line' sketch by Lew Wallace.

Duck thumbed back through the sketchbook. "I had some friends who were sent to Andersonville and were never seen again," he said. "Thank you for being part of the court that gave them a small measure of justice."

Wallace said, "Thank you for your appreciation, but it was no more than any man would have done with evidence of such barbaric cruelty."

"Is it true that 10,000 died there?"

"The records showed 45,000 went in and 32,000 survived. Most who came out were never the same men again."

He described the prisoners' testimony about mass graves, lack of food and water, epidemic dysentery, typhus and lice, men who died of exposure because they were not given firewood. Some prisoners preyed on weaker men and took clothes from the dying.

"What was that camp commander's name?" Gillespie asked. It was Duck's turn to be silent, alone with his thoughts.

"Captain Henry Wirz," Wallace answered.

"Hanged."

"Yes. That was our verdict. A lot of the civilians throughout the South were starving as well, but that could not excuse how Wirz refused to exchange suffering prisoners to relieve the horrible crowding."

Duck pointed to one of Wallace's drawings titled "Over the Dead Line." Wallace explained, "It had its beginning in this wise: one of the witnesses before the Wirz commission testified that a poor prisoner, half dead with thirst in the Andersonville pen, crawled under the bar called the 'dead line' to reach a brook outside where the water was not so poisonous. The sentinel on duty shot him dead, and the tin cup dropped from his hand beyond the boundary. That is my scene. Only the fallen figure in faded-blue uniform, the stream for which the starving man longed, a portion of the stockade, the bar, the cup."[55]

Wallace got up, went to his trunk again and retrieved another notebook. He sat down on the ground again and began to read:

"The proof under the second charge shows that some of our soldiers, for mere attempts to escape from their oppressors, were given to ferocious dogs to be torn in pieces; that others were confined in stocks and chains till life yielded to the torture, and that others were wantonly shot

Captain Henry Wirz

---

55 *Lew Wallace; An Autobiography. Vol. II - Scholar's Choice Edition.* 2015.

down at Wirz's bidding, or by his own hand. Here, in the presence of these pitiless murders of unarmed and helpless men, so distinctly alleged and proved, justice might well claim the prisoner's life. There remain, however, to be contemplated crimes yet more revolting, for which he and his co-conspirators must be held responsible.

"The Andersonville Prison records contain a roster of over thirteen thousand dead, buried naked, maimed and putrid, in one vast sepulcher. Of these, a surgeon of the Rebel army, who was on duty at this prison, testified that at least three-fourths died of the treatment inflicted on them while in confinement; and a surgeon of our own army, who was a prisoner there, states that four-fifths died from this cause. Under this proof, which has not been assailed, nearly ten thousand, if not more, of these deaths must be charged directly to the account of Wirz and his associates."[56]

He paused, took a drink of water from a tin cup, cleared his throat and continued to read from his notes.

The boss of hell on earth

"This wide-spread sacrifice of life was not made suddenly or under the influence of wild, ungovernable passion, but was accomplished slowly and deliberately, by packing upwards of thirty thousand men, like cattle, in a fetid pen, a mere cesspool, there to die for need of air to breathe, for want of ground on which to lie, from lack of shelter from the sun and rain, and from the slow, agonizing processes of starvation, when air and space and shelter and food were all within the ready gift of their tormentors.

"This work of death seems to have been a saturnalia of enjoyment for Captain Wirz, who amid these savage orgies evidenced such exultation, and mingled with them such nameless blasphemy and ribald jests, as at times to exhibit him rather as a demon than a man. It was his continual boast that by these barbarities he was destroying more Union soldiers than Rebel generals were butchering on the battlefield.

---

56   Ibid.

He claimed to be doing the work of the Rebellion, and faithfully, in all his murderous cruelty and baseness, did he represent its spirit. It is by looking upon the cemeteries which have been filled from Libby, Belle Isle, Salisbury, Florence, Andersonville, and other Rebel prisons, and recalling the prolonged sufferings of the patriots who are sleeping there, that we can best understand the inner and real life of the Rebellion, and the hellish criminality and brutality of the traitors who maintained it. For such crimes human power is absolutely impotent to enforce any adequate atonement."[57]

He closed the book with a gentle clap that seemed louder in the stunned silence.

Finally, Gillespie stated more than asked, "You wrote that as president of the commission that hanged him."

"Correct," Wallace replied.

Duck said, "I reckon hanging might have been too good for Wirz. But I can't abide that rough talk about hellish criminality and traitors of the South. My brother didn't die at Antietam as a traitor or a criminal. He believed in the cause and the War of Northern Aggression and Southern Independence. They just wanted to be left alone, but the Northern states held the whip hand in Washington and set out to destroy the Southern economy for their factories. We had many a discussion. That's how he saw it, and he was a good, honest man."

Gillespie said, "I would imagine the governor has mellowed a bit since that was written right after the trial." He glanced at Wallace, who said nothing, but nodded. "For my part, there were times when I thought the most fanatic John Brown abolitionists were as dangerous as the worst secessionists of the South."

"Such as Senator Sumner," Duck said. Sen. Charles Sumner of Massachusetts was nearly caned to death on the floor of the Senate in 1856 by South Carolina Representative Preston Brooks, after Sumner used a speech in the Senate to slander and ridicule Brooks's elderly, infirm cousin, Sen. Andrew Butler.

---

57   Ibid.

"A lot of men might have done as Brooks did," Gillespie admitted.

"It's easy to do wrong in the name of right," Duck said.

"Twain again?" Gillespie asked.

"No, that's Ezra Mason," Duck said, pointing a finger in his own chest and stating his seldom heard, God-given name.

Wallace raised his eyebrows. Gillespie smiled and asked, "Do you mean Sumner or Brooks did wrong in the name of what's right?"

"Both," Duck said. "Abolition of slavery was the greatest blessing we gave to the future by all that dying and suffering. But I am not ashamed to say that the honor and independence of the South was a good cause, too. And that has been lost."

"Please expound on that," Wallace said.

"Beware what you ask for," Gillespie quipped.

Duck smiled at Gillespie, then said, "First, the Articles of Confederation that preceded the Constitution said, I quote, that the states had 'sovereignty, freedom, and independence, and every power, jurisdiction, and right, which is not by this Confederation expressly delegated.' Those limits on the federal government were added to the Constitution or it never would have been ratified. All powers not specifically delegated to the central government were retained by the states. Three states even demanded that the right to secede be included before they would ratify the Constitution. Ipso facto, all states had that same right to secede if the federal government became oppressive."

"I warned you," Gillespie said. "Now you've got him talking like Julius Caesar."

Wallace laughed. "You make a strong case, counselor," he said. "All true. But among other things, the Union won control of the 'official record,' as they say in Washington. Back in 1860 before it all started, I wrote that 'However we go into the war, we shall come out of it abolitionists.' That case is now closed."

After a pause, Gillespie said, "I take some comfort to believe that our grandchildren and great-grandchildren will no longer be divided by hostility over race. Then our friends and brothers did not die in vain."

Duck nodded his grudging agreement. "Napoleon said, 'What is

history, but a fable agreed upon.' And history will say the casus belli—
that's 'cause of war' for Andrew—was abolition, because that looks better
in books than plundering cheap Southern cotton for the Northern textile
mills. But I fear we have unloosed the tyranny of central government
that our Founders feared. Soon the reach of Washington will wrap its
greedy fingers around the last free land here in the West."

Wallace gave Duck a fresh appraisal but chose to say nothing.
Gillespie hunkered down, drew up his blanket against the cooling desert
air and said, "I begin to see why lawyers are so often misunderstood.
Wherever two or more are gathered, they begin to speak in tongues.
Good night, gentlemen. Long ride tomorrow again. We start at sunup."

The next evening, they rode into Lincoln. The town was subdued,
guilty, ashamed like a wifebeater, eager to forget and be forgiven. They
stopped by the Tunstall store to reprovision. It was a long, desert-brown
stucco building with bullet marks on the outside and inside, still showing
scars of the shootout. Tunstall and McSween were buried side by side
behind the store under crude wooden crosses framed by a lonesome

The Torreon in Lincoln, New Mexico, built by Spanish
settlers for protection from Apache raids.

desert sky and low foothills dotted with stunted juniper scrub and sun-tortured snakeweed, mesquite and creosote.

"Word travels fast," Duck said, noting the cold glances and furtive stares from the locals.

"If this goes wrong, we're outnumbered by cutthroat store clerks and outlaw schoolmarms," Gillespie winked.

"I will make a dash for that stone silo," said Duck, nodding down the road in the direction of a squatty round stone tower with narrow gunports, called the Torreon. "We could hold out there until we run out of cartridges."

The store clerk grudgingly directed them to the home of Squire Wilson, conveniently across the dusty street from the Torreon, where Dolan's gang took cover to shoot at McSween's gang. John B. "Squire" Wilson, the justice of the peace who had lent an occasional legal veneer to the recent bloodshed, lived in a modest house. He had the last word on frontier justice in a county that was bigger than some states and covered a quarter of the New Mexico Territory.

But first they took rooms at the Worley Hotel, a long, low building of mud-colored adobe that looked like a bunkhouse, with a shaded wooden porch behind square white pillars.

That night after dinner, as the governor waited in Wilson's parlor, he took the opportunity to cross examine Judge Wilson about events in the past 13 months since the Lincoln County War broke out in February 1878. He found some of the answers less than persuasive. Just after 9:00 p.m., right on time, there was a knock at the door. It was Wilson's home, but it was the governor who said, "Come in."

The man who entered was alone, as agreed. Wallace had warned him by letter to tell no one about the meeting and come by himself. The Kid stood in the doorway, looking uneasy, holding his Colt .44 in one hand and a Winchester rifle in the other. He wore his sombrero, a dark shirt and a weathered vest over dark, chalk-striped pants tucked into tall boots. A bright red bandanna was tied around his neck.

"I was sent for to meet the governor at nine o'clock. Is he here?"

Wallace stood, extended his hand and said, "I am Governor Wallace."

The Kid introduced himself as "Kid Antrim," but explained that that was his stepfather's name. Wallace assured him his promise of protection would be kept. The Kid holstered his pistol and took a seat, and the negotiations began over cups of Wilson's coffee. Wallace knew the Kid was not a drinker.

Wallace had seen more than his share of random slaughter and senseless evil. He was not impressed by the young shootist. But he needed the Kid's testimony to prosecute the men who had murdered Susan McSween's lawyer, Huston Chapman. That would not be the last indictment and trial, but it was a good start. Chapman had been gunned down in cold blood almost immediately after Wallace had issued an amnesty to call a truce in the range war.

The ambush of Huston Chapman

The Kid agreed to talk and candidly described the killing. James Dolan and others, including Billy Campbell of the Jesse Evans gang, had been drinking to celebrate the range-war truce when they saw Chapman walking down the street in the dark at about 10:00 p.m. They stepped in front of Chapman to block his way and Campbell demanded to know who he was.

"I am Huston Chapman," was the brusque reply. "What do you men want from me?" Chapman had been riding all day and was tired.

Campbell pulled his Colt pistol and poked Chapman in the chest with it. He ordered Chapman, "Dance!"

Chapman coldly replied, "I don't propose to dance for a drunken mob."

Dolan and Campbell answered with gunpowder and lead. Both fired their guns—Dolan from behind and Campbell point-blank into Chapman's chest. As he collapsed in the street, Chapman cried out, "My God, I am killed!"

The gunshots were so close his clothing caught fire and lit the boots and faces of the men who had killed him.

Yes, the Kid said, he was certain the gunmen were Campbell and Dolan. He described how Chapman's body burned in the street while Dolan laughed and Campbell crowed about finally killing Huston

Chapman. Then they stumbled off to the nearest saloon for another drink.

The Kid joined them at the bar and offered to go put a pistol in Chapman's hand so it would look like self-defense. Instead, he used the excuse to slip away and rode out of town with his Regulator friend from Texas, Tom O'Folliard. The truce between Dolan's gang and the McSween Regulators had lasted only a few hours.

Once he got started, the Kid poured out details of other killings, hideouts and crimes by the Dolan gang. By the end of the meeting, Wallace offered the Kid a deal: He would be "arrested" for show and held in jail for his own protection while he testified in court, then released despite two warrants for his arrest on charges of murder.

The Kid thought it over, and agreed. His court testimony led to the arrests of Dolan and Campbell, and Wallace followed up by obtaining indictments of more than 50 locals who had been involved in the Lincoln County War on both sides.

By the time he got back to Santa Fe, General Hatch, commander of the Military District of New Mexico and the 9th Cavalry, had removed Colonel Dudley.

But Wallace didn't reckon with the corruption of New Mexico and the Sante Fe Ring. Campbell escaped from the Lincoln County Jail. Dudley was found not guilty of arson. And Dolan was acquitted of murder and remained a powerful business and political leader in the Territory.

When the Lincoln County prosecutor ignored Wallace's amnesty and threatened to hang the Kid for murder, the outlaw killed a deputy, broke out of jail and went on another murder spree, claiming at least four more lives, including three lawmen, before he was finally hunted down by a posse and shot to death in 1880 by Lincoln County Sheriff Pat Garrett. Wanted posters offering a $500 reward were circulated on orders from Gov. Wallace, who had signed the death warrant for the Kid.[58]

---

58 In 2002, New Mexico Gov. Bill Richardson announced that he would investigate granting a pardon to Billy the Kid. In 2010, as he left office, he decided a pardon was not justified. He was unable to find that Gov. Lew Wallace had ever promised one.

Before he was shot down, the Kid swore he would kill the governor.

Wallace wrote to his wife Susan: "The Lincoln County reign of terror is not over, and we hold our lives at the mercy of desperadoes and outlaws, chief among them 'Billy the Kid,' whose boast is that he has killed a man for every year of his life. Once he was captured, he escaped after overpowering his guard, and now he swears when he has killed the sheriff and the judge who passed sentence upon him, and Governor Wallace, he will surrender and be hanged. His own words: 'I mean to ride into the plaza at Sante Fe, hitch my horse in front of the Palace, and put a bullet through Lew Wallace.'"[59]

Looking back years later, Wallace summarized the range war and his efforts to finally end it by declaring martial law with permission of President Hayes and the help of the US Cavalry:

"I could not possibly have stopped that trouble by civil means, and, accordingly, I was forced to resort to arms. I received the statements of the judges why they dared not hold court in certain districts. The United States marshal told me that he had a large number of warrants which he dared not serve and could not find deputies rash enough to attempt service, when they knew their lives would pay the penalty. The military commander at Fort Stanton sent a list of the murders that had been committed in his part of the county.

"I forwarded these combined statements to President Hayes, and asked him to proclaim an insurrection in New Mexico, which he did. That was the only way for me to have the use of the troops for the purposes I desired. I finally had four companies of cavalry for two months, and at the end of that time the desperadoes were driven out of the country, the armed factions were broken up, and the best grazing section of country in the United States was opened to immigrants." [60]

In November of 1878, the Santa Fe *New Mexican* reported, "Thanks to the energy, tact and superior executive ability of Governor Wallace,

---

59   *Lew Wallace; An Autobiography.* Vol. II - Scholar's Choice Edition. 2015.

60   Ibid.

peace and order has been again restored to our much-abused sister Lincoln County."

Wallace had less success with the powerful Santa Fe Ring, which blocked his efforts to reform the corrupt politics of the Territory. And the members of the powerful Ring were only slightly less threatening than the Apaches and Comanches, of whom he said, "Kindness makes no impression upon them. They are what they were when the Spaniard found them—cunning, bloodthirsty, untamable."

In 1880 he wrote to Washington, requesting more troops to fight Indians.

"I suppose very few people in the East know that there is an Indian war now in progress in New Mexico, but such is the fact. Last year an Apache chief, Victorio, a man seventy-five years old, became hostile and took to the warpath.... With a band of seventy-five warriors, he succeeded in uniting tribes always hostile to one another before, and in a few weeks he had three hundred well-armed followers. He has held his own against us from that day to this, in open conflict, and he has murdered about one hundred men, women, and children in the most horrible manner. He is an enemy not to be despised."

More than 400 were killed by Victorio's renegades, including an incident Wallace described vividly:

"I set out from Santa Fe to investigate difficulties in a remote region of the Territory ... with a strong guard armed with Winchester rifles. After a few hours, Indians began to appear in the distance. My men held up their Winchesters, and the savages were careful not to approach within range.

"When we reached the town, the people came out and greeted us with amazement; had we been newly raised from the dead, they could not have shown greater awe. We presently learned the cause. After returning the salutations of the officials, we followed them to the church. There was the explanation. Before the altar were 16 corpses, men, women, and children, some of them shockingly mutilated. The head of one little child had been crushed to pieces by beating it over the wheel of a wagon. In view of all this butchery, it is no wonder that they considered our escape little short of a miracle."

Wallace finally left New Mexico in the spring of 1881, glad to shake the dust off his heels and take a more civilized post as Ambassador to Turkey for President James Garfield.

In his autobiography, he wrote, "Every calculation based on experience elsewhere fails in New Mexico."

His wife Susan agreed. "General Sherman was right," she wrote. "We should have another war with Old Mexico to make her take back New Mexico."

BOOK III:
WARRIORS, SPIES AND COPPERHEADS

'Buffalo Hunt on the Southwest Prairies' by John Mix Stanley, 1845.

A FIRST-RATE SOLDIER
'Buffalo chips are scarce'

In 1850, America flooded the vast empty spaces of the West like a rain-swollen river spilling over its banks. Hundreds of thousands of frenzied prospectors were pouring into California to strike it rich in the Gold Rush. New territories larger than most European countries beckoned "pilgrims" to sink their sod-busting plows into lands that were conquered in the recent Mexican-American War. The young nation stretched its legs out all the way to the Pacific.

Lt. Henry Heth, age 25, fresh out of West Point in the Class of 1847, found himself far beyond the ragged edge of civilization in a huge, wild, empty place on the map that had no name yet other than Indian Country. The land was so desolate, barren and treeless that the US Army had to build its fort out of layered sod.

Heth was happy to be there. He welcomed the adventure.

He was temporary commander of Fort Atkinson, west of Dodge City in the Kansas Territory, the newest military base on the Sante Fe Trail in the unmapped frontier. It was the kind of assignment that would make most men's knees rattle like dice in a cup: Protect wagon trains of hopeful, naive, often defenseless settlers from merciless tribes of Plains Indians, whose methods of torment were as exotic as their names—Apache, Comanche, Kiowa, Pawnee, Cheyenne and Arapaho.

Defeating Mexico had thrown open the gates on almost half of the North American continent. But the excitement and dreams of the homesteaders were more than matched by the hostility and violence of Indians, who killed casually and carried off whatever they could take in raids, including wives, daughters and children.

The most savage attacks and battles during the post-Civil War westward expansion were still 15 years away, provoked by predatory Indian agents and the lies and betrayals by the "White Fathers" in Washington. But the clash of cultures was already throwing sparks, deadly enough to require US Army outposts to protect wagon trains and the families they carried.

At times, Fort Atkinson—called "Fort Sod" by the troops who had to endure it—was surrounded by thousands of hostile Indians who circled like sharks around a sinking prairie schooner. Inside the low walls of the fort, Heth had only 80 soldiers in his command.

To complicate the miseries of life in Fort Sod, all supplies, including firewood, building materials, clothing and the meager, rough comforts of military life, had to be hauled out on wagons from Fort Leavenworth nearly 400 miles away. Heth saw dozens of rattlesnakes wherever he rode. They were nearly as common as prairie dogs, and prairie dogs outnumbered the people. But even thousands of snakes and gophers combined could not match the legions of field mice that infested the sod mess halls, offices, sleeping quarters and stables.

Heth's requests for more troops were ignored or rejected. Only the mice, snakes and Indians seemed able to draw on inexhaustible reinforcements. During bitterly cold winters of impassable snow, subzero temperatures and howling winds, it could take months to hear even a scrap of news from cities such as St. Louis and Cincinnati. In the springtime, clouds of grasshoppers darkened the sky like smoke from grass fires and would descend like a biblical plague for days, covering everything, inside and out, and leaving no scrap of anything green behind. The soldiers breathed, ate and slept in dirt; it sifted from their sod walls, filtered through doorways and windows on the breath of a relentless prairie wind and settled on every surface, even on their eyelids as they slept.

Visitors to Fort Atkinson described what they saw in 1852:

> Our eyes were first greeted some ten miles distant from the post with a sight of the stars and stripes, waving over and among what appeared to be a close encampment of huge tents, but on nearer approach proved to be buildings of earth, the roofs of which were

covered with tent canvass or duck, to keep out the drifting snow in winter and the dust in spring and summer.

The scarcity of fuel and grass is the chief inconvenience experienced by this fort, though in other respects it is by no means agreeably situated—its location having been chosen solely with a view to the accommodation of the neighboring Indian tribes and the protection of the Santa Fe trade. The Arkansas River flows within a few rods of its walls, having a depth of three or four feet at certain seasons of the year; but in summer, like most of the prairie streams, its bed is generally nearly dry. The surrounding country is a barren waste, without vegetation, save a few shrub bushes and the crispy buffalo grass, diversified only by innumerable sand hills. No wood is to be had within thirteen miles; and "buffalo chips" once found in great abundance, are now quite scarce.[61]

Lieutenant Heth, as always, was undaunted and relished the hardships.

He requisitioned a dozen cats from Fort Leavenworth to control the mice, bought a pair of greyhounds to hunt jackrabbits, killed hundreds of rattlesnakes, protected the settlers when he could and earned the respect of the tribes as he hunted with the Indians.

"I had hunted buffalo so much with the Indians, who, as I have said, used only the bow and arrow in their hunts, and it seemed so easy to kill buffalo in that manner that I determined to try that method of hunting," he wrote almost 50 years later. "I found it to be the most difficult job I had ever undertaken."

Heth was the son of a wealthy Richmond, Virginia family, an aristocrat of the South, educated at the finest boys' schools and West Point. His family would have been scandalized to see him ride after the buffalo bareback, with only a rope for a bridle and reins, wearing nothing but a breechcloth. After missing with more than 100 arrows, he finally killed a buffalo cow. And his legend began to grow throughout the Army.

---

61   Leo E. Oliva, Fort Atkinson on the Santa Fe Trail, 1850-1854, Kansas Historical Society, summer 1974.

Henry Heth

On one jackrabbit hunt, his horse stepped into a prairie dog hole at full gallop and threw him across the plains, breaking his saddle like a pistol shot. The horse, his favorite, snapped its leg and had to be killed. He also lost the use of his left arm for 18 months. Probably a broken collarbone, but there were no x-rays, no pain medications except alcohol or laudanum made from opium.

By modern standards, Heth would be a superb athlete. He was known as the Army's best horseman, best rifle shot and most daringly reckless (and only) bow-and-arrow buffalo hunter in the West. On a bear hunt, he narrowly escaped being killed and eaten by a grizzly bear by climbing a tree like a cat. As they heard rumors of his exploits, his classmates from West Point probably shook their heads and smiled—or cursed.

An abominable student

He had finished dead last in his class of 1847, but first in popularity among most classmates, who loved him for his wild streak and the apoplectic fits he gave to their stiff-necked instructors and exasperated, high-collar commanders.

The words they used to describe him were hellion, instigator, rascal, reprobate, scamp, troublemaker, scoundrel, buffoon, prankster, rapscallion, rogue and incorrigible frolic. And others seldom spoken and never printed in those days.

His first roommate was removed and reassigned because the two "bad boys" were such a terrible influence on each other. His new cadet roommate was Ambrose Burnside.[62] "Burnside had but few demerits when he came to live with me," Heth wrote of his lifelong friend. "In a few months he had over a hundred. I must say I found Burnside a very ready pupil."

Henry Heth had an uncommon gift: He could laugh at himself. "My four-year career at West Point as a student was abominable," he said. "My thoughts ran in the channel of fun." He racked up 683 demerits for absences, pranks, smoking, "devilment" and vulgar language that was said to dishonor the moral standards established by George Washington.

He once taunted a classmate until the enraged cadet hurled a musket at Heth—with the bayonet attached. Heth was stabbed in the thigh within inches of his femoral artery. He was hospitalized, but not punished. The cadet who hurled his musket was not so lucky. Heth recalled that the young man was "severely punished—not because he had hurt me, for he would have been justified in killing me, but for a soldier to part with his gun was criminal."[63]

He must have laughed so hard he almost tore his stitches.

If Heth had stayed even another month at West Point he probably would have been booted out in disgrace, but he graduated by a whisker with his class of future Civil War officers and generals—and the entire faculty heaved a weary sigh of relief that he was finally gone.

The Army he joined was remarkably feeble following its recent victory in the Mexican-American War (1846-48): Just 9,640 enlisted men and 945 officers. He was too late to take part and win glory in that war, but was sent to Mexico anyway, where he served with the future military nobility of the Civil War: Winfield Scott; Lewis Armistead; Heth's cousin George Picket, who led the gallant and tragic Pickett's

---

62   Burnside's side-whiskers started a fashion known as sideburns.

63   Heth, Henry. *The Memoirs of Henry Heth*. Praeger, 1974.

Charge at Gettysburg; and a nondescript, sloppy, taciturn captain named Ulysses Grant.

Heth may not have crossed paths with Lew Wallace in Mexico. But they were destined to meet in 1862 in one of the most dramatic encounters of the looming War Between the States.

Like Wallace, Heth seemed to be everywhere. Indian fighter in Kansas and New Mexico Territory (1850-53); commander at Fort Kearny in Nebraska Territory (1853-60); officer on the Harney Expedition against the Sioux (1855). In one Indian battle, he fought alongside a first lieutenant named John Buford. The two would meet again as enemies across a historic battlefield as their troops fired the opening shots of the Battle of Gettysburg.

In 1858, he served in a campaign to restore peace to warring Mormons in Utah. His commander was Albert Sidney Johnston, who would be the greatest loss for the South at Shiloh.

In 1861, the curtain rose on the Civil War when South Carolina cannons opened fire on federal troops at Fort Sumter in Charleston. As a man of the South, Heth saw no other choice: He reluctantly resigned his commission as a captain in the 10th Regiment, *United* States Infantry, and offered his services to the president of the new Confederate States of America, Jefferson Davis.

Gen. Robert E. Lee. Mathew Brady, 1865.

"No act of my life cost me more bitter pangs than mailing my resignation as Captain of the US Army," he said.

Davis was happy to have Heth join the cause. "This is a first-rate soldier," he wrote in pencil on Heth's letter that he forwarded to his secretary of war.

Within two years—in 1862, the same year Wallace was fighting at Shiloh as the Union's youngest general at age 35—Heth was promoted to Brigadier General of the Confederate States Army, a few days after his 36th birthday.

He led his troops in several minor but bloody battles and endured the appalling, petty incompetence of two generals whose prewar political rivalry made them incapable of fighting anybody but each other.[64] After brief duty in Chattanooga, Tennessee, Heth was transferred in March of 1863 to join Gen. Robert E. Lee and his Army of Northern Virginia, reporting to Gen. A.P. Hill.

"Robert E. Lee was so far ahead of our other soldiers that our war produced that it appears a travesty to institute a comparison," Heth said after the war. "When God made Lee, he rested himself."[65]

In May he led his brigades into combat at Chancellorsville, where Lee defeated the Union although outnumbered two to one. The losing Union commander was Maj. Gen. Joseph Hooker,[66] who had replaced Heth's friend Gen. Ambrose Burnside as leader of the Army of the Potomac.

On July 1, Heth sent one of his brigades to a little Pennsylvania town, where they hoped to find shoes to replace boots that were so worn out many marched on bare feet.

As the troops came down dusty Cashtown Road that hot, dry

---

64   Confederate Jefferson Davis told one of the feuding generals "I think I will have to shoot you." The general replied, "Shoot me, that is all right, but for God's sake let me see you hang that damned rascal first."

65   Heth, Henry. *The Memoirs of Henry Heth*. Praeger, 1974.

66   "Fighting Joe" Hooker was a courageous veteran of the Mexican-American War and numerous battles during the Civil War, but he was indecisive and too cautious as a commander at Chancellorsville. He was buried in Spring Grove Cemetery in Cincinnati. Services were conducted at Newport Barracks in 1879.

summer day, they were greeted by rifle shots and a hail of bullets fired by a company of dismounted Union Cavalry, led by Heth's friend from Utah, Gen. John Buford.

The town was Gettysburg. The troublemaker Heth had ignited the biggest battle of the Civil War.

Old friends, new enemies

Buford's unexpected welcome stalled Heth's Confederates just long enough for the Union Army to take the high ground on the other side of town, which proved to be decisive in the three-day battle that followed. General Lee had issued orders to avoid engagement until he could scout the countryside. His cavalry "eyes and ears," led by Gen. James Ewell Brown "Jeb" Stuart, was supposed to give Lee the intelligence he needed. But they were missing somewhere to the east and had not reported for days.

Now it was too late to avoid a fight. Heth and his men had literally stumbled into the equally surprised Yanks. Buford's carbine rifles opened the battle, joined quickly by Heth's muskets and cannons. The bloodiest, most historic battle of the war had begun, and Heth was in the hot, deadly thick of it.

He was severely wounded in the head that day, but his division continued to fight on without him, and joined General Pickett in his futile assault of Cemetery Ridge two days later. Pickett's Charge on July 3, assisted by the remains of Heth's brigades, was nearly annihilated. Lee was forced to retreat in defeat.

From *The Memoirs of Henry Heth,* 1897:

My division was the leading division of the III Corps. My men were sadly in want of shoes. I heard that a large supply of shoes were stored in Gettysburg. ... General A.P. Hill said, as I had done, that he did not believe that there was any force at Gettysburg. ... I said to Hill, "If there is no objection, I will march my division tomorrow, go to Gettysburg and secure those shoes." Hill replied, "Do so."

Heth soon found himself battling an elite unit of the Union Army.

I struck the Iron Brigade and had a desperate fight. I lost 2,300 men in thirty minutes. I was struck by a Minié ball on the head which passed through my hat, and the paper my clerk had placed there [the hat was too large] broke the outer coating of my skull and cracked the inner coating, and I fell senseless.

Heth's North Carolina regiment went looking for shoes with 800 men that morning. They lost 86 killed and 502 wounded before noon. After Pickett's Charge, only 80 of the 800 were left walking. The head wound probably saved his life.

After Gettysburg, Heth recovered and fought on with Lee, as the Confederates waged a slow and bloody withdrawal back to the South. The Wilderness Campaign, Cold Harbor, the Siege of Petersburg (just 20 miles from his family home in Richmond, Virginia), the Battle of the Crater—Heth was there to the bitter end.

Along the way, he met his old friend Burnside—now Gen. Burnside of the Union Army. At the Battle of Spottsylvania Court House in May 1864, Burnside's troops came within 30 yards of Heth's trenches at a landmark of terrible brutality known as the Bloody Angle.

"My infantry poured a shower of lead into Burnside's troops," Heth said. "Burnside made three assaults at this angle; each was repulsed with great loss."

Heth reported that he lost one man. Counting bodies left on the field, he estimated Burnside's losses at 1,800.

About three months later, Burnside nearly got his revenge on Heth. At the Battle of Petersburg, Heth was in the Confederate line directly over a massive, buried mine Burnside was ready to detonate. But Heth and his troops were moved just before the Battle of the Crater erupted like a volcano on July 30.

Burnside's troops and a former mining engineer on his staff had tunneled under a fort that anchored the Confederate defenses. The end of the tunnel was packed with 320 barrels of gunpowder, making 8,000 pounds of explosives.

The fuse was lit, set to go off at 3:45 a.m., when all but the Union pickets were fast asleep. But somewhere down that dark tunnel, the

Gen. Ambrose Burnside

fuse fizzled and went out. As Burnside and the Union soldiers cursed the shabby materials they were given and waited and waited… nothing. Finally, two soldiers with nerves of steel volunteered to crawl back through the three-foot-wide tunnel entrance and follow the faulty fuse that might still be smoldering and could detonate at any second. They found the break, spliced it, lit it again and ran for their lives.

At 4:44 a.m., just before dawn broke, a deafening roar shook the earth and the sky was filled with flying bodies, arms, legs and fragments of men, riles, cannons, canteens, shoes, hats and fountains of blood-stained red Georgia dirt, as the underground mine exploded like a Civil War version of an atomic bomb. It was as if the sky was raining the disintegrated inventory of a butcher shop and armory.

The blast was so powerful, both armies were paralyzed and sense-less for 15 minutes. As they looked on, dazed and shocked, the smoke gradually cleared, the dirt pattered and thumped to earth, and they beheld a massive, smoking crater that was 170 feet long, 20 feet wide and deep enough to bury a three-story building.

The blast killed 278 Rebels almost instantly. They never had a chance to wake up before being vaporized. A huge hole was opened in the stubborn Rebel defensive line, big enough to drive regiments through to flank the position and end the siege. But the Union troops missed their chance. They had been briefed by a drunken officer who failed to warn them what to expect and how to exploit their rare opportunity. The officer was later court-martialed. But that was no comfort to the men who were killed by his derelict incompetence.

Hoping for cover from Confederate rifles as the enemy regrouped, they made a fatal mistake and scrambled down *into* the crater. As the soldiers in blue spilled into the crater like lemmings, they became easy targets for a Rebel "turkey shoot." The pit was so crowded with men, a bullet could hardly miss.

When it was over, the Confederates had 1,491 casualties including 361 killed, 727 wounded and 405 missing. But the Union side lost more than twice as many: 3,798 casualties, with 504 killed, 1,881 wounded and 1,413 missing.

Burnside's mine had blown up in his face.

Among the Union losses were most of two brigades of US Colored Troops, who were supposed to lead the assault, but were swapped at the last minute for white troops who had not been trained for it. General Grant had approved the last-minute swap to avoid the appearance that the black troops were being used as cannon fodder. He admitted later that his decision to substitute unprepared troops was a fatal mistake.

Many of the black troops were captured and brutally executed by the Confederates or shot down without mercy as they tried to surrender.

Burnside, already under a cloud for his lopsided loss to Heth at Spotsylvania Court House, was relieved of his command. The decision that doomed the attack was Grant's. But the scapegoat was Burnside.

Heth was spared by fate and missed the Battle of the Crater. But he followed Lee to the end of the line. They both offered their swords to Grant at Appomattox Court House, where "General Lee surrendered a famished regiment of his once-great army, April 9, 1865," Heth recalled.

As the Confederates marched in columns to surrender their arms, the hero of Little Round Top at Gettysburg, Brig. Gen. Joshua Chamberlain, ordered his Union soldiers to salute the defeated Rebs—and the men from the South returned the salute. It was a stirring expression of respect and honor on both sides.

One nation, under God

After the surrender, Grant shook hands with Heth and invited him to his headquarters to talk about their carefree days together before the war. [67] As they parted, Grant sent Heth off with two gallons of good whiskey—a generous gift. Confederate officers were paroled to go home and stay there, so Heth found a wagon and horses and returned to his home in Richmond, the former Capital of the Confederacy, now under Union occupation.

Typical of their era, men such as Heth and Grant lived by the code of a gentleman. Faith in God was their rock-solid foundation; grace and honor were the reins that guided their conduct. They fought bitterly and did their best to kill and maim each other. But when the war was over, it was truly over. Most found a way to forgive what they could not forget.

At the 50th reunion of Gettysburg in 1913, veterans in their 70s and 80s met again on the battlefield to swap stories in tart Northern accents and buttery Southern drawls. The only spark of rekindled hostility was a fight that broke out in the Gettysburg Hotel dining room when Southerners expressed their unchanged opinions of Abe Lincoln. Seven men were stabbed, all Yanks. None were seriously injured.

But that was the exception among more than 50,000 veterans who shook hands, put their arms around each other, took off their Stetsons, derbies and straw hats, tucked their chins into flowing white biblical beards and shed tears together at the landmarks where they had battled so fiercely and so many of their friends and brothers had died.

Ironically, the number of veterans at the reunion from every corner of the United States roughly equaled the total Gettysburg casualties of more than 51,000.

---

67   They recalled an incident when Grant was nearly killed by running his horse into a cow. Heth said, ":During the past three years I have wished a thousand times that you had broken your neck when you ran into that cow."

Most who had been in combat packed away their hostilities in the attic with their motheaten uniforms, tarnished swords and rusting muskets.

A dinner party in Washington, DC in 1877 was typical of their forgiveness, grace and honor.

It was hosted by Ambrose Burnside and Henry Heth at Burnside's home. The guest list was composed of top generals of the Union Army. President Grant was ill and unable to attend, but Heth sat down at 7:00 p.m. next to General William Tecumseh Sherman—whose name was hated in the South. Champagne and spiked punch flowed like rain gutters in a spring storm as the war stories stretched past 3:00 a.m.

As they dined, Sherman turned to Heth with a muttered remark about "You damned Rebels...."

"Stop, Sherman, and think," Heth interrupted. "If there are two men in the world that should go on their knees and thank the Almighty for raising up the Rebels, those two men are Grant and yourself. But for the Rebels, you would now be teaching school in the swamps of Louisiana and Grant would be tanning bad leather at Galena."

Sherman, the relentless fighter who famously said, "War is hell and you cannot refine it," clapped a hand on Heth's shoulder and replied, "That is so, old fellow."[68] Heth's good humor and biting wit had won that battle, at least.

A couple of weeks later, Burnside and Heth organized a second party for Confederate generals. "We had a delightful time, the dinner lasting about as long as the Federal dinner and quite as much champagne and punch were consumed," Heth said.

The Kentucky Campaign

But in 1862, five months after Shiloh, memories of their defeat at Corinth were still fresh wounds for the Confederate Army. Determined to avenge those losses, they had won decisive battles that summer at Murfreesboro, Manassas, and Second Bull Run. The Yankees were on the run and Heth

68   Heth, Henry. *The Memoirs of Henry Heth*. Praeger, 1974.

was now leading his troops under the command of another West Point graduate and Mexican-American War veteran, Gen. Edmund Kirby Smith. Smith, the son of a judge in Florida, had piercing eyes framed by receding hair and an advancing bushel of dark beard. His nickname in the Army was "Seminole."

A new counterattack by the South was being led by the Shiloh veteran Gen. Braxton Bragg and his Army of The Mississippi, to avenge Shiloh and Corinth and drive a wedge through the middle of the Union.

They would invade Kentucky.

PANIC IN CINCINNATI

'I hope to have God on my side, but I must have Kentucky.'

– President Abraham Lincoln

Abraham Lincoln in 1860.

As the whole nation watched, Kentucky balanced precariously on the knife-edge of neutrality during the Civil War. North and South wooed the Bluegrass State, but Kentucky pushed them both away with a firm "no." Louisville and Lexington were in the arms of the South, but the northern part of the state was married to Cincinnati, for better or worse.

It was a slave state that was the birthplace of the nation's most anti-slavery president, Abraham Lincoln. It was Southern in manners and culture but sent twice as many men to fight for the Union. Then, as if to atone after the war, all but a dozen of the state's nearly 70 Civil War monuments were dedicated to the Confederacy.

Northern Kentucky was the prize most coveted by North and South, because it was the gateway to the sixth largest city in the nation, the largest inland city, the critical manufacturing center that was strategically located on the Ohio River and along railroad lines that fed the growing nation: Cincinnati. The Queen City of the West was the hub where Western agriculture, the Southern slave economy and Northern industry met and shook hands on business.

And it was Kentucky that became the first line of defense for Cincinnati and the Union.

President Lincoln knew Kentucky was critical. "I think to lose Kentucky is nearly the same as to lose the whole game," he wrote in 1861. "Kentucky gone, we cannot hold Missouri, nor, I think, Maryland. These all against us and the job on our hands is too large for us. We would as well consent to separation at once, including the surrender of the capital."

The South saw it just as clearly. What Robert E. Lee hoped to capture in his campaign to Gettysburg in 1863—surrender of the nation's capital—could have been achieved in 1861 if Kentucky had eloped with the South, taking along Maryland and Washington, DC.

Jefferson Davis and his generals still coveted Kentucky from their side of the Mason-Dixon Line in 1862. It would give them a foothold in the heart of the Union, with a base to take Cincinnati and then march north through Ohio, on to Michigan, and seize or cut off the entire Great Lakes region from the Union, with all its resources and supplies. The gut punch of losing Kentucky could be fatal to Union morale, handing power to Copperheads and Democrats who wanted peace at any price. Lincoln could be checkmated. The North would be forced to accept a new nation in the South. Sweet victory would fall into their arms if Kentucky would only say "I do."

Lexington and Louisville harbored strong Southern sympathizers. President Davis and his generals hoped that when his troops in gray marched into Kentucky, the whole state would rise up in rebellion against the North. A new government could be formed in Frankfort, and the South would win by force what it could not have by consent.

Kentucky's most ardent secessionists included its governor, who strongly believed that the right to secede was implicit and explicit in the Constitution.

The lines dividing Cincinnati from Kentucky were as muddy as the banks of the Ohio River.

Kentucky had voted overwhelmingly against Lincoln in the 1860 presidential election,[69] while he narrowly carried Cincinnati, thanks to support in the growing German population of refugees from the failed 1848 revolution in Germany. But Cincinnati was not a Union city as much as a free-enterprise city. It was no coincidence that the leading daily newspaper was named *The Commercial Appeal*.

"Commercial appeal," defined the city's entrepreneurial spirit.

The hog slaughterhouses that gave Cincinnati its nickname "Porkopolis" were feeding the nation. Foundries on both sides of the river were booming, putting steel in the backbone of America. Riverboats built in Cincinnati transported local manufactured goods up and down the Ohio River on an interstate river pipeline of profits, rivaled only by expanding railroads that connected in a tangle of tracks in Cincinnati.

The editorial voice of the *Cincinnati Commercial Appeal*—speaking for most Cincinnatians—was to avoid war if at all possible, to protect strong business ties to the South. Most businessmen and merchants relied on Kentucky and other Southern states; slaveowners and traders were among the wealthiest customers for downtown hotels, restaurants, saloons and emporiums.

But Kentucky came within a blade of bluegrass of joining the South.

Kentucky says no

As Secessionist Fever swept the Southern states, Kentucky Gov. Beriah Magoffin called a special session of the legislature to consider secession in January 1861. It was rejected by a pro-Union majority of lawmakers who refused to meet.

---

69 The most Northern counties, Kenton and Campbell, which also had the lowest slave ownership, voted for Lincoln. *The impact of the Civil War on Northern Kentucky and Cincinnati, 1861-1865*, Elrod, Matthew, 2006 Thesis.

A few months later, President Lincoln called for troops from Kentucky. He was rejected too. "I will send not a man nor a dollar for the wicked purpose of subduing my sister Southern states," Governor Magoffin replied, defying the new President.

A few weeks later the South tried its luck and asked for troops from Kentucky. Magoffin said no again, just as emphatically. Although he was in favor of secession, he vowed to honor the wishes of Kentucky lawmakers, who ratified neutrality in May 1861.

But by the following year, their speeches and declarations would be empty words on paper. Both armies, North and South, crossed state borders to fight more than two dozen bloody battles in the state, including Perryville and Richmond.

On August 14, 1862, Gen. Kirby Smith entered Kentucky from Tennessee with 15,000 combat veterans. But when his Army of Kentucky arrived at the small town of Barbourville four days later, they were dismayed to discover that there was no uprising in support—in fact, hardly any support at all.

With supplies running short and the fear of demoralizing disaster for the South if he retreated to Tennessee, General Smith informed General Bragg, "I have therefore decided to advance as soon as possible upon Lexington."

Waiting near Lexington was another Army of Kentucky, led by Union Gen. William Nelson, a six foot two, 300-pound Kentuckian nicknamed "Bull"—the same general who was the first of Buell's Army of the Ohio to arrive at Shiloh.[70]

On August 30, 1862, the two armies fought at Richmond, Kentucky, just south of Lexington. They were evenly matched, with about 6,500 Confederates against 6,850 Union troops. It was one of the worst Union defeats of the war. The Yankees were routed and fled, throwing away weapons and supplies as they ran. General Nelson was shot in the thigh

---

70   Nelson also served at Corinth, and was the first Union general to enter the city when the siege was broken. He was shot and killed in a dispute with another Union General at the Galt House Hotel in Louisville in 1862. Nelson slapped and insulted Union General J. C. Davis, who went after a gun, returned, and shot Nelson to death. Davis was never prosecuted or court martialed. He was reinstated and returned to duty by General in Chief Henry Halleck.

as he tried to rally terrified raw Union soldiers who had never seen combat. They lost 5,553 casualties, including 206 killed, 844 wounded and 4,303 taken prisoner or missing.

That was more than 10 times the loss to the Confederates: 451 casualties: 78 killed, 373 wounded or missing.

The Union troops were reported to be "hopelessly broken and scattered." On September 2, General Smith led his Confederate troops into Lexington. "We come not as invaders but as liberators," he announced.

His next stop was Frankfort, where he raised the Confederate flag over the state capitol and began to form a new government.

News of the fall of Kentucky was eclipsed in the Eastern newspapers by another battle on August 30 in Manassas, Virginia—the Second Battle of Bull Run.

But in the Ohio River Valley and throughout Ohio and Kentucky, there was no bigger headline and no bigger panic. If Lexington and Frankfort could fall, there was nothing to stop the South from taking Cincinnati.

Cincinnati's second leading paper, *The Cincinnati Gazette*,[71] let loose the dogs of war:

> **"To Arms! To Arms! The time of playing war
> has passed. Let us prepare to resist an army of
> 100,000 men bent on our destruction."**

---

71   *The Gazette* had 22,000 circulation in 1865, vs. 25,000 circulation for the Republican *Commercial Appeal*. Third was the *Cincinnati Enquirer*, at that time the city's Democratic Party paper, with 14,000. The *Cincinnati Times* had 10,000.

HETH MARCHES NORTH

'Let me take Cincinnati'

In the scorching, dusty late August and early September of 1862, the "liberator" of Lexington quickly discovered it was easier to crush the Union Army than to organize a new Confederate government. Besieged by a relentless stream of politicians who were eager to claim a comfortable perch of power in the new Confederate State of Kentucky, General Smith welcomed a visit from one of his most promising commanders, Gen. Henry Heth.

Heth had just arrived in Lexington, bringing up the rear of Smith's army, guarding trains and supplies with 4,000 men. Smith closed his door on the restless, milling herd of political pleaders and sat down to discuss strategy with Heth.

Their plan to capture Frankfort would be the first time—and last—the Confederates took any state capital that had not voluntarily joined the rebellion. As they shared a glass of whiskey, their talk turned to how they could harvest the "fruits of victory," a phrase that sparked the imagination of Kirby Smith, an amateur botanist.

Heth recalled recent victories and argued that the South had failed to follow up any of them with something significant and permanent. But he had exactly that kind of ripe fruit in mind.

"I feel certain you can capture either Louisville or Cincinnati," Heth said. "There is no force at present in either of those cities."

Smith smiled, nodded and agreed. But he was pinned down by politicians, who insisted he had to stay to help them set up the new state government. He was entangled in the mangrove swamp of political favors and the spoils of patronage. If the seedling state government wilted because he was not there to water and cultivate it, he would be blamed. As a Florida native, he knew the swamp of politics contained more alligators, snakes and quicksand than the Everglades.

"But taking Cincinnati will do more to organize a new state of Kentucky than staying here in Lexington," Heth argued. With that border secured, the rest of the state would be set free to rise up and join the rebellion.

Heth's memoir doesn't have much to say on the subject of slavery, but it seems evident that if he was asked, he would say he was not fighting for slavery but for his state, for the South and for glory, not necessarily in that order. As a man of Virginia, he was comfortable with the concept of owning slaves, but he also had demonstrated humanity, friendship and compassion for the Plains Indians. Taking Cincinnati could be the decisive blow the South needed to end the war.

Smith considered Heth's arguments, but also thought about the trouble he would stir up from Jefferson Davis in the Confederate capital of Richmond, Virginia if their first state by conquest was lost. He had plans to go to Frankfort, fly the flag and show the world that the Confederates now had Kentucky, the prize that would break Lincoln's heart and break the back of the Union.

'The Seminole,' Gen. Edmund Kirby Smith

Heth argued that seizing some of the biggest cities in the nation from the Union would do more for the cause than passing out political posts or waving flags in Frankfort.

Smith hesitated.

Finally, Heth said, "If you cannot go and take Cincinnati or Louisville, let me go and take one of the two places."[72]

Smith thought it over and replied, "I will let you know tonight what I will do."

About midnight, Heth heard a knock on the door of his hotel room. Smith had made up his mind. The answer was yes. The target would be Cincinnati.

Heth wasted no time. On September 4, he led his troops north from Lexington. The worst fears of panicked Cincinnati were now true. A Confederate army was on its way to attack the Queen City of the West.

Heth was right. There was nothing that could stand between him and his force of 8,000 combat veterans. While Heth took Cincinnati, General Bragg had vowed that he would crush the Yankees in Kentucky "like an eggshell" and take Louisville. Smith promised to reinforce Heth to seize Cincinnati.

The man who had tamed the Santa Fe Trail and hunted bareback with an Apache bow and arrows was confident. Cincinnati would fall like a wounded buffalo.

---

72   Heth, Henry. *The Memoirs of Henry Heth*. Praeger, 1974.

RUMORS OF WAR

'The situation was not at all reassuring'

Vivid descriptions of attacks by Sioux and Chippewa Indians in Minnesota led the news in *The Cincinnati Enquirer* on September 2, 1862. One survivor described being shot twice, then buried under logs by Indians who said they would come back later to cut him up. Another told of losing his daughters, wife and sons.

Readers must have been puzzled. By then, the city was already in the cold grip of panic. Richmond, Kentucky had fallen. Lexington was in Confederate hands. Cincinnati was defenseless. But the front page seemed almost oblivious.

Finally, on page 2, halfway to the bottom, was a small headline announcing the biggest news of the day. A surprising proclamation:

"It is but fair to inform the citizens that an active, daring and powerful enemy threatens them with every consequence of war; yet the cities must be defended and their inhabitants must assist in the preparation. Patriotism, duty, honor and self-preservation call them to the labor and it must be performed equally by all classes.

All business must be suspended at nine o'clock today. Every business house must be closed.

Under the direction of their Mayor, the citizens must ... at ten o'clock A.M. assemble in their convenient public places ready for orders. As soon as possible they will be assigned to their work.

This labor ought to be that of love, and the undersigned trusts and believes it will be—*any how it must be done.*

The willing shall be properly credited—the unwilling promptly visited. The principal adopted is, citizens for the labor, soldiers for the battle....

Martial law is hereby proclaimed in the three cities [Cincinnati, Covington, Newport]; but until they can be relieved by the military, the injunction of this proclamation will be executed by the police.

Lew Wallace
Major General Commanding

Whether the newspaper knew it or not, Cincinnati was at war. Another story on Page 2 reported the evacuation of Lexington—days after Lexington was already occupied by Confederates—and a Rebel army just 45 miles from Cincinnati, in Cynthiana, Kentucky.

Even given the primitive communications of the times, telegraphs were available and rumors traveled just as fast. Most of Cincinnati was already on edge, feeling the first tremors of panic. Families buried their silver, sent wives and children to Dayton, out of harm's way, and began organizing militias. The Indian attacks in the West were no more scary than hordes of Rebels pillaging Cincinnati.

"Not an armed man was left between Kirby Smith's victorious army and the city of Cincinnati, where a large supply of army stores had been collected for the use of the Western armies, a most tempting prize, as well as the plunder of a wealthy city by the ill clad, poorly fed Confederate troops," wrote Cincinnatian William Howard Neff in 1891.

Bankers, store clerks, street-sweepers, barbers, dockworkers, businessmen, teachers and pastors, who had been left behind when local volunteers marched off to war, were suddenly on the front lines. They thought about their homes, their loved ones, their property, their bank deposits, their city and their country.

"It is not too much to say that the moral and material effects of the capture of Cincinnati might have tipped the scale at this critical time, and assisted in the dismemberment of the Union," said Neff, who manned the trenches to defend the city as lieutenant colonel in the Pearl Street Rifles volunteer militia.

"The situation in Cincinnati was not at all reassuring. The mayor of the city was a Democrat of doubtful proclivities and was strongly suspected of a desire to find a good pretext for the surrender of the city."[73]

Wallace had arrived late the day before and immediately summoned Mayor George Hatch to a midnight meeting at his headquarters in the city's finest hotel, Burnet House. Hatch was a well-known Southern sympathizer, probably described behind his back as a Copperhead, the more colorful name for "peace Democrats" who wanted to end the war at any cost to the Union.

In 1863, *Atlantic Magazine* reporter and poet Thomas Buchanan Read explained a Copperhead for his readers:

"Loosely defined, this term referred to northern Democrats who criticized Lincoln's war policies. They condemned such policies as the confiscation acts, arbitrary arrests, suspension of the writ of habeas corpus, the Emancipation Proclamation, federal conscription and violation of free press and speech."

Read insisted that "only a small number of extremists were actually disloyal to the Union. Those extremists did encourage desertion and resistance to the draft."

But Read's guess was too low. In 1863 the group claimed as many as 500,000 members who used secret handshakes, codes and rituals to plan their overthrow of the government with thousands of stockpiled weapons.

Bitter medicine

Copperheads were not uncommon in Cincinnati and Ohio. One of the most infamous Copperheads in the nation was Congressman Clement Vallandingham of Dayton.

In 1863, the former newspaper editor ran for Governor of Ohio as a peace protestor. He was against the war, opposed the draft, detested abolitionists and believed that the Southern states had a constitutional right to secede and form their own nation, just as the colonists broke from Britain in the American Revolution.

---

73 Lt. Col. William Neff's History of the Pearl Street Rifles, 1891. Cincinnati History Library and Archives at the Cincinnati Museum Center.

The arrest of Rep. Clement Vallandingham in his pajamas, Dayton, 1863.

Lincoln had already suspended civil rights and declared martial law in Baltimore and New York to suppress rioting against the Union Army and against the draft.[74] During the war, more than 14,000 citizens in the North were arrested for "disloyalty" to the Union. Vallandingham called Lincoln a "king" tyrant who was violating the Constitution and civil rights.

In March, Lincoln appointed Gen. Ambrose Burnside as commander of the Department of Ohio, shortly after Burnside's defeat by Confederate Henry Heth and the disaster at Petersburg, Georgia. Burnside, head-quartered in Cincinnati, declared martial law and issued Order No. 38: "The habit of declaring sympathies for the enemy will not be allowed in this Department." He claimed authority to arrest civilians, try them in military court and execute them by firing squad.

---

74 The draft riots in New York were in response to mandatory conscription, but also resembled the riots in Cincinnati in 1862: poor immigrants, mainly Irish, targeted blacks who competed for scarce jobs. The law allowed those who could afford it to buy their way out of the draft for $300—more than most immigrants could afford.

Vallandingham blasted Burnside for violating "Order No 1—the Constitution of the United States." While giving a campaign speech to a crowd of 20,000 in Mt. Vernon, Ohio, he said, "The sooner the people inform the minions of usurped power that they will not submit to such restrictions upon their liberties, the better."

That was more than Burnside could take. He sent 100 soldiers to Vallandingham's home to break down his door at 2:30 a.m. and haul him out, under arrest, in his pajamas. The former congressman and candidate for governor was thrown in jail in Cincinnati and put on trial for disloyal statements that aided the enemy.[75]

Thousands of armed Vallandingham supporters who were Copperheads and Sons of Liberty protested in Dayton, shouting "Release Vallandingham." They burned buildings, looted stores and fired random shots that left hundreds wounded by stray bullets.[76]

When confronted about violations of the First Amendment and Bill of Rights, Lincoln replied that suspending civil rights in wartime was like prescribing an emetic—harsh medicine for a sick man, not used for someone who is healthy. He had his own private misgivings. When he was urged to go further, he replied, "Would I not thus give up all footing upon Constitution or law? Would it not lose us the very cause we seek to advance?"

Most newspapers, Vallandingham's jury and even the Supreme Court had no objections. Editorials supported Lincoln. Vallandingham was found guilty and sentenced to prison for the rest of the war. And the Supreme Court refused to consider the case, claiming they had no authority over military justice.

As Ben Franklin would have said, "Those who would give up essential liberty to purchase a little temporary safety deserve neither liberty nor safety."

Lincoln's conscience or his political sense prevailed, and he released Vallandingham and ordered a military escort to deliver him

---

75 Bill of Rights Institute, *Clement Vallandingham and Constitutionalism.*
76 Miller, Dr. John W., Copperhead Activities, Cincinnati Civil War Roundtable, February 21, 1960.

to the Confederacy. He was turned over to Gen. Braxton Bragg in Murfreesboro, Tennessee.

After the war, the Supreme Court reversed itself and said it was the military that had no authority over civilians outside a war zone. Newspaper editors suddenly rediscovered the First Amendment that protects freedom of the press as well as unpopular opinions.

Vallandingham eventually made his way to Canada and ran his campaign for Ohio Governor from a hotel in Windsor, Ontario. He lost by a landslide and came back to Ohio. After the war, he was in court in Hamilton, Ohio, defending a man accused of murder. As Vallandingham demonstrated to the jury how the victim could have committed suicide, he accidentally shot himself in the stomach and died.

He was wrong about slavery, but right about the abuse of civil rights by Lincoln and Burnside.

Oxford's wild Moon sisters

Burnside also arrested a more sensational Copperhead in Oxford, Ohio. Unfortunately for him, the suspect was a former fiancé who had jilted him at the altar before the war.

The intended bride, Cynthia Charlotte "Lottie" Moon, was asked, "Do you take this man, Ambrose Burnside, to be thy lawfully wedded husband?"

Lottie Moon

Guests and groom who expected to hear "I do" were shocked to their shoes by her reply.

"No siree, Bob, I won't," she chirped, then turned her back on the pulpit and walked out with a defiant spring in her step as Burnside and the wedding party stood stunned and stammering.

Burnside was probably a bit relieved to remain single and free. His best friend, Henry Heth, described in his memoirs the scandalous escapades of his roommate "Burn," including a "perfect daisy" of a girl in Mexico who tried to cut his throat, chased him through two houses with a knife and attacked another woman who was a rival for his affections. Burnside told Heth, "She pulled enough hair out of that girl's head to stuff a pillow, and then drew out a stiletto—they all carry stilettos, I believe—and made for me. I took to my heels."[77]

Burnside was likewise lucky to escape marriage to Lottie Moon. She boasted later that she had been engaged a dozen times, as part of her patriotic duty to raise the spirits of Confederate officers by promising to marry them.

When she finally did marry, her husband held a gun on her at the altar and warned, "There will be a wedding here tonight or a funeral tomorrow."

Her flamboyant sister Virginia "Ginny" Moon was even more scandalous. Ginny was engaged 18 times and was booted from Oxford Female Institute for Women after she shot the stars out of a United States flag and scratched "Hurrah for Jeff Davis" on Oxford storefronts.

Both were spies for the Confederates.

They posed as mourners accompanying a coffin that was stuffed with medical supplies for the South, pretended to be an invalid in a wheelchair and carried coded messages to Gen. Kirby Smith in their hoop skirts. When Ginny was caught carrying secrets to Confederate Gen. Bedford Forrest, she pulled a pistol to buy time and swallowed the note.

A $10,000 reward was offered for Lottie Moon, "Dead or Alive."

---

77 Heth, Henry. *The Memoirs of Henry Heth*. Praeger, 1974.

She was finally arrested in Oxford and put under house arrest at the Burnet House in Cincinnati by Burnside. His headquarters was also conveniently at Burnet House.

During her arrest, the Army listed the contents of a trunk that Lottie Moon was smuggling to the South. It included four corsets, four pairs of cotton hose, six skirts, several bolts of fabric—and a valise that contained six balls of opium and 40 bottles of morphine. The bolts of fabric were probably intended as bandages.

Lottie complained bitterly that the men who arrested her were not "gentlemen," but Burnside was unmoved. He finally had his revenge for being jilted at the altar. He made her sign a parole promise to behave and sent her to the Confederates. The "Lottie Moon House," a square, white-brick home behind an iron fence at 220 East High Street in Oxford, is a local and national landmark.[78]

Cincinnati's violent history

Martial law was a handy tool for government leaders in the 1860s. With one stroke of a pen, they could suspend civil rights, arrest their enemies, muzzle their critics, stop the presses and squelch dissent—including protests about martial law. They could arrest anyone on suspicion of treason, then arrest anyone who dared to complain about the arrests.

They could even have "traitors" shot by firing squads. [79]

Mayor Hatch used it during the first scare by Morgan's Raiders in the summer of 1862. But now he would find out how it felt to be on the wrong end of the whip. Once General Wallace imposed martial law, Hatch had no choice but to salute, say "Yes sir" and obey.

Wallace didn't want to be in Cincinnati. He had been on his way to the battle for Lexington and Louisville, hoping to redeem his reputation with gallantry and glory. But he only got as far as Paris, Kentucky, when

---

78 After the war, Lottie Moon, who claimed to be a ventriloquist, became a journalist. Her sister Ginny became an actress in early silent films.

79 One man, William B. Mumford of New Orleans, was hanged for treason in 1862. His crime was to tear down a Union flag. In Ohio, two leaders of the Sons of Liberty Copperheads were sentenced to hang, but their sentences were commuted by President Lincoln. One of the men was Dr. William Bowles of French Lick, Indiana.

he received a telegram from Gen. Horatio Wright, ordering him back to Cincinnati as fast as possible to defend the city.

One of his aides told Wallace the mission was doomed. "Do you mean to accept this request?" he asked.

"Yes," Wallace replied."

"You are not bound to."

"No," Wallace agreed.

The aide shook his head. "There is nothing at Cincinnati with which to make a defense—not a soldier, not a gun, not a fort. To try must end in failure."

The rest of Wallace's staff agreed, and one of them told him to remember that he had enemies at the highest levels of the Army who would like to see him disgraced by failure. The assignment looked like a setup. The Confederates had taken Lexington, and now threatened Louisville. Union Gen. Don Carlos Buell demanded every man available to defend Louisville. So Wallace was sent to defend Cincinnati with no troops. The order came from General Wright, but it had the fingerprints of Halleck. If Wallace failed, they could be rid of him. And if he somehow succeeded, all the better.

Wallace understood the political games behind the orders. "Still," he said, "to leave the city to the enemy without an effort to save it would be cowardly."

He had compassion for the citizens of Cincinnati. "The war had been a horror to them, read of as so distant it could not be brought to their doors. Now, suddenly, here it was, and with demands that did not stop with a mere appropriation of their time and a blockade of their business—it actually ordered them to go to work in unaccustomed ways or take arms and be ready to fight."[80]

He imagined the average Cincinnati businessman, corpulent and comfortable, opening his newspaper over breakfast: "Dwelling in a land of peace and plenty, he had been accustomed to cream for his coffee and hot rolls for breakfast; now the milkman was shut out and the baker shut in."

---

80   *Lew Wallace; An Autobiography. Vol. II* - Scholar's Choice Edition. 2015.

Wallace knew the city. He had visited many times, most recently to give a recruiting speech earlier that year while he was "on the shelf" as the scapegoat for Shiloh. As a Hoosier from Crawfordsville, born in Bellevue in southeastern Indiana, he knew and loved the Queen City as his nearest "Athens" of arts, learning and culture.

He also knew the local history. This was not Cincinnati's first brush with violence. Just that summer the city had been torn apart by panic, then violent riots, in July and August.

When the war began in 1861, Cincinnati's lucrative commerce with the South was choked off and the city fell into a recession. Except for military shipments, river traffic slowed to a trickle and jobs loading and unloading riverboats on the docks became scarce.

Meanwhile, Confederate Gen. John Hunt Morgan, a Shiloh veteran, led the first of his cavalry raids into the Ohio Valley in July, 1862, invading Kentucky with 867 mounted troopers. Fear spread through the region like a debilitating flu.

Panicked, the city of Cincinnati foolishly sent 120 of its policemen to defend Lexington from Morgan, leaving only 40 to enforce the law in a city of nearly 200,000. It was a futile gesture and a costly mistake.

While the city was left without police protection, trouble was brewing on the riverfront in a cutthroat competition for jobs between Irish immigrants and blacks, both on the lowest rungs of the poverty ladder. Former slaves set free by the advancing Union armies, called "contrabands," migrated north to Ohio and were hired as cheap labor to replace Irish immigrants throughout the city, including 50 Irish workers who were dismissed and replaced by contrabands at Burnet House.

As usual, the worst hostility of the underclass came from the layer only one step above. Those at the top could afford to be more enlightened. For the Irish, the fight for jobs could mean life and death for their families.

When Irish stevedores on the docks were replaced by black contrabands on July 15, gangs of Irish workers rioted. They drove black workers off the boats and attacked "Bucktown," the squalid neighborhood of tarpaper shacks and shanties between Sixth and Seventh streets, east of Broadway, populated by blacks, Irish and other immigrant groups. Bucktown was the worst—except for Rat Row and Sausage Row in the muddy, stinking riverfront area known as The Bottoms, where all of the city's waste trickled downslope to the Ohio River, or was pushed back into the city by floods that spread deadly outbreaks of cholera and dysentery.

The rampaging, drunken Irish mob burned homes in Bucktown and severely beat any black men they could find.

There were not enough police to enforce the law, and most of the "coppers" who remained were Irish, inclined to look the other way. Most in the rioting mob were friends and relatives. The attacks on blacks continued for seven days.

The *Commercial Appeal* and *The Cincinnati Enquirer* staged their own street fight by hurling insults like rocks and bottles. The *Appeal* condemned "gangs of miscreants in this community who degrade the name of man and disgrace the community ... led on by cunning and designing knaves and covert traitors who are ... too ready to attribute poverty and distress to any but the real cause." Those "knaves and traitors" were understood to be the editors at the competing newspaper.

The *Enquirer* fired back that the riots were a conflict of two economic systems that escalated to "cudgels and paving stones," but saved the harshest scorn not for rioting mobs, but for the *Appeal* and the *Gazette*. The Democrat *Enquirer* blamed Republicans and the Republican *Gazette* for welcoming the "incoming hordes" of freed slaves.

The local *Catholic Telegraph* urged forgiveness and sympathy—for the poor, misunderstood, Catholic Irish.

The real shock to the city was that the black residents took up arms and fired back at the Irish mobs.

Being black in Cincinnati

Black residents didn't have a voice in the leading newspapers. But if they had, they might have said that Cincinnati was *almost* free.

As of the 1860 Census, there were 3,731 blacks in Cincinnati, making up just over 2 percent of the population of 161,000. Both numbers grew rapidly, as immigrants flooded into the city and slaves set free during the war migrated north.

Cincinnati abolitionists were proud that the city was part of the Underground Railroad. But they seldom mentioned that Cincinnati was not the preferred *destination* for smuggled slaves. Freed slaves were quickly hustled on to Canada. And well into the mid-1800s, Black Laws were still in effect that required new black residents to post a $1,500 bond and get two white sponsors to guarantee they would behave.

As far back as 1829, race riots forced 1,200 blacks—probably more than half the city's black population—to flee to Canada.[81]

Yet Cincinnati was not completely segregated and had no real black ghetto. Bucktown, despite the pejorative name, was home to poor families of all races. Many blacks lived in clusters within or surrounded by white neighborhoods. Ironically, the first ghettos were created after the Civil War, when increasing industrialization required more skilled jobs that were reserved for whites. The percentage of blacks with skilled jobs in Cincinnati actually decreased from 1860 to 1920.[82]

But in 1862, leading black residents included the owner of a coal business, a successful tailor, photographers, a manufacturer and many barbers, whose trade in those days was monopolized by blacks for customers of all races.[83]

Blacks held skilled jobs, such as carpenters and riverboat mechanics, but most unskilled black laborers worked on the docks. Slave owners in Northern Kentucky also sent workers to the docks and profited from their income.

Cincinnati was divided like the rest of the nation. For every abolitionist who sang "John Brown's Body," there was a Copperhead secessionist who sang "Dixie" and hated Lincoln.

---

81 Cincinnati riots were diverse. In 1855, anti-immigration Know-Nothings and Germans clashed over elections. As an angry mob marched toward the German neighborhoods in Over-the Rhine, the German immigrants barricaded the streets and fired a cannon at the mob, which quickly reconsidered and dispersed.

82 Elrod, Mathew, *The Impact of the Civil War on Northern Kentucky and Cincinnati, 1861-65,* Thesis, 2006.

83 Ibid.

The city was home to Harriet Beecher Stowe, whose book *Uncle Tom's Cabin* was such a powerful argument against slavery that when Lincoln met her he said, "So you're the little woman who wrote the book that started this great war."

But Cincinnati also was headquarters for the Knights of the Golden Circle, a (not very) secret society that schemed to create a "golden circle" of legal slavery that encompassed the 11 Confederate States, Havana, Mexico, Central America, parts of South America and the Caribbean. Some of its members plotted a coup to depose or assassinate Lincoln and overthrow the Union.

Lew Wallace was well read and knew the divided, violent history of Cincinnati. He had already angered many in Cincinnati by daring to suggest in his recruiting speech on Market Square (later Fountain Square) that blacks should be enlisted in the Union Army to free up soldiers for combat. He even argued that they should be armed for self-defense. By the end of the war, it was accepted. But in 1862, even Wallace admitted that was a radical idea.

As Wallace finally crossed the Ohio River and arrived in Cincinnati on his "doomed" mission, he found a city out on the ledge of a nervous breakdown.

"You can fancy the consternation in every corner—the rushing here and there—the demand to know what was the matter," he recalled. "The whole city was involved—all doors were shut and held closed—the entire population, men, women and children, were on the streets. They heard of the danger to the town. They only wanted to know what they could do."

Wallace knew he would have his hands full with Copperheads and Southern sympathizers on both sides of the Ohio River. He also had probably heard about a strange and embarrassing chapter in the history of the Queen City—that Cincinnati had done its best to cover up and forget.

A HOUSE DIVIDED

'A grenade of the most destructive character'

Cartoonists showed the new president Abraham Lincoln in disguise, fleeing secessionists who plotted an assassination before his inauguration. *Harper's Weekly*, **1860**

The election of 1860 was like the contest described in Mark Twain's short story *The Celebrated Jumping Frog of Calaveras County*. Candidates were leaping randomly in all directions while voters placed their bets, and the outcome looked as slippery as a bullfrog's belly.

As Leonidas W. Smiley said in the story, "It might be a parrot, or it might be a canary, may be, but it an't, it's only just a frog."

Several frogs jumped into the presidential contest in 1860. Four made the ballot: John Bell, a curmudgeonly carpetbag of confusion from Tennessee, who represented the Constitutional Union Party, which was for slavery *and* the Union; Democrat Stephen Douglas, an incontinent orator from Illinois who could speechify for hours without mercy; incumbent Vice President John C. Breckenridge of Kentucky, a square-jawed, stiff-necked lawyer representing the hardline "slavery or war" Southern Democratic Party; and Abraham Lincoln of Illinois, a gangling, homely, soft-spoken Republican from a background so humble dirt floors were a luxury.

Americans had never elected a Republican before. Nobody knew which way the hopelessly divided, angry nation would hop. Among the factions gathered around the political pond were the anti-immigration Know Nothings, conservative Whigs, secessionists, abolitionists, the Free Soil Party, the Liberty Party, the People's Party, young Republicans called Wide Awakes, and a flock of squawking politicians and voters who chose sides according to slave states and free states.

But it was no friendly wager. The nation's political battle would soon escalate from ballots to bullets.

In the final four-way race, Lincoln won a plurality with less than 40 percent. Breckenridge won the South, where Lincoln was not allowed on the ballot. The outcomes in five states were so close that winners had "victory" margins of less than 1 percent. The election proved again that the nation was a house divided that could not stand. Americans were headed for a violent divorce over irreconcilable differences on slavery and states' rights.

Lincoln carried Ohio with 51 percent. Cincinnati narrowly voted for him. But Kentucky would not even give him 1 percent of their votes.[84]

During the campaign, he promised he would not abolish slavery: "If I could save (the Union) by freeing all the slaves, I would do it; and if I could save it by freeing some and leaving others alone, I would also do that."

But most voters didn't believe him.

When Lincoln was declared the winner of the November 6, 1860 election, seven Southern states declared that they would secede from a nation led by the "cursed abolitionist." They would rather break up the nation than call Abraham Lincoln "President."

In the weeks and months before he was inaugurated in March, Southern senators and congressmen emptied their desks, locked their

---

84 Support for Lincoln followed slave ownership. Boone County had 1,745 slaves; Kenton County, 567; Campbell County, 116. Source: *The Impact of the Civil War on Northern Kentucky and Cincinnati, ,1861-1865*, Elrod, Matthew, 2006 Thesis. Cincinnati History L:ibrary and Archives.

offices, packed their bags and left Washington, resigning in protest or ejected for refusing to accept the election. Some plotted to derail Lincoln's election by forcing a vote in the House, stealing ballots or kidnapping or killing the president-elect.

On his way out the door of the White House, President James Buchanan, a Democrat from Pennsylvania, tried to sabotage the new Republican President with a last-minute compromise on slavery. It was a failure like the rest of his presidency. Buchanan was remembered for bank failures, corruption, abysmal leadership and incompetence. [85]

During the presidential campaign, Lincoln said of Buchanan, "He is thrown aside as unfit for further use."

On February 11, 1861, Lincoln left Springfield, Illinois to go to Washington and replace Buchanan. He boarded a train for a winding, 2,000-mile whistlestop tour of the North on his way to his inauguration on March 4, which was also his 52nd birthday. As he tied a rope around his baggage and addressed it to "A. Lincoln, White House, Washington, DC," stacks of hate mail and threats addressed to him were already pouring in. A lot of Americans did not want him to see that next birthday.

The gleaming new "Special" train, painted in red and yellow, sped down the tracks nearly as fast as rumors. Some said there were sharpshooters waiting down the line. Bombs. Poison. Armed gangs who would infiltrate the crowds, surround him and knife him to death like Caesar in the Roman Forum.

As he stopped in Indianapolis, Cincinnati, Columbus, Pittsburgh, Cleveland, New York, Philadelphia and Baltimore, new threats waited at each train station. Huge crowds came out to see the first Republican president, sometimes pressing so close in such a seething mass that they

---

85　Buchanan, a former Senator, Congressman, Secretary of State and ambassador, was the ultimate Washington insider and career politician. As president, he was nearly impeached. An investigation by Republicans in Congress exposed his attempts to bribe members of Congress to vote for slavery in Kansas. Buchanan claimed to be against slavery, but was also anti-abolition. His absence as a leader during the growing national hostilities over slavery led many to call the Civil War "Buchanan's War."

threatened to crush him in their enthusiastic embrace. [86]

One letter addressed to "Sir, Mr. Abe Lincoln," warned, "If you don't resign we are going to put a spider in your dumpling." Lincoln probably laughed, but other threats were more troubling.

Just as his train was leaving Illinois and approaching the Indiana border, the primitive brakes squealed and took nearly a mile to bring it to an emergency stop. A railroad worker had discovered a piece of equipment "fastened upon the rails in such a manner that if a train at full speed had struck it, the engine and cars must have been thrown off and many persons killed."[87]

That was just the beginning.

A balding, bearded, redhaired Scotsman named Allan Pinkerton was chosen by the railroad as chief of security for the new president. He reported to Lincoln that his Pinkerton detectives had "decisive" information about an assassination plot hatched in Baltimore, the major city of slave-state Maryland. Lincoln had to go through Baltimore to get to DC. Pinkerton went to Baltimore to investigate, disguised as a Southern businessman. "The opposition to Mr. Lincoln's inauguration was most violent and bitter," he wrote, "and a few days' sojourn in this city convinced me that great danger was to be apprehended."[88]

The Abe Lincoln train rolled on.

As it passed through North Bend, Ohio, the family of President William Henry Harrison stood by Harrison's tomb to greet him. It was the first of many historic connections with former and future presidents along the journey.

In many of the cities that had supported him, he stayed overnight, greeted dignitaries and gave dozens of speeches to massive crowds that cheered, jeered, heckled him and shook his hand until his bones ached.

At one hotel, a suspicious package was removed by police.

---

86 Lincoln Inauguration Attracted Death Threats, Kidnapping Plot, *The Washington Post*, January 15, 2021.

87 Widmer, Ted. *Lincoln on the Verge*. Simon & Schuster, 2020.

88 Stashower, Daniel, The Unsuccessful Plot to Kill Abraham Lincoln, *Smithsonian Magazine*, February 2013.

Burnet House in 1860. A Forbriger lithograph. Library of Congress.

Welcome to Cincinnati

He arrived in Cincinnati at 3 p.m. on February 12, greeted by massive, unruly crowds that were held back by police "with great difficulty," according to newspaper reports. At one stop, a member of his military escort had his shoulder dislocated as he tried to hold back the mob.

As his train pulled into Cincinnati, the crowds hoorayed, and cannons were fired—an ominous preview of the war to come. He made his way slowly through the jammed streets. It took two hours to get to Burnet House at the northwest corner of Vine and Third streets.[89] But the hotel's luxurious steam-heated rooms were worth the wait in February.

He spent the evening and following day shaking hands and giving speeches. That night a large crowd of Germans from Over-the-Rhine gathered in front of the hotel, waiting to hear from the president they had helped to elect. They were America's most recent immigrants, and

---

89 Now a parking lot and garage.

had seen enough of division, revolution and violent bloodshed before fleeing Europe for America. The "Dutch Planks" in the Republican platform for 1860 protected homesteaders and citizenship, making the Germans ardent supporters of the Union and Lincoln.

At 9:00 a.m., just before his train left the next morning, Lincoln was greeted at the station by a crowd that newspapers said was more than 100,000 in a city of 160,000. "The Germans were particularly enthusiastic," the *Cincinnati Daily Press* reported.

But the day had begun with more disturbing news. Early that morning, Lincoln had been briefed by one of Pinkerton's agents on the latest assassination plots in Baltimore.

While Lincoln and Pinkerton worried about Baltimore, Cincinnati nearly killed him.

As Lincoln's train coughed clouds of steam in the station, boilers stoked, ready to leave for Columbus, an alert security inspector found an abandoned carpetbag sitting in Lincoln's private car. According to scarce news reports, it was opened by police, who found "a grenade of the most destructive character ... so arranged that within fifteen minutes it would have exploded, with a force sufficient to have demolished the car and destroyed the lives of all the persons in it."[90]

Lincoln would have been sitting in his car, unpacking or stretching his long legs in an easy chair, rubbing his aching hands. And then… KABOOM. That would have been the end of Abraham Lincoln before he even set foot in the White House as president.

The incident was quickly suppressed. Most in Cincinnati and the rest of the nation never heard about his close brush with assassination. One local newspaper alluded mysteriously to his "escape from danger," but no details were offered. The assassination attempt was buried. Blowing up the new president would not reflect well on the proud image of the Queen City of the West, which was already self-conscious about comparisons to more sophisticated cities such as New York, Boston and Philadelphia.

---

90   *New York Times*, February 18, 1861.

Disaster was averted. The bomb was quietly removed, closing the door firmly on a frightening alternate history: Lincoln killed. The nation thrown into chaos. A new president chosen by Congress who might negotiate to accept slavery, or go to war—but certainly without the strength, patience, faith and unique, visionary, rail-splitter character that enabled Abraham Lincoln to end slavery and save the Union. [91]

Could a divided, weakened America have saved Europe and the rest of the world in two world wars? What nation would have taken the place of the USA as the dominate empire of the 20th century? Germany? Japan? Russia?

It's impossible to know. But a grenade hidden in a carpet bag in Cincinnati came within minutes of blowing American history to smithereens on February 13, 1861.

'The better angels'

When Lincoln finally arrived in Baltimore, the threats and menacing crowds were so serious that one of his bodyguards offered him a pistol and Bowie knife to defend himself. But the man whose nicknames included "grand wrestler" and "young Hercules" declined. What would the American people think if their new president had to enter the capital armed to the teeth? Lincoln said, "I have no fears."

Instead, he disguised himself in a huge overcoat and soft wool hat, pulled down over his eyes, and switched trains by a back door to his sleeper car. His route was changed at the last minute to throw off assassins, and he made it safely, secretly into Washington where he checked himself in to the Willard Hotel.

When his "undercover" arrival was discovered, the same newspapers that called him a "long-armed baboon" mocked him in cartoons as an ape-like fugitive, running from a mob. He was a coward, they said. Most Democrats and their partisan megaphones in the press loathed Lincoln with irrational, visceral hatred.

---

91   The First Secret Plot to Kill Abraham Lincoln, *Time Magazine*, April 30, 2020.

Some even suggested that the plots to kill him were fiction, made up by Lincoln to win sympathy and create drama. But not Gen. Winfield Scott, who accompanied Lincoln on his train. Scott sat behind Lincoln at his inauguration, expecting a rifle shot any second. He called it "the most critical and hazardous event with which I have ever been connected."

As the train reached DC, Scott warned, "'If any of the Maryland or Virginia gentlemen who have become so threatening and troublesome show their heads or even venture to raise a finger, I shall blow them to hell."

But Lincoln did not return evil for evil or insult for insult. More than most presidents since George Washington, he lived his deep faith in the manner of Proverbs 12:16 ("A fool shows his annoyance at once, but a prudent man overlooks an insult."), and Matthew 5:39 ("Whoever slaps you on your right cheek, turn the other to him also.")

He was more likely to deflect scathing insults with one of his humorous, homespun frontier stories and a good laugh. The stories were like parables with a punchline. They drove his advisers and enemies crazy with frustration. But he replied, "With the fearful strain that is upon me night and day, if I did not laugh I should die."

In Cincinnati, he turned the other cheek to his native state of Kentucky:

"We mean to leave you alone, and in no way to interfere with your institution [slavery]; to abide by all and every compromise of the Constitution. We mean to remember that you are as good as we; that there is no difference between us, other than the difference of circumstances. We mean to recognize, and bear in mind always, that you have as good hearts in your bosoms as other people, or as we claim to have, and treat you accordingly."

And in his inaugural speech, he said the hope of the nation was found in "Intelligence, patriotism, Christianity, and a firm reliance on Him who has never yet forsaken this favored land."

"We are not enemies, but friends. We must not be enemies. Though passion may have strained, it must not break our bonds of affection. The mystic chords of memory, stretching from every battlefield and patriot grave to every living heart and hearthstone all over this broad land, will yet swell the chorus of the Union when again touched, as surely they will be, by the better angels of our nature."

Six weeks later, the nation was at war.

BOOK IV:
SHOWDOWN

By Winslow Homer for Harper's Weekly, 1862.

THE SIEGE BEGINS
'I found there was no need for spies'

**Gen. Lew Wallace leads troops across the Pontoon Bridge to Kentucky.
Sketch by A.E. Mathews, Ohio 31st Volunteers. 1862.**

Under clear blue skies, heated by the early September sunshine that still blazed like a baker's oven, the small army led by Gen. Henry Heth raised clouds of dust that could be seen for miles as they marched north to Cincinnati in 1862.

To the rural Rebels, it smelled like home: farm work, horse manure, ditch weeds, honest sweat and the late-summer music of locusts buzzing in the trees.

As they moved up Lexington Pike, they passed to the west of Cynthiana, where Morgan's Raiders had humiliated about 400 Union troops and militia in July. Among the prisoners Morgan captured were a platoon of firemen from Cincinnati and their brass cannon, sent by the Cincinnati City Council to defend Lexington.

Morgan ran off the Yankees, burned the train station and reported to General Bragg that local support showed Kentucky was ripe for an uprising against the Union. Generals Kirby Smith and Henry Heth had seen that report, and it was one of the strongest arguments for Smith to send Heth to take Cincinnati.

As Heth's snaking line of 8,000 soldiers, mounted officers and wagonloads of supplies trudged and trundled its way up the bone-dry dirt road, they brought along 20,000 extra rifles to arm all the fresh recruits they expected were waiting for a chance to join the War for Southern Independence. But as they passed little towns named Biddle, Sadieville, Corinth and Hells Halfacre, only a trickle of young men joined the march. Most of the extra rifles stayed packed away.

There was still good news for Heth. Before leaving Lexington, he had seen reports from spies who said Cincinnati was almost paralyzed by fear of an attack. And now, as they got closer to the city, the reports were even more encouraging.

"I sent a number of spies ahead," he recalled. "I marched from twenty to twenty-five miles a day. I found there was no need for spies; half a dozen or more men met me each day, just from Cincinnati, representing that the utmost panic prevailed in that city; there was no organized force there."[92]

Heth must have smiled at the news. "The authorities were impressing [drafting] the lawyers, the doctors and shopkeepers to defend the city. Some had guns, some pistols. They had some cannons but no ammunition, and on the improvised breastworks, wooden logs were painted black and put up; and that at the first shot fired, they would break for the river."

The spies also gave him a shopping list for plunder: "a complete inventory of the government stores and property in the city."

---

92   Heth, Henry. *The Memoirs of Henry Heth*. Praeger, 1974.

Every day he sent at least two reports back to Gen. Kirby Smith. Cincinnati was defended by clerks and "Quaker cannons" made from painted logs. It was almost too easy. All those supplies, millions in Union cash and gold in bank vaults, riverboats, weapons, food to fuel the Confederate Army, a critically strategic transportation hub—all ready to be plucked from drooping branches, defenseless.

"Smith gave me permission to attack," Heth said.

Before Wallace arrived, Cincinnati Mayor George Hatch called an emergency meeting of city leaders at Burnet House, including the mayors of Covington and Newport. He proposed surrender, "to avoid pillage and destruction." Hatch's political compass was already wiggling more South than North. And when he contemplated the death, damage and terror of an army turned loose on Cincinnati like Romans sacking Carthage, he chose the white flag. Better to be ruled by the South than to see Cincinnati looted and burned, he argued.

That was Sunday, August 31.

"The moral effect of this [surrender] would have been most inspiring to the Confederate cause and equally disheartening to the National troops," wrote Lt. Col. Willaim Neff in his 1891 history.

As Wallace hurried to Cincinnati to take command, one of his officers asked him, "Do you believe the enemy will come?"

"Yes," he replied. "He is an idiot if he does not. Here is the material of war—goods, groceries, salt, supplies, machinery—enough to restock the whole bogus Confederacy."

Wallace arrived at 10:00 Monday night and immediately dragged the city by its collar from the brink of surrender to defiant defense. His first midnight meeting with Hatch and the mayors of Newport and Covington made it very clear: There would be no more foolish talk of white flags.

"I had been told he sympathized with the South," Wallace said of Hatch. So he showed the mayors his letter from General Wright, giving him military command of their cities. Their cherished authority was immediately null and void. One man was now mayor, general and commander of everyone, military and civilians: Lew Wallace.

No matter how it rankled, they had to follow orders.

Hatch objected, "You are to put us in a state of defense, are you? How are you going about it? Have you a plan?"

Wallace calmly replied, "Yes."

"What is it?" Hatch demanded.

"It is to make the city defend itself."

As the mayors shook their heads, wide-eyed in disbelief, Wallace told them what he said to his skeptical staff: "Cincinnati has two hundred thousand inhabitants, and they ought to be able to defend themselves. They *can*, and I believe they *will* do it. What they want is direction."

Hatch tried to protest, but Wallace put up a hand. "Say, however, that I am mistaken," he said. "That the city is lacking in the right spirit. Behind it are the great states of Ohio and Indiana; the two together have a push the force of which is unknown, because it has never been tried. I mean to try it. If Gen. Kirby Smith will give me one week in which to get ready, I believe we can all lie back and laugh at him."

Then he read them his proclamation of martial law.

"This is martial law," Hatch grumbled.

"Yes, sir," Wallace replied.

"You suspend all business?"

"Yes, and all civil authority as well."

"And then what?"

"Every able-bodied man to work or to fight. I give him his choice."[93]

The proclamation went out.

Some in Cincinnati stayed locked behind doors of denial and scoffed at the fire-drill preparations for a siege.

Their confusion was understandable. The local papers were reporting that Kirby Smith and his Confederates were routed and on the run. It was typical of the propaganda published on both sides. Every battle was a victory—until the papers were forced to admit defeat and find a scapegoat for their wildly inaccurate headlines.

"Thousands did not believe in the impending danger," the *Atlantic*

---

93   Wallace, Lew. *Lew Wallace; an Autobiography*, New York; London, Harper & brothers, 1906.

Monthly reported from Cincinnati at the time. Wallace was warned, "If the enemy should not come after all this fuss, you will be ruined."

"Very well," he answered. "But they will come. And if they do not, it will be because this same fuss has caused them to think better of it."

Hatch challenged him, "Without soldiers, how can you enforce that proclamation?"

Wallace thought about it, then summoned the mayor to his headquarters at Burnet House for another meeting. When Hatch arrived, Wallace got right to the point.

"Will your police enforce?" he asked.

"Yes, you may have them," Hatch replied.

Wallace shook his head. "No," he said. "I won't direct them. I want you to control and direct them."

That decision led to one of Wallace's greatest legacies of the 10 days that followed.

But on that Tuesday morning, September 2, the arguments, debates and quibbling were over. The Defense of Cincinnati had begun. The city went to war.

Within a few hours of imposing martial law, $5,000 was offered by the city council for supplies, guns, ammunition and payrolls for the defenders.

Wallace wrote a letter to Ohio Gov. David Tod and Indiana Gov. Oliver Morton, asking for aid and troops, "the only hope of saving the city from capture, contribution in money [ransom] or fire."

He called a meeting of newspaper editors and publishers. They agreed to support his proclamation—declaring a brief truce in their acrimonious war on each other to defend the city.

The 89th Volunteer Infantry at Camp Denison northeast of the city was called out and reported for duty. Next came the 103rd Ohio Volunteer Infantry from Northeast Ohio. Soon on the way were the 7th Ohio Cavalry from Ripley, the 45th Ohio from Columbus, the 50th Ohio from Camp Dennison, and the 96th Ohio Infantry from Delaware, Ohio.

Everywhere in the city, neighborhood militias sprang into action, eager to show their courage. Most were formed at the outset of the war and again when Morgan's first raid threatened the city in July.

They had names like The Pearl Street Rifles, named after a business district where merchants pooled their money for rifles and organized their owners and employees to drill and defend the city.

Other volunteer militias that rallied to the defense were the Guthrie Grays, Captain Bard's Independent Infantry Company, Wallace Guards Independent Cavalry, the Ohio River Guard Force and the Steamboat Flotilla under command of Captain John Duble.

The Burnet Rifles were formed by members of the Literary Club of Cincinnati[94] and named after West Point graduate Robert Burnet, son of Burnet House owner Jacob Burnet. The Literary Club's account:

> After the firing on Fort Sumter, an episode in which member Larz Anderson's brother was the hero,[95] the Club called a special meeting and all who came agreed to volunteer, including those disqualified by disability or age, such as Alphonso Taft, and others who served in the Home Guard.

The literary club led by an innkeeper turned out to be some tough hombres.

That special meeting was called to order by Rutherford B. Hayes, the future 19th president of the United States. Hayes soon enlisted in the Union Army, fought and was wounded at the Battle of South Mountain in Maryland and rose to the rank of brigadier general.

Burnet Rifles drills were supervised by John Pope, who became one of the foremost Union generals, was defeated by Robert E. Lee at Manassas, then went on to command US Cavalry troops in the Indian Wars in the West.

Fifty-one members of the club joined the Union Army. Their ranks included a major general, five brigadier generals, eight colonels, four lieutenant colonels, 11 majors, 14 captains, seven lieutenants and one private. Among the 50 club members who went to war was Manning

---

94   The Literary Club of Cincinnati was formed in 1849 and still is active today.

95   One of the cannon batteries built in Northern Kentucky was named Battery Larz Anderson.

Force, Colonel of the 20th Ohio at Shiloh.

Colonel Neff of the Pearl Street Rifles was first to report to Wallace on the first day of martial law. He saluted and announced: "General Wallace, I have eighty men armed with Colt's revolving rifles,[96] well drilled, uniformed and fully equipped, ready to march."

"Sir," Wallace replied, "you are Company 1 of the 1st Regiment. If your people respond in this way, your city is safe."

Within two days, 14,000 Cincinnati men were organized and armed with Springfield rifles, Neff said. Soldiers took an oath of allegiance and were mustered in at Eighth Street Park.[97]

Wallace sent word that he needed any civil engineers in the city to report to him. He asked them if any had any military experience. None raised a hand. He asked if they knew how to build a rifle pit or where to put the ditch for defense around a battery of cannons. Again, silence. So he gave them detailed instructions, put them under command of an officer on his staff and sent them on ferry boats across the river to begin building batteries and trenches in the hills of Northern Kentucky. Following a basic principle of military strategy, Wallace took the high ground before Heth and his army could seize it. If Heth held the hilltops, his cannons could devastate the city.

Next, Wallace created the Cincinnati Navy.

"To keep in communication (and) patrol the river night and day and to assist in holding the fords, I had impressed 16 steamboats and, organizing them into a flotilla, put it in command of an old river captain, John Duble by name, as perfect a type of his class as the time afforded. While but a commodore by grace, he was of the stuff admirals are made of. Duble defended his boats with bales of hay securely lashed in place, and for each of them he had two six-pounder brass pieces and ammunition in plenty."

More than 2,000 men were stationed aboard the gunboats to fight or rush into battle as reinforcements.

---

96   A dangerous gun that sometimes discharged all chambers at once, injuring or killing the man using it. However, they could fire much faster than muzzle-loading rifles.

97   Garfield Place.

Cincinnati gunboats Lexington and Tyler saw action at Shiloh. Similar boats were used in the Defense of Cincinnati, clad in timber or cotton bales. *Harper's Weekly*, 1861.

It seemed as if there was nothing the city could not do.

"One spirit possessed them," Wallace recalled in his memoirs. "The drilled companies assembled in their armories and organized themselves into regiments. The air throbbed with the beat of drums. Unnumbered flags on the housetops, suddenly flung from the windows, freshened the beauty of the sunshine. The women were alike taken with the spirit; before the day expired every ward had its club of them determined to do what they could for the common defense."

The women distributed supplies and clothing and fed thousands of men in mess halls on Market Square, where the city's landmark Tyler Davidson Fountain would find its home in 1871.

But Wallace had a problem. There were no bridges across the Ohio River. Only the stump-like piers of the Roebling Suspension Bridge had been built. Getting all those shovel-toting civilians, soldiers and militias to the defensive line in Kentucky would take too much time using ferries.

Wallace called on the city's leading builders. Together with a group of riverboat captains and architect Wesley Cameron, they offered to build a pontoon bridge using coal barges that were sitting idle in the Licking River on the Kentucky shore.

Wallace asked how long it would take. It was already midweek, and it felt as if Heth was close enough to look over his shoulder and read his mail.

He was stunned when Cameron and the rivermen cooly replied, "Forty-eight hours."

Nothing like it had been done on the wide Ohio River. Wallace couldn't believe it was even possible but encouraged them to try.

"Within the forty-eight hours—my recollection is thirty hours—the enormous structure was reported ready and a city regiment crossed in platoon front," he recalled years later.

Once the barges were lashed together, they were lined with timbers and planked, making a bridge 25 feet wide. In the following days, whips cracked, shouts rang out and the bridge creaked and groaned under the weight of thousands of marching men, heavily loaded supply wagons pulled by six-mule teams, and heavy cannons and caissons of ammunition.

A second Pontoon Bridge was built across the Licking to connect the defenses from Covington to Newport.

The rush was frantic. At Court and Vine Streets, a man was run over by a gun carriage and both legs were crushed. [98]

Many of the troops who rushed across the river carried haversacks stuffed with souvenirs from home, but not enough blankets. When reports came back to Cincinnati that the troops were shivering in the chilly September nights, "Ladies stripped the blankets from their beds and came to their front doors with arms full of blankets for the men across the river," Colonel Neff reported.

He described his own unit's call to service.

"On Thursday evening, marching orders came for our regiment. We were to cross the Ohio River on the Pontoon Bridge and take position in defenses constructed the year previous at the outbreak of the war. General Ormsby McKnight Mitchell had been placed in charge in 1861. He proceeded at once to fortify the city by a chain of forts on the

---

98   Wimberg, Robert J. *Cincinnati and the Civil War*. 1992.

Kentucky hills about three miles south of the Ohio River. The most prominent and important fort was named Fort Mitchel in honor of its founder."

Cheers in Cincinnati, jeers in Covington

It was the same Ormsby Mitchel who built the Cincinnati Observatory in Mount Lookout. He was best known for The Great Locomotive Chase of April 1862. General Mitchell devised a plan to steal a Confederate train loaded with supplies for Corinth. He chose 23 raiders, who hijacked a train in Georgia, cut telegraph wires, tore up track and burned bridges until they were discovered and chased.

Out of fuel, they ran for the woods and were captured. Six men escaped, six were exchanged, and eight were hanged as spies, including Alfred Wilson of the 21st Ohio Volunteers, who was a railroad mechanic from Cincinnati. An 1890 collection of Civil War stories, *Sparks From the Camp Fire,* recounted Wilson's last words on the gallows:

> "He told them that though they were all wrong, he had no hostile feelings toward the Southern people, believing that not they but their leaders were responsible for the rebellion; that he was no spy, as charged, but a soldier regularly detailed for military duty; that he did not regret to die for his country, but only regretted the manner of death; and he added, for their admonition, that they would yet see the time when the old Union would be restored and when its flag would wave over them again. And with these words, the brave man died."[99]

Before the war, Mitchel was a math instructor at Cincinnati College, educated at West Point. One of his former students was Colonel Neff, who called him, "One of the most intelligent and accomplished officers. A gallant leader, second to none in ability and patriotism."

The defenses were being supervised by General Wallace and one of his best officers, Col. Charles Whittlesey, who fought alongside Wallace

---

[99] Morton, Joseph W. *Sparks from the Camp Fire.* 1892.

as commander of the 20th Ohio at Shiloh.[100] Whittlesey, an engineer and West Point graduate, insisted it would take 100,000 troops to defeat his defenses once they were finished.

Wallace was not so optimistic.

Colonel Neff described the scene as his 1st Company of the 1st Regiment for the Defense of Cincinnati marched off to battle:

> Then came word of command, "Forward March," and amid the deafening cheers and hurrahs the regiment moved down Vine Street to the river. The windows were filled with ladies' handkerchiefs waving, and amid tears and many a "God bless you, boys," we passed through the streets and crossed the Pontoon Bridge into Kentucky.
>
> Here a different reception awaited us. The sidewalks of Covington were lined with crowds of Rebel sympathizers who jeered and hooted as we passed. Taunts and curses, loud and deep, were heard on all sides. "Steady, boys, steady, forward march. Pay no attention."
>
> For many, that night was their first sleep on the ground in the open air. The colonel felt anxious for the situation. We were on the Lexington Road, without support, liable from the intelligence to be attacked at any moment.[101]

The 103rd Ohio Volunteer Infantry had a similar experience, according to their official history:

> The 103rd remained in Covington from September 4 to the 6th. Friendly citizens offered the men hot coffee and food. The regiment drew additional clothing—trousers, jackets and overcoats—and received $50 in bounty money. Life was very comfortable. The men bathed in the Ohio River, which they said was sluggish. The 103rd moved out on September 6 at 9:00 p.m. and marched a distance of three miles—all uphill in excessive heat on the dusty Lexington Pike.[102]

---

100 Whittlesey was part of the military guard that accompanied President-elect Abraham Lincoln on his train journey from Illinois to Washington, DC for his inauguration.

101 Lt. Col. William Neff, History of the Pearl Street Rifles and the Siege of Cincinnati, 1880.

102 Later named the Dixie Highway,

The troops were loaded down with three days' rations, excessive clothing and souvenirs from home. At one point along the pike, some thirsty men asked a man at the gate of his house, apparently a Confederate sympathizer, for drinks of water. After received an insulting answer, Lt. Luty J. Neville, of Company D., drew his revolver and told the man that he came down South to shoot Rebels and that this would be a good place to start. However, nothing more came of the incident.

The 103rd was armed with several siege cannons, 24 and 32 pounders, each with a range of 2,000 yards at a five-degree elevation.[103]

Almost more astonishing than the 48-hour bridge, an overnight Navy of gunboats and thousands of troops invading Kentucky in those early days, was the sight of bankers, businessmen, doctors, lawyers, clergymen, professors and teachers—indoor men with soft hands and clean nails—swinging pickaxes and wielding shovels alongside dockworkers, factoryworkers, coalmen, carpenters, bricklayers and blacksmiths.

Irish, Germans, English, Catholics, Protestants, Jews, wealthy, middleclass, poor—all rolled up their sleeves and sweated together, side-by-side in the hot September sun, digging trenches, manhandling wagons and mules, carrying ammunition and supplies.

For two weeks, class distinctions, pretensions, snobbery, prejudice and artificial social boundaries were dropped like a red-hot spoon, left behind along with all the other trivial demands of "normal" daily life. Cincinnati was united to fight a common enemy, bonded in a brotherhood and sisterhood of crisis.

They shared their misery and humor, blisters and new friendships born in the rocky trenches they dug. They liberated "secessionist chickens" for lunch and took pride in being members of "the motley crowd known as the Shovel Brigade."

"Every man had his choice of weapon," Colonel Neff wrote. "He

---

103 History of the 103rd Ohio Volunteer Infantry, 1865.

must fight with either a musket or a shovel, whichever he preferred, but it must be one or the other."

He described a wealthy businessman who owned a large clothing manufacturing company, who came across the river in a carriage to get vouchers signed so he could be paid for the supplies he delivered.

"A patrol saw him enter and he was then told to 'Fall in.' The command was given, 'Forward march,' and he was escorted to the fortifications where he labored faithfully with his shovel for a day or two."

According to the unflinching orders from General Wallace, none was spared. Artists, actors, musicians and poets were spared from hard labor, but were ordered to entertain the officers each night. Everyone shared the burden, and the spirits of the city were never higher.

But there was more to come.

ONE SQUIRREL, ONE SHOT
'Like the ghost of Daniel Boone'

An army of Union troops and irregulars crosses the Pontoon Bridge. The piers of the unfinished Roebling Suspension Bridge can be seen in the right foreground and center-left background.

Nehemiah Woods climbed down from the train at the Little Miami Railroad Depot in Cincinanti. His legs were unsteady. He had never been on a train. And in all his 67 years, he couldn't recall ever sitting in any one place so long, or being caged by glass and steel, surrounded by more people than he had laid eyes on in the past ten years combined.

As the crowded station swirled around him like a river current around a sunken tree, a little boy stared at him with wide eyes and an open mouth. He stared back. The boy was wearing shoes with buckles, short pants and a ruffled white shirt like a miniature English Lord on a can of chewing tobacco.

"Watch out, sonny," he finally said in a rumbling growl. "You'll catch flies if you don't close that mouth." The kid kept staring.

So Nehemiah patted his pockets to make sure he had everything he had started out with the day before when he walked out of the forest near Chilicothe. It was not much: a rolled, dirty blanket wrapped around his shoulders, a tomahawk and knife on his belt and his flintlock .54 caliber, muzzle-loading Hawken Rifle in his right hand. The rifle was more valuable than everything he owned rolled up in the blanket.

He wore deerskin leggings that were mostly gray and blackened in the knees from tending campfires. His shirt was buckskin too, with fringe at the bottom he could tear off and use to tie things together. His hat was ancient, with a flat, drooping brim and a dented round crown that had lost any shape it once had when it belonged to a soldier in the Revolutionary War. His feet were covered in tall Indian moccasins that climbed up over his leggings. A broad belt with a powder horn and cartridge box wrapped around the outside of his shirt.

He gave up on the kid, who seemed paralyzed like a stone statue, and turned to a black porter who was wheeling a stack of carpet bags and boxes on a handcart. He asked, "Sir, can you direct me to the head-quarters of General Lew Wallace?"

The porter stopped in his tracks, first out of astonishment at being addressed as "sir," then out of curiosity. He had seen hundreds of these untamed frontiersmen arrive, as wild as black bears and wolves, but none had been such a perfect museum exhibit. This one looked as if he had stepped out of history, directly from the previous century.

"Yes, *sir*," the Porter replied with a smile, returning the honor. "Just take Third Street to the corner of Vine. Look for a castle. That's the Burnet House. You can't hardly miss it."

"My name's Nehemiah Woods," the museum exhibit said, extending a calloused hand blackened by woodsmoke, dirt and who knew what else.

The porter paused, unaccustomed to such a cordial introduction. "Nehemiah," he repeated, extending his hand. "Ain't that the man who stood up to fill a gap in the wall when his city was invaded?"

"That's the one. Book of Nehemiah," Woods replied.

"You are right on time, Mr. Woods. That gap across the river is big enough to hold the New Jerusalem with room for King Solomon's Temple. I'm Moses, but my friends call me Mose."

A man standing by a carriage shouted, "Porter!" and Mose jerked his head in that direction, waved and nodded an "I'm coming" signal.

Nehemiah said, "I can see you know your Good Book, Mr. Porter. Thank you for pointing the way."

As he walked off, Mose watched briefly and shook his head with a smile. *Mr. Porter!* He would have quite a story to tell Abigail tonight over dinner. *Does that man even know they make rifles now that are not longer than a fence rail?*

He pushed his handcart stacked with luggage to the waiting carriage, where an impatient, frowning man in a derby was pointedly looking at his pocket watch. As Mose loaded the luggage, he wondered again, *Where do all those wild men come from?"*

They came from southern Indiana towns such as French Lick, Columbus, Connersville and Batesville and all the unmapped forests that had no name. They came from Ohio towns such as Wapakoneta, Minster, Gallipolis, Ripley and Snow Hill, and from counties named Tuscarawas, Muskingum, Coshocton, Seneca and Vanwert. They walked out of the pages of James Fenimore Cooper novels about the frontier past; men who remembered the days when Southern Ohio was called "The Miami Slaughterhouse," a "dark and bloody ground" ruled by fierce Shawnee warriors, whose favorite entertainment was torching cabins and torturing homesteaders.

The backwoods men were from an earlier, harder species that pushed back the thick forests, built their own log cabins in the wilderness and wrestled a life from thin crops and abundant deer, occasional bear and whatever else they could trap, shoot or hook.

When Ohio Gov. David Tod read the letter from General Wallace asking for urgent help, he immediately ordered all the troops that Columbus could spare to be rushed to Cincinnati. He sent 5,000 obsolete rifles from the city's armory to arm Cincinnati militias. And on September 2 he called on any armed man in Ohio to help defend Cincinnati and their state. They would get free transportation on the railroads, reimbursed by the State of Ohio. Then he boarded a train for Cincinnati himself.

In the following days, 16,000 men climbed aboard trains or walked to Cincinnati from 65 Ohio counties, Indiana and throughout the Great Lakes region. Cincinnati was overwhelmed.

Churches, warehouses and public buildings were used for barracks and the Fifth Street Markethouse was transformed into a giant mess hall.

As Nehemiah Woods approached the turreted palace called Burnet House, he saw a line of men winding down the street and joined them. The line, he found out, took him two blocks north to the Markethouse, where he was handed a plate that was quickly filled with fresh bread, boiled potatoes and slabs of ham.

"Boys," said a rough-looking man down the table, "this is better than we have been used to at home."[104] Nehemiah laughed and nodded with the other men, tucked his long gray-white beard into his homespun shirt and put his knife and fork to work, adding to the clinking, clanking music of hundreds of men eating and talking at once. Nehemiah had never heard anything like it.

As he took a break to gulp some coffee, a man at his elbow asked, "Where's home?"

He answered, "Near Chillicothe. You?" He learned that the man had a place on the Mad River near Buck Creek, northeast of Dayton. "Wyandots, Senecas, some Mohicans," the stranger said.

Nehemiah nodded and answered with his own geographic coordinates: "Shawnees. Some Cherokee." He paused, tore off another chunk of bread and asked, "Peaceful?"

"Mostly," was the reply. The man looked to be in his 40s, but it was hard to tell age among people who spent all their waking hours outdoors, regardless of the weather. "I believe the Western tribes have been taking advantage of our distractions."

"The army has been busy elsewhere," Nehemiah agreed. "My own son was at Shiloh."

---

104 Remarks of James Ramage on Battery Hooper and the Confederate Invasion of 1862. August 20, 2005.

The Squirrel Hunter. Artist unknown.
From Ohio in the War, by Whitelaw Reid, 1893.

His new friend inquired sympathetically, with raised eyebrows. Nehemiah understood the silent question and shook his head. "Missing, presumed dead."

"I am sorry to hear of your loss. My boys are with Buell's Army of the Ohio, somewhere near Louisville. I pray they are safe."

"Amen to that," Nehemiah said. He introduced himself and the man said his name was Amos Breyer, "like the thorn bush."

"I admire that Hawken Rifle you carry," Amos said.

"Thank you," Nehemiah replied, glad to change the subject. "That looks like a Kentucky Rifle," he said, pointing to the long gun leaning against the table next to Amos, stretching about three feet above their heads.

Amos nodded. "I hear tell they are offering Springfield rifles, but I think I will decline. I have never seen the like of a Kentucky Rifle for accurate shooting. I inherited it from my pa, who carried it at the Battle of Fallen Timbers."

It was Nehemiah's turn to raise his eyebrows. The gun was six feet long with a four-foot barrel. Amos lifted it up to show him the stock of polished walnut, burnished by years of shooting, with a pine tree-shaped inset of polished brass that shined like sunshine on a still pond.

"Two rounds a minute?" Nehemiah asked.

"Maybe a bit more in a scrap," Amos replied. "How about that Hawken?"

"About the same. It will hit the eye of a dragonfly at two hundred yards."

"Then old Jeff Davis better go shopping for a glass eye," Amos smiled as he polished his plate with his last crust of bread. "I hear they are sending all that's ready across that new bridge in an hour. Want to join me?"

"It would be my pleasure, sir," Nehemiah replied. "Allow me to collect my belongings from the presidential suite at the Burnet House and I will be ready to march."

Amos looked uncertain, then laughed as he caught the twinkle in Nehemiah's eyes. "In that case," he said, "let me summon my footman and have him bring up the carriage."

They both laughed, adding to the raucous, rising and falling waves of voices, laughter and the rough shouts of men in high spirits, crowded together by chance, eager to get started on a great adventure.

Both men joined hundreds more outside the Markethouse and held up their right hands to swear to God and give their oath of service. The huge, shifting mass of frontiersmen looked as comfortable in the city as badgers, raccoons and coyotes, Nehemiah thought. *And what kind of critter does that make me?* He knew what his late wife would say: "A bear with a sore tooth."

After the mustering in was completed along with lots of blatherskite about rules and whatnot, they hiked down to Burnet House, the latest "Eighth Wonder of the World." It did not disappoint them.

The floors were adorned with Turkish rugs that looked and felt like walking on deep red moss. Staircases built from enough sawn trees to build a dozen of their cabins and barns seemed to reach into the sky.

Amos nearly swallowed his chaw when he saw a cast-iron bathing tub with clawed feet, like some mythical beast of purification from the Book of Revelation.

Liquor was banned by martial law, leaving the city parched dry, but Amos reached into his rolled blanket that was tied around his neck and drew forth a small bottle of crystal clear firewater that he declared to be from the finest still along Buckskin Creek—his own.

They took turns taking a pull as they raised the bottle to each other and made toasts.

"To the Union and our sons," Nehemiah said, taking a swig.

"To claw-footed tubs," Amos said, tipping the bottle.

Nehemiah gave him a puzzled frown and Amos explained, "Any city that can feature such marvels is worthy of rescue."

With a chuckle, they capped the bottle and were soon lost in the moving crowd, crossing the Pontoon Bridge. As they passed over the wide river, men in the crowd began to sing "John Brown's Body," and more voices picked up the song that swelled like a mighty men's chorus, with "Glory, glory hallelujahs" rolling across to Kentucky and back up into the hills of Cincinnati.

The 'Cincinnatus' spirit

"They call them squirrel shooters," someone said. "Farm boys that never have to shoot at the same squirrel twice."

Others said they got the name when a few of the woodsmen shot squirrels out of the trees from the Pontoon Bridge before they even set foot in Northern Kentucky.

Whatever the source, the name stuck like tar on a bootheel.

They were an unexpected, undisciplined, spontaneous army of rough and ready farmers and homesteaders. They reminded the city of its fabled Cincinnatus Tradition, based on the story of the Roman general Cincinnatus, who stepped away from his plow, saved the Republic, then refused to become emperor and returned to his modest farm.

The turnout of Squirrel Hunters was so enthusiastic, after only a couple of days Governor Tod called for Ohio to please stop sending them before Cincinnati was crushed under an invasion of frontiersmen before the Confederate Army arrived.

Each trainload of federal troops called out by Tod was thrilling, but nothing raised goosebumps of gratitude and lifted the spirits of nervous Cincinnati like seeing the shambling buckskin brigades, with rifles like flagpoles across their shoulders, marching south across the river to save the city.

The *Atlantic Monthly* reported, "They came in files numbering thousands upon thousands, in all kinds of costumes and armed with all kinds of firearms, but chiefly the deadly rifle which they knew so well how to use.

"Old men, middle-aged men, young men, and often mere boys, like the 'Minute Men' of the old Revolution, they left the plow in the furrow, the flail on the half-threshed sheaves, the unfinished iron upon the anvil—in short, dropped all their peculiar avocations and with their leathern pouches full of bullets and their oxhorns full of powder, poured into the city by every highway and byway in such numbers that it seemed as if the whole State of Ohio were peopled only with hunters, and that the spirit of Daniel Boone stood upon the hills opposite the town beckoning them into Kentucky."

Most of the Squirrel Hunters declined to set down their rifles to pick up a shovel, but some offered their skills with an axe to clear acres of timber and make an open field of fire. The defenses stretched eight miles in an arc across the Kentucky hills, anchored on the Cincinnati side to the west at Price Hill and to the east on Mount Adams.

The downed trees were cut again into logs for revetments around artillery batteries and stacked in front of rifle pits to protect the artillery crews from infantry assaults.

Wallace's letter to Indiana Gov. Oliver Morton was nearly as effective as the one he sent to Tod. Both governors quickly grasped the dire situation: They could fight now to defend Cincinnati, or they might have to fight later on the outskirts of Columbus and Indianapolis. Confederate flags flying over Lexington and Frankfort were all the motivation they needed.

Morton sent ordinance—cannons, rifles, ammunition. He ordered the railroads to clear the tracks and give right-of-way to trains that carried men and weapons to Cincinnati.

By the end of the week, Wallace could not believe the morning reports. They showed he now had 72,000 men standing shoulder to shoulder to protect the Queen City.

"Of these, fully sixty thousand were irregulars," he wrote. "Such a gathering, if only on account of its numbers, begets a multitude of inquiries. The irregulars, so called, were in most part from Ohio, but with a supporting force indefinitely large from Indiana. Coming with pistols, shotguns, sporting rifles—in short, all the arms usual to the unwarlike citizen—we called them 'Squirrel Hunters.'

"Seventy-two thousand men! What did I do with them? Fifty-five thousand of the best armed, including the Cincinnati regiments, I posted behind the breastworks and rifle pits, which by that time were complete and stretching almost continuously from bank to bank of the great bend of the Ohio River, centering on Covington and Newport. With these were the garrisons of Fort Mitchell and its three supporting works down on the Lexington Pike, drawn from the regulars at Newport Barracks. About fifteen thousand were stationed as guards at fordable places above and below Cincinnati, for the river was in its lowest stage."[105]

On paper, Wallace's defense sounded invincible. But as a veteran of Shiloh, the general knew it was not that simple. Nearly all of his men were civilian militias or Squirrel Hunters. For all their spirit, they would be no match for combat veterans.

His 12,000 regulars outnumbered Heth's army that had swelled to 9,000 with recruits and volunteers. But very few of Wallace's troops had "seen the elephant" or heard a shot fired at them. They were green, like the men who broke and ran at Richmond, Kentucky.

At his peak of strength, Wallace's regulars included 26 regiments

---

[105] *Lew Wallace; An Autobiography.* Vol. II - Scholar's Choice Edition. 2015.

representing Ohio, Indiana, Michigan and one unit of cavalry from Kentucky.

The Confederate Army led by Heth had 24 regiments from Alabama, Georgia, Maryland, Arkansas, Texas and Tennessee. Heth's troops were hard men. They had seen the elephant, shot it, ate it and lived to boast about it. They were battle-tested, handpicked by Heth for their courage and combat experience.

Worse for Cincinnati, they were the same troops who routed the untested Yanks in Richmond. The Confederates were spoiling for a fight and had momentum and confidence on their side.

The anti-Lincoln *Cincinnati Times* spoke for many in the city: "The news from all quarters today is disheartening. Every waft of wind is ladened with disasters and in all quarters our brave men are being crushed."[106]

The Union was losing the war.

Wallace had seen how fighting spirit and blood in the eye could terrorize and rout larger armies. He didn't like to imagine what those warriors in gray would do when they turned loose their blood-chilling Rebel yells on skittish recruits, civilian store-clerk militias and back-woods Squirrel Hunters with antiquated guns.

What if his defense was a "pair of threes" poker-bluff, like those black-painted logs pretending to be cannons? That wouldn't fool anyone, much less a fighter like Heth.

About 20 miles south on the Lexington Pike, General Heth was pleased with the cards in his hand. He had decided he would hold Cincinnati hostage for $15 million. And if the city was foolish enough to refuse to pay the ransom, he would sack the city. Or Cincinnati might even burn itself just to keep all those valuable supplies out of the hands of the South—and the Union as well.

Whatever happened, he would win. Ransom, sack or civic suicide. Three aces.

---

106 *Cincinnati and the Civil War: Under Attack,* Wimberg, Robert J., 1999, Ohio Book Store, Cincinnati.

LET MY PEOPLE FIGHT

'You ain't citizens'

Courtesy of the Ohio History Connection, Columbus, Ohio.

Moses W. Williams did not get a chance to tell Abby about the grizzly-bear man who got off the train and called him "Mr. Porter."

Late that afternoon while he was sweeping the platform, a group of police showed up at the station carrying rifles bristling with bayonets that looked longer than Shawnee arrows and twice as sharp. He figured they were there to escort some rowdy passengers off a train. Like that time a few weeks ago in late July, when a trainload of 800 drunk, paroled Union prisoners pulled into the station. They had strange accents from Michigan and Pennsylvania, and it took all the city's 200 policemen to escort them at gunpoint aboard their next train to Camp Chase in Columbus.

Half of Cincinnati turned out that day as rumors flew that the prisoners were captured Confederates from Morgan's Raiders—only to be disappointed to find out they were Union soldiers set free after the battle of Murfreesboro in Tennessee.

This war was full of surprises like that.

But while Mose looked down the tracks to see if an unexpected train was coming along, he realized he was suddenly surrounded by three of the policemen, who formed a circle and pointed their bayonets at *him*. His first thought was that they must have mistaken him for some other man who had robbed a store or killed someone.

He knew some policemen were not especially careful about who they grabbed off the street, as long as they could arrest a suspect. And he had heard some say that men like Mose "all look alike."

And so do you, he thought.

One of the coppers who looked to be barely 16, wearing the patched and torn pants and jacket of a street gang, jabbed a bayonet at his stomach and said, "Come along now, boy. Don't give us no trouble."

Boy! Mose thought. *I'm old enough to be your father.* But he made his voice calm and friendly and said, "I don't want any trouble. Are you sure you have the right man? What's going on? How can I help you?"

They ignored his questions and an older big man with stripes on his sleeve said, "Come with us." This one didn't have to act tough like the kid. His voice carried all the menace of a man who is accustomed to being obeyed.

A few, like the older policeman, wore uniforms, but some of the others looked like the troublemakers who loitered around the railroad station and riverboat docks, looking for odd jobs or unattended luggage they could "confiscate" from its owners. They were rough and handled their rifles as if they had never held one.

"Pat," said the big officer, "pick yer head up. Hold that musket straight, like you see Liam doin'. Mary and Joseph, I can smell the liquor on ye like ye been bathin' in it, which would not be such a bad thing come to think of it. Don't breathe near a match or ye'll blow us all to kingdom come."

Another voice shouted from inside the station, "We caught three more in here, Captain." They came out pushing two more porters and a train mechanic—all black men Moses knew well—and herded them into a huddle, using their bayonets and fists and rifle butts. A kid who had freckles barely outnumbering his pimples tied them all together at the waist.

"Sir, can you please tell us what's going on?" the mechanic asked of the captain. A large man, not in a uniform, slapped him hard with the back of his hand and said, "You will keep your mouth shut, boy, if you know what's good for yeh."

Moses never got home to Abby and his girls that night. He and hundreds of other black men were crowded into a stinking mule pen paved with manure on Plum Street.

Mose joined other men who gathered scraps of lumber and bricks to sit on so they would not have to sit in manure. But then the big man with stripes on his sleeve came back and told them all to get up. He marched them out of the shade and into the hot sun and ordered, "Damn you, squat!"

As some of the men hesitated, he shouted, "Corporal, if any of these men stands up, shoot him."

Mose could tell most of the men were scared like he was, but a few glared back at the captain with eyes like hot coals that could start a fire in a bucket of water. The captain smirked. He seemed to enjoy the defiance.

Mose was also worried sick that Abby and his daughters would be afraid he was killed or injured. He had no idea what was going on. Would his family be rounded up? Were they already in a pen for women and children? Were they all going to be killed or sold into slavery across the river?

He thought about the proclamation from the new military commander, General Wallace. Along with everyone else in Cincinnati, he had read it yesterday morning. It said "all able-bodied men" would be put to work. And the mayor's proclamation said "every man of every age, be he citizen or alien, who lives under the protection of our laws, is expected to take part."

But Mose was not foolish enough to think that included black men. After Fort Sumter fell, he had joined a meeting of men who organized a group called the Home Guards. They were not foolish enough to think they could invade the South. They only wanted to defend their homes, their families, their property and their city. But when they offered to serve, they were told to keep out of it: "This is a white man's war." And when they tried to organize a second meeting, the police were there first and took away their keys to the schoolhouse.

Mose's friend Peter Clark still couldn't believe that the proclamations were for whites only. Although he was a well-educated teacher and soft-spoken, respected superintendent of the black school, Mose could easily picture Clark among the defiant men in the mule pen who dared to glare back at the police or even physically resist being herded into a pen like dumb beasts.

The men who resisted were easy to spot by their bleeding heads, bayonet wounds and purple bruises.

Clark told Mose how he had approached a policeman the morning of September 2, after the proclamation of martial law, and asked, "Please, sir, can you tell me, does the mayor desire colored men to report for service in the city's defense?"

The answer made Clark's blood boil and still made Mose angry too, although it should have been no real surprise. The cop replied, "You know damned well he doesn't mean you. You ain't citizens. All he wants if for you to keep quiet."

Except the way Clark described it, the answer was peppered with racial insults worse than curses.

"Everyone else will be allowed to volunteer," Clark said hotly. "But that privilege is denied to us. Permission to volunteer would imply some freedom, some dignity, some independent manhood."[107]

He remembered what Clark said at the first Home Guards meeting: "Colored men of the North are everywhere contemptuously being refused permission to participate in the great struggle which is opening the prison doors to their brethren in the South. In no community is this exclusion more generally ratified by public sentiment than in Cincinnati."[108]

---

107 Clark, Peter, The Black Brigade: A History of its Labors, 1868.

108 Ibid.

Mose was not so sure. Cincinnati gave more rights to blacks than any of the 11 states in the Confederacy—or Kentucky, for that matter. They could own property. They had a right to trial by jury. Freed blacks had protection from being dragged off the streets and sold into slavery in the South. They could not be imprisoned indefinitely or without explanation.

Then again, here he was, dragged off the street, imprisoned without explanation, indefinitely. Were they going to be sold off to the South in trade for Union prisoners?

And what about the riots? The city didn't seem to care much when mobs of Irishmen burned homes and beat black men half to death, until Morgan and his Raiders threatened Cincinnati again. *Then* they finally demanded an end to the riots.

Mose wondered about that. He decided being a border state made the city more hostile and divided than people in the South, who were settled on slavery, or people in the North, who were determined to end it. Cincinnati had its abolitionists, but the last time they tried to speak, one was pelted with stones. And Rev. Henry Beecher was locked out of the meeting hall because he might incite violence.

The anger and resentment was hotter in Cincinnati. Same in Maryland, from what he heard. And in border states such as Missouri and Kansas, people had been killing each other long before the Civil War started.

Apparently, the promises of free speech, assembly and other civil rights were as hard to catch as fireflies. Like that promise that "all men are created equal" and have the right to "secure the blessings of liberty."

He had laughed out loud when he read the part of the martial law proclamation instructing all citizens to assemble at their "usual places of voting." *We don't have usual places of voting because we don't have any usual right to vote,* he thought.

Finally, late that night, Mose and the rest of the men were taken out of the mule pen and marched across the river into Kentucky. It was the last place any of them wanted to go.

All of the men were familiar with the story of Ben Chelsom, whose story was reported by the Anti-Slavery Society in 1861. Chelsom was set free in his owner's will in 1840, and left slavery in Lexington for freedom in Cincinnati. But, "The heirs of his master were unwilling to lose so valuable a piece of property, and tried various schemes to get possession of him."

A gang of kidnappers "pounced upon Ben, who fought with the desperation of a man who had tasted the sweets of liberty, after having spent half a life in slavery, and it was not until he had been several times brought to the ground with a stick, and his head severely cut and bruised, that he yielded to his captors, who bound him, and took him to Covington jail, whence he was sent to A. M. Robinson, Estil County, Kentucky." Back into slavery.

As soon as they set foot on the Pontoon Bridge and touched the northern border of Kentucky—the edge of the Ohio River—the captives could lose their freedom.

They were finally halted south of Covington on Lexington Pike, and put to work immediately with shovels and picks. Under armed guards, they labored all night and all the next day. But they didn't know what to believe. Left without blankets, lacking food and water, they had been forced to cross into the slave state they feared most, where their rights, liberty, property and families all could be lost as soon as some slave trader rode up with a fistful of money.

Their fears were justified. Almost immediately after arriving at their new camp, 300 of the men were kidnapped—not by slave traders or Rebels, but by Union soldiers, who saw them as "abandoned property" they could use any way they wanted.

'A sad sight'

Three years after the war, Peter Clark turned his anger and resentments loose in his history of the Black Brigade.

> If the guard appointed to the duty of collecting the colored people had gone to their houses and notified them to report for duty on the fortifications, the order would have been cheerfully obeyed. But

the brutal ruffians who composed the regular and Special Police took every opportunity to inflict abuse and insult upon the men whom they arrested. The Special Police was entirely composed of that class of the population which, only a month before, had combined to massacre the colored population....

The Special Police was, in fact, composed of a class too cowardly or too traitorous to aid, honestly and manfully, in the defense of the city. They went from house to house, followed by a gang of rude, foul-mouthed boys. Closets, cellars and garrets were searched; bayonets were thrust into beds and bedding; old and young, sick and well, were dragged out and, amidst shouts and jeers, marched like felons to the pen on Plum Street, opposite the Cathedral. No time was given to prepare for camp-life; in most cases no information was given of the purpose for which the men were impressed. The only answers to questions were curses and a brutal "Come along now; you will find out time enough." Had the city been captured by the Confederates the colored people would have suffered no more than they did at the hands of these defenders. Tuesday night, September 2, was a sad night to the colored people of Cincinnati. The greater part of the male population had been dragged from home, across the river, but where, and for what? None could tell.[109]

Mose and Clark didn't know it, but at 2:00 a.m. that morning, Mayor George Hatch had issued the orders to round up all the black men in the city. He was the same mayor who had locked them out of their own schoolhouse when they tried to organize a Home Guard.

Many in Cincinnati were disgusted by Hatch's orders, according to an 1894 history of Cincinnati and Hamilton County:

Henry Howe of the Cincinnati Emergency Volunteers described the scene: "The colored men were roughly handled by the Irish police. From hotels and barber shops, in the midst of their labors, these helpless people were pounced upon and often bareheaded and in shirtsleeves, seized, driven in squads at the point of the bayonet, and

---

109 Ibid.

gathered in vacant yards and guarded. What rendered this act more than ordinarily atrocious was that they, through their head men, had at the first alarm been the earliest to volunteer their services to our mayor for the defense of our common homes. It was a sad sight to see human beings treated like reptiles. After being detained a few hours, they were taken across the river.[110]

On Thursday, September 4, the *Cincinnati Gazette* protested the harsh treatment of the city's black men. "Let our fellow soldiers be treated civilly," the editor pleaded, "and not exposed to any unnecessary tyranny, nor to the insults of poor whites." The *Gazette* maintained that Cincinnati blacks should have been invited to volunteer, "then there would have been an opportunity to compare their patriotism with that of those who were recently trying to drive them from the city."

The pro-Southern, Democrat *Cincinnati Enquirer*, had a different opinion. Their editors stoked the fires of racial resentment with an editorial warning Cincinnati that "Hundreds of thousands, if not millions of slaves will come North and West, and will either be competitors with our white mechanics and laborers, degrading them by the competition, or they will have to be supported as paupers and criminals at the public expense."

But if the mayor thought he finally had the whip hand, he was wrong. Once again, Hatch met his match.

Outraged citizens came to Wallace's headquarters to protest the way the mayor and his police were terrorizing black men and their families.

Wallace listened and got just as angry. He immediately appointed Judge William Martin Dickson to take command and form a Black Brigade, the first use of black men in military service during the war— something Wallace had advocated since the beginning of the war.

The choice of Dickson was a gut punch to Hatch and his police. The judge, educated at Miami University and Harvard, was a vocal abolitionist who argued publicly for freedom, enlistment of black soldiers and equal civil and political rights.

---

110   Wimberg, Robert J. *Cincinnati and the Civil War*. 1992.

Every man was ordered to fight or work on the Defense of Cincinnati. Workers felled trees, stacked logs and dug rifle pits and roads. H. Mosler, *Harper's Weekly*, 1862.

Colonel Dickson wasted no time. He rode across the Pontoon Bridge to inspect his new troops and reported what he found:

"I found them at work on the rifle pits and trenches about Fort Mitchel, on the Lexington Road, in the rear of Covington. They had been faithfully laboring during the previous night, and had already been commended by the engineer in charge, for efficient work. They were, however, weary from long labor, and anxious about their families. They were also alarmed because of the treatment they had received from the regiments of soldiers near them.

These seemed to look upon the colored men as abandoned property, to be seized and appropriated by the first finder. They detailed squads of soldiers, who appeared among the negroes at work, selected from them the number they wanted and, at the point of the bayonet, marched them off to the camps of the regiments, there to be employed as cooks, or in some menial capacity, for the officers.

A corporal's guard was engaged in this business when I reached Fort Mitchel. The colored men objected to this. They justly apprehended that they might be carried off with the regiments, or abandoned in Kentucky, where their presence as freemen was one of the most grievous crimes known to that state's laws, punishable with the enslavement of them and their posterity forever. They expressed entire willingness to labor on the fortifications under proper protection, but they desired to first return to their families and make preparations for camp-life.[111]

First, Colonel Dickson rode among the camps and rescued all of the black men who had been kidnapped. Then he marched them all back to his headquarters at Sixth and Broadway. By then, the sun was setting. The men had worked for 36 hours nonstop and had not seen their families for two days.

As he sent them home, Dickson gave them welcome news. They would be kept together with "the same protections and treatment as white men."

The men broke out in tears and cheers, with "grateful emotion," as Dickson described it. He told them they could go home but to report the next morning at 5:00 a.m.

"They felt some apprehension that the police would arrest them," Dickson said. "I told them that they could go home without fear in this respect, and dismissed them. In this I was, however, mistaken. Scarcely had these men, wearied with thirty-six hours of constant labor—upon half rations, and without sleep—broken ranks, when they were set upon by the police, and numbers of them, with blows and imprecations, dragged to the nearest cells. I reported the matter to General Wallace."

Wallace laid down the martial law again to Hatch. He sent his chief of staff, Nathaniel McLean, to deliver an order to the mayor:

"You will instruct the city police to arrest negroes only for crimes or disorderly conduct or when directed to be arrested by orders from these headquarters, or the orders of the military commander of the city."

The mistreated men were freed from jail late that night.

Colonel Dickson's head count showed that 400 men went home. What would happen the next day was anyone's guess. Could they really expect men who had been beaten, abused and insulted to defend a city that was unwilling to defend them?

Mose was not sure what would happen, either. He went home to the grateful, tearful arms of Abby and his daughters and shared his odyssey:

---

111   Dickson, William, Enrollment and Report of the Black Brigade of Cincinnati, 1864.

dragged from the railroad station, penned like an animal, herded across the forbidden river deep into Kentucky, sentenced to hard labor like a prison convict with no trial, bullied, humiliated, bruised and blistered, bone-weary from lack of food and sleep...

"What will you do?" Abby asked.

Mose didn't hesitate. "I will report in the morning."

That brought a fresh flood of tears. His wife implored him not to give up his liberty again, but he was determined, there would be no debate.

"Don't you see?" he said. "This is my chance to defend you and the girls, my home, my city, *like a man*. I may never get this chance again."

"But what if nobody else shows?" she asked.

"Then Moses W. Williams will be there."

He was able to get to bed for a few hours, but as tired as he was he could hardly sleep. The events of the past days kept spooling through his head in jumbled scenes. He saw the trenches, the bayonets, the Pontoon Bridge in moonlight, the hard, menacing faces of the Special Police, the frightened and angry eyes of the men in the mule pen.

Just before he finally drifted off, he saw Judge Dickson, a handsome man, sitting straight-backed on his horse, his head held high as he spoke loudly to reach all of the crowd gathered in the darkness lit by the glow of streetlamps, telling them something they almost couldn't believe. They would have *"all the rights and protections of the white man."*

Could it be true? He had to find out for himself. If there were rights to be given, he had to be there to get his share.

He was up and out of his house before daybreak, kissed Abby good-bye, wiped away her tears and promised he would come home again, although he was hardly sure of it himself.

As he headed west to Colonel Dickson's headquarters, he was glad to see men, alone or in small groups, just like him, walking in the same direction. It made him feel better to know that there were at least a few as crazy as he was.

As he got closer, the groups grew to dozens, then scores. He wanted to shout with joy and run, but just kept walking until he rounded the corner to Sixth and Broadway.

The crowd of volunteers was huge and growing.

About 400 men had gone home the night before. All of them came back. Plus hundreds more.

When heads were counted, Dickson couldn't believe it. More than 700 men had reported for duty. "They were glowing with enthusiasm," he reported, "ready for anything."

Capt. James Lupton stepped forward and presented the new Black Brigade with their own flag. "On its broad folds is inscribed 'The Black Brigade of Cincinnati,'" Lupton said, holding it aloft for the men to see. It was the Stars and Stripes, with 34 white stars on a midnight-blue background. Beneath the field of stars in one of the white stripes was the name of their new regiment.

"I am confident that in your hands it will not be dishonored," Lupton said.

A mighty cheer erupted that woke up the downtown neighborhoods, bouncing off the buildings and down the streets and alleys from Broadway to the mayor's office, the police headquarters and down to that filthy mule pen on Plum.

Mose kept shaking his head in disbelief.

"Men of the Black Brigade, rally around it!" Captain Lupton shouted. "Assert your manhood; be loyal to duty, be obedient, hopeful, patient. Slavery will soon die; the slaveholders' Rebel lion, accursed of God and man, will shortly and miserably perish. There will then be, through all the coming ages, in very truth, a land of the free—one country, one flag, one destiny."[112]

The cheers rose higher and louder. *He called us men!* Mose thought. This soldier in the crisp blue tunic was shouting things that were almost forbidden in Cincinnati. *The end of slavery!*

Lupton paused to let the cheers dwindle, held up a hand for quiet and concluded:

"I charge you, men of the Black Brigade of Cincinnati, remember that for you, and for me, and for your children, and your children's

---

112 Clark, Peter, The Black Brigade: A History of its Labors, 1868.

children, there is but one flag, as there is but one Bible, and one God; the Father of us all."

Tears of joy streaked Mose's face. He wished Abby and his girls could hear it. *Maybe they did,* he thought. *It was loud enough!*

The cheers that followed Lupton's closing words would have lifted the roof off the city if it had one. He looked around for his friend Peter Clark and picked him out standing close to the steps where Capt. Lupton stood with Dickson. Even Clark was smiling, his face lit with joy.

"I never saw so many men so happy to dig ditches," a man near him grumbled. Then he broke out laughing and cheered with the rest of them.

Courage and grace

There was still friction in the days ahead.

The following day, the Black Brigade was marched out a mile in front of the defenses, with nothing but scouts between them and the Confederates. They had no weapons to defend themselves, only shovels and picks. But they did not retreat or complain; they showed more courage than some Union officers.

Col. Jonah R. Taylor of the 80th Ohio lost his nerve and decided they must be Heth's army. In a panic, he ordered his artillery battery to fire on them.

Fortunately, the commander of the battery knew better and refused. Colonel Taylor insisted and again shouted the order to "Fire!" But the artillery crew loaded their cannons only with black powder and fired blanks. Finally, a rider came up in a cloud of dust and shouted at the fool Taylor to cease fire.

Later that week, Gen. Horatio Wright decided Louisville was safe from Confederate Gen. Braxton Bragg and came back to Cincinnati, taking command from Wallace, who moved his headquarters to Covington.

Once again, the army nearly found a way to turn victory into defeat.

As soon as Wallace moved out of Cincinnati, Colonel Dickson was disgusted to see the mayor and police take advantage of the change in command to resume arrests of the Black Brigade.

And once again, Hatch and the police had to be shaken by the neck and reminded that *they* could be arrested and jailed for disobeying orders.

But during the critical days of the Siege of Cincinnati, the men of the Black Brigade distinguished themselves with courage, perseverance and grace.

"They labored cheerfully and joyfully," Dickson reported. "They made miles of military roads, miles of rifle pits; felled hundreds of acres of the largest and loftiest forest trees; built forts and magazines.

"The section of work assigned to their special care lay between the Alexandria Road and Licking river, along the Cemetery Ridge and Three-Mile Creek."

Most in Cincinnati showed their appreciation. As the Black Brigade marched off to defend the city on September 4, Mose and the other men got choked up again to see Cincinnati citizens, white and black, crowding the sidewalks to cheer for them.

"Their march was enlivened by strains of martial music, from a band formed from the ranks," Dickson reported. "They were cheered on their way to their work by the good words of the citizens who lined the streets, and by the waving handkerchiefs of patriotic ladies. As they passed the different regiments in line of battle, proceeding to the fortifications, mutual cheers and greetings attested the good feeling between these coworkers in the same cause."

One Member of the Brigade, Joseph Johns, was killed by a falling tree.

Many members went on to fight for the Union. Some enlisted in the famous 54th Massachusetts, because Ohio would not permit black enlistments at the time. Some were killed at the Second Battle of Fort Wagner, depicted in the 1989 Oscar-winning film *Glory*. And Black Brigade member Powhatan Beaty became one of 23 black soldiers who won the Medal of Honor in the Civil War, by taking command to lead his regiment after all the officers were killed at the Battle of Chaffin's Farm in Virginia on September 29, 1864. Beaty is buried at Union Baptist Cemetery in West Price Hill, Cincinnati. [113]

---

113   Clark, Peter, The Black Brigade: A History of its Labors, 1868.

In his *History of the Black Brigade*, Peter Clark eloquently described its inspiring historic significance:

The shame meant to be inflicted upon them rebounded upon their enemies, and the members of the Black Brigade returned to their homes with the proud consciousness that, while the fortifications erected by their own hands had deterred the enemy from attacking in front, their uniform good conduct had completely routed the horde of Rebel sympathizers in the rear, who had vented upon the Brigade the spite they felt toward the Union and Liberty.

But they hope for more: they wish to be numbered among the children of the nation, to be invested with the privileges wherewith she endows her sons, to feel the heart throb when gazing upon the country's flag; to say with proud joy: We too are American citizens! Is this too much to hope for?

When the siege was over, the Black Brigade returned to Cincinnati. They marched across the Pontoon Bridge, through streets lined with cheering crowds. A barrier of prejudice had been broken down, at least temporarily. Just as the men of the Black Brigade were set free to fight for the city, the city was set free from its bigotry to embrace them as men, with dignity and courage.

A time of great crisis had brought out the "better angels of our nature," as Lincoln said.

For at least a few days, a welcome truce was called in the hostilities between the races in Cincinnati. Threatened with destruction, the city looked North, not South, for its salvation and future. The advocates of slavery and the Confederacy were being washed away like dead branches floating down the Ohio River to the Deep South.

As they were mustered out, Colonel Dickson offered the gratitude of the city. He wouldn't let Cincinnati forget what it had done to the men, but urged them, "In your hours of adversity, remember that the same God who has numbered the hairs of our heads, who watches over even the fate of a sparrow, is the God of your race as well as mine. The sweat-blood which the nation is now shedding at every pore is an awful warning of how fearful a thing it is to oppress the humblest being. Until our country shall again need your services, I bid you farewell."[114]

The Black Brigade returned that blessing with the highest honor of the times: A ceremonial sword, "knowing that whenever it is drawn, it will be drawn in favor of freedom."

As they went home, the men knew their own freedom was still in doubt—from the mayor and his minions in the police, from gangs and mobs fueled by racist hatred and resentment, from the southern half of America that would rather die than set its slaves free.

As the first week of martial law came to an end, Cincinnati's freedom was still in doubt too.

---

114 Report of Col. William Dickson, 1864.

FROM SIEGE TO SAVIOR

'Harsh measures are required.'

Gen. Horatio Wright, 1862. Mathew Brady.

The life of Horatio Gouverneur Wright was as thrilling as novels about Horatio Hornblower. Wright seemed to be everywhere at every pivotal battle in the Civil War: Bull Run, Gettysburg, Cold Harbor, the Siege of Petersburg, Appomattox Court House.

As an engineer, he worked on the Brooklyn Bridge, finished the Washington Monument, built forts in Key West and St. Augustine, Florida, and planned the defenses of Washington, DC and Cincinnati. Fort Wright in Kentucky was named after him, first as an artillery battery, then as a city.[115]

He was second in his class at West Point, a brilliant student who stayed on after graduation in 1841 to teach French and engineering.

---

115   Fort Wright's neighbor is Fort Mitchell. The city was named after Gen. Ormsby McKnight Mitchel of Cincinnati, who spelled his name with one "L," so the battery named after him was Fort Mitchel. Somehow, the city of Fort Mitchell installed an extra "L."

He was commanding troops in Florida in August 1862 when he was sent to command the Department of Ohio. That put him right in the middle of the Confederate invasion of Kentucky.

It was a consolation-prize assignment. His commanding officer in Florida had recommended him for promotion to major general and battlefield glory, but the Senate never confirmed him. Something in Wright's record seemed to follow him at a distance like a stray dog, never getting close enough to identify its owner. Being part of Union defeats at Bull Run and other battles didn't help. He may have lacked the right connections or made political enemies.

Or maybe he just didn't look the part. He was a heavy-set Yankee from Connecticut with a mild, agreeable, placid face and the soft eyes of a thinker, not a warrior. His downturned mouth looked like he expected disappointment, and his goatee and mustache were already showing gray at age 42. But among Union generals, he was greatly respected for his integrity and uncanny ability to organize the legions of logistics, details and paperwork of an army at war.

By the time he arrived in Cincinnati, Confederate Gen. Braxton Bragg's army was on the march to take Lexington and Frankfort. Louisville was in jeopardy when Wright reported under the command of his West Point classmate Gen. Don Carlos Buell, who was ordered to defend it.

A battle that could exceed Shiloh in savagery seemed inevitable to everyone—except Bragg and Buell. Both generals stalled and dithered like nervous boys at a dance, afraid to make the first move.

Bragg blustered that he would crush Buell "like an eggshell." Then a few weeks later he lost his nerve and fretted that his army would be "totally destroyed" by Buell.

"Bragg's management of this campaign was as faulty and badly managed as any military operation of the war," said Gen. Henry Heth in his memoir. Heth and Gen. Kirby Smith were so dismayed at Bragg's incompetence they both agreed that "General Bragg had lost his mind." Smith even sent Heth to report Bragg's mental incapacity to Confederate President Jefferson Davis.

If Bragg lost his mind, Buell lost his way. On August 25, shortly after arriving in Cincinnati, General Wright received a telegram from the overall commander of the Union Army, Maj. Gen. Henry Halleck. It played the biggest trump cards in the deck: It said that Halleck, Secretary of War Edwin Stanton and President Lincoln were "greatly displeased with the slow movements of General Buell. Unless he does something very soon, I think he will be removed."

Both Bragg and Buell had been in the most brutal fighting at Shiloh only three months before. They had seen mangled bodies, bloated corpses and broken men enough to last a lifetime. Perhaps they hesitated because they were still sleepless with nightmares and couldn't bear to feed more innocent, promising young sons into the meatgrinder of dismemberment and death.

But Wright must have been shocked to learn that his new commander was about to be sacked as soon as someone in Washington shouted, "Off with his head!" It was not an encouraging situation for anyone in command, and especially unsettling for Halleck to slander Buell to his subordinate. [116]

Halleck's telegram said, "I can hardly describe to you the feeling of disappointment here in the want of activity in General Buell's large army." The scheming Robespierre[117] of the Union Army added, "The government seems determined to apply the guillotine to all unsuccessful generals. But perhaps with us now, as in the French Revolution, some harsh measures are required."[118]

The message to Wright was written between the lines: Make the right moves and Buell's "large army" could be his. All he had to do was betray his classmate and join Halleck's clique of toadies.

Goaded by the political bayonets in Richmond and Washington,

---

116   Lew Wallace wrote later that Wright was being "ground into dust" by opposing political and military pressures, "Yet the result proved him the good soldier and excellent man he certainly was."

117   A political leader of the French Revolution who instigated the purges that became known as the Reign of Terror, Maximillien Robespierre was beheaded by the revolution he incited.

118   Smith, David, The Defense of Cincinnati: The Battle that Never Was, Cincinnati Civil War Round Table, January 15, 1998.

Bragg and Buell finally fought each other in October at the battle of Perryville, Kentucky, the bloodiest battle in the state. More than 20,000 Union troops fought 16,000 Confederates. Buell had another 30,000 men in reserve, but refused to commit them and was defeated that day.

But then Bragg, fearing Buell's huge reserves, chose to retreat from Perryville and Kentucky, ending the Confederate Kentucky Campaign. Perryville was the "high water mark" of the South in the Western Theater of the Civil War. After that, the Dixie tide receded.

For General Wright, though, the political, tactical and practical problems in late August 1862 were overwhelming: defend Louisville under a general who was reluctant to fight, yet somehow also defend Cincinnati from General Heth's approaching army without any troops.

By September 4, Bragg's plans to take Louisville had evaporated along with his confidence. The city was safe under Buell, so Wright returned to Cincinnati.

Mistakes were 'instantly apparent'

Wallace was already looking over his shoulder, waiting for Halleck to roll out the guillotine. Friends brought him rumors of Halleck's schemes to replace him, and he was demoralized. The sudden return of Gen. Wright to take command did not go well. Wallace wrote:

"General Wright returned to Cincinnati, and by his order, as the situation was becoming critical, I transferred my headquarters to Covington. Immediately a great pressure was brought to bear upon him by certain individuals to permit them to open their shops and stores and, yielding, he modified my proclamation according to their wishes. The bad effect became instantly apparent."

Those "certain individuals" probably included the mayor and local businessmen. Just two days earlier, the *Cincinnati Times* had published an editorial calling the defense of the city a fraud, a foolish "big scare." The mockery of the threat was reckless and damaging to the morale of the city, so Wallace shut the paper down.

The bigger, leading newspaper did not rush to defend freedom of the press for the *Times*. Instead, the *Cincinnati Commercial* gloated that "for the present they cannot proceed in their favorite role of common scolds, raving like bedlamites about things great and small, fatally and foolishly bent on mischief."

America's liberties were still fragile new growth, easily trampled. But the harm by the *Times* and General Wright's concessions was done.

By Saturday, September 6, "The trenches were almost abandoned," Wallace said.

Heth on Lexington Pike

Meanwhile, in addition to spies who reported to him daily, Heth also had help from Cincinnati newspapers that reported battery positions, work on the defensive networks, troop arrivals and the decaying morale of the city.

Farmers who pretended to deliver hay to the city while collecting intelligence told him Cincinnati's hasty defenses were collapsing. Heth was close enough to feel victory in his grasp.

"Undoubtedly, had Heth moved with directness of purpose from Lexington, it had not been possible to have saved the city from him," Wallace said. "Its very defenselessness, however, helped thwart him. In excessive confidence, he journeyed leisurely along, helping himself to cattle and horses on the way."

Heth would have disagreed. His men were covering 20 to 25 miles a day.

As Heth approached, General Wright reconsidered his leniency. He had reports that 30,000 to 40,000 men were marching with Heth, bringing as many as 40 cannons. So he called out another 3,000 civilians to return to the trenches.

But time was running out.

Wright also telegraphed the governor of Kentucky in Louisville that both cities could not be defended at once. "We had better give the Rebels temporary possession than to risk all while the chances are against us."

It was clear which city would be sacrificed to "temporary possession." It was not Louisville.

By Sunday, September 7, Heth was only a few miles from Covington.

As his men, horses and cannons trudged up Lexington Pike, bystanders described them, as "ragged, greasy and dirty, and some barefoot, and looked more like the bipeds of pandemonium than beings of this earth." [119]

The men who waited ahead in the trenches—soldiers, civilians, Squirrel Hunters and the Black Brigade—had been on a wild carousel of hard labor, cold nights, hot days, bad food, rain, frustration, mutiny, pranks, sunstroke, boredom and panic.

Sgt. T. B. Marshall of the 83rd Ohio described one of the false alarms. His regiment was marched across the river without rations or rest on a scorching, humid day and ordered to form battle lines immediately at Camp King in a cloud of dust so thick they could not see where they were. "Captain Cornell of Company E rushed in front of his company waving his sword frantically over his head and cried, 'It is victory or death' at the top of his voice. Most of us were so badly frightened that if the enemy appeared it would have met with but a feeble resistance."

Their commander, the excitable Colonel Taylor who had tried to fire cannons on the Black Brigade, saw men in the distance and declared, "It is either our men or the Rebels." And with that brilliant observation, he scurried back to his safe quarters. Sgt. Marshall reported, "The affair was ever after facetiously called 'The Battle of Camp King.'"[120]

Cincinnati Archbishop John Baptist Purcell came out to bless the men, followed by a surprising entertainment. Colonel Neff of the 103rd Ohio described it:

"Just then a performing elephant, escorted by its keeper, Corporal Seely of Company A, was making the rounds of the camp and appeared at headquarters to honor our guests.

"The unwieldy animal knelt down, rose again, raised the right foot, then the left, and finally reared up on his hind legs. The keeper was quite encouraged and said, 'The elephant will now stand upon his head.' But this interesting performance was indifferently performed. A portion of

119   David W. Smith, Cincinnati Civil War Round Table, January 1 5,1998.

120   Wimberg, Robert J. *Cincinnati and the Civil War*. 1992.

the elephant remarked in a stage whisper that when he got from under his cover he would thrash the keeper."[121]

The soldiers inside the elephant suit were not as amused as the crowd.

Crowds of curious onlookers rode out in carriages and wagons, as if the thousands of men who cleared trees, built forts, marched, drilled and dug rifle pits were all performers in a circus that came to town. One wagon was owned by a sutler who sold cigars and tobacco at "exorbitant prices," Neff wrote.

An officer learned about it and ordered, "Unload the wagon and fill it with ammunition," and two dozen men "sprang to obey the order." Within minutes, the cigar sutler had made his own involuntary contribution to the Defense of Cincinnati.

Confederate sympathizers also came out to heckle and insult the men as they worked. But they were soon forced to work, too.

"The Rebel sympathizers of Newport and Covington were marched out under guard to dig entrenchments," Neff said. "They did not relish the work. It was bad enough for hands unused to tools to dig at all, but to throw up entrenchments against their friends was adding insult to injury. Curses loud and deep expressed their anger.

"In passing along the line, one of our men asked permission to prick one of them with his bayonet: 'He is so abusive, flesh and blood cannot stand it. I will only give him an inch. It will do him so much good.'"

The answer was a firm "No." Stabbing the future congressman from Newport with a bayonet would not be allowed, no matter how much "good" it would do him.[122] The loud curses continued, but so did the work.

Neff, like many of the men, discovered he liked sleeping outdoors, and had a hard time returning to the comforts of a soft bed and roof over his head when the siege was over. And going back to "normal" life was dull after all the excitement on the front lines.

As he worked in the makeshift headquarters one afternoon, a cavalry

---

121   William Neff, History of the Pearl Street Rifles.

122   Rep. James Beck, Democrat, elected and served 1867-1890.

scout rode up and said in the elaborately understated, wry style of the times, "I do not wish to alarm you needlessly, but yonder battery of artillery is trained directly upon your headquarters. The captain is gone to the city and the lieutenant is nervous. It would not take much to blow you beyond the Southern Confederacy."

"He was right," Neff wrote. "We could look into the muzzles of the guns. An orderly was dispatched forthwith, and the guns were elevated to the proper range over our heads."

Disaster was averted.

One Wednesday night, "Word came that the long-expected attack would come at daylight the next morning," Neff wrote in small, elegant handwriting. "Everything was in readiness. At three o'clock Thursday morning, the long roll sounded and the entire army, now numbering eighty thousand men, was under arms and in line of battle. No attack was made.

"In the afternoon we were again ordered out in full assurance of an imminent attack."

A Presbyterian pastor rode up in his carriage to tell them the enemy would emerge from the woods at any second and the shells would fly immediately. A father rushed out to demand his son, but the young man refused to go home with him. "The boy would not budge an inch."

Across eight miles of defensive lines, men and boys, soldiers and civilians, black and white, wealthy and poor, all shared a common thought: Would this be their last day on earth? How would they handle their fear when the bullets swarmed? Would they run or fight? Each was alone with his fear, quiet, afraid to give voice to doubt, convinced he was the only one so frightened. Still, nearly all of them stood firm and waited for whatever might come.

But back in the city, the spirit of unity and determination had begun to melt away like sugar cubes in hot coffee.

General Wright let the banks open on restricted hours, sent teachers back to school, opened the bakeries, butcher shops and grocery stores, released doctors to see their patients and let the anti-Lincoln, "big scare"

Times crank up its presses again. Drugstores were opened and funerals resumed. Only liquor sales remained suspended—at least on paper.

All of these were necessary in a city that had grown to more than 200,000, but they also sent a message that life could go back to normal, that there was no threat, the city was safe.

It was not. Cincinnati would have been alarmed to learn that earlier in the week, while Heth and his army were in Georgetown, Kentucky, marching north, General Kirby Smith had sent him word that he would send reinforcements under the command of Col. Preston Smith, who would rush his men north from Cynthiana.

Heth and the Confederates were dead serious even if Cincinnati was not. By September 10, he was just a mile south of Fort Mitchel and Smith himself was making plans to march north in support with the rest of the army that had taken Richmond, Lexington and Frankfort.

Wallace knew the crisis was coming. He had sent one of his aides, Col. Ben Spooner of Lawrenceburg, Indiana, to scout the Heth army. Spooner and two handpicked men posed as Southern slaveowners chasing a runaway. The ruse worked so well Heth even invited them to dinner. The spies brought back a detailed report of his cannons and regiments of infantry and cavalry.

Left to General Wright, that valuable intelligence would never have been known. Wright wanted nothing to do with dishonorable spying and refused to approve the mission.

But Wallace knew Heth was very close. At night, he could see lanterns in Cincinnati windows, sending signals to Heth and his scouts.

"The hours were of sharp anxiety," Wallace wrote. "For ever since the completion of the bridge, I had been subject to a dread. If Heth rushed our works with all his might and my citizen soldiery fell into a panic, each of them would betake himself to the bridge and then what wholesale drowning would occur."

He had seen routed, panicked troops run at Fort Donelson and Shiloh. He could easily imagine the scene as thousands of soldiers and civilians jammed the bridge entrance, easy targets for slaughter by Heth. Even if the bridge did not come apart, the river would have been clogged by floating bodies as the men were pushed off its sides like water from a bursting pipe.

He could imagine the Confederates sacking and burning the city, plundering food, bank vaults and military supplies. Then the Rebels could gather all of the recruits Kentucky could offer and march north, to Columbus, Indianapolis and other cities that might fall like Lexington.

All it would take would be one thrilling victory to make Gen. Kirby Smith's call to join the rebellion irresistible to the southerners in Kentucky. Cynics said the state was "just waiting to see which side won." When he entered Lexington, Smith had reminded them how the American colonists had seceded from Great Britain: "We call upon you to take up arms and join with us in hurling back the Northern hordes who could deprive us of our liberty."

Even General Grant knew the crisis was dire. He sent word to his parents to leave their home in Covington and go north, where they would be safer.

But most of Cincinnati had slipped into a false confidence in the work they had done. By September 8, they had eight forts and batteries in Kentucky, fortified with logs and trenched rifle pits, containing 15 cannons.

They were named after local leaders (Battery Burnet, Battery Hatch), war heroes (Battery Phil Kearney), and generals (Fort Mitchel, Fort Wright).[123] Some had no cannons at all.[124]

It looked like a formidable defense. But Wallace knew better. He was sleepless and constantly worried that his lines would collapse when the first shots were fired.

On Wednesday, September 10, the local press was panicked. The *Cincinnati Times* went from scoffing at a "big scare" to being just plain

123 Gen. Kriby Smith may have been surprised to learn that one of the batteries—Battery JLK Smith—would be named after his nephew, Joseph. L. Kirby Smith, who fought for the Union and was killed at Corinth that October. Another was named after an old friend of Heth, Gen. John Buford of Kentucky (Battery Buford). Battery Burnet was named for the commander of the Burnet Rifles, Robert W. Burnet of the Burnet House family.

124 By 1864, the defensive line had 24 batteries and four forts, added under supervision of Major James Simpson.

scared. "It is probable that before this reaches our city, the roar of artillery may be heard from the Kentucky hills," the paper said.

"A fight is expected this evening," said the *Gazette.*

For the men across the river, that was not news. They had been told to form battle lines for an imminent attack no less than seven times. Each time the adrenaline would rush, making their hands shake as they loaded their rifles, standing in assigned battlelines, expecting hordes of Rebels to come roaring out of the woods at any second. And then they would wait. And wait.

After several episodes, their fighting edge was as dull as a rusty spoon.

Nehemiah and 'Mr. Porter'

Nehemiah Woods was curious about all the commotion. Drums were making a racket, men were shouting orders, wagon drivers were cracking their whips and dust was swirling everywhere. It looked like something big was about to happen, so he told Amos he was going yonder over the hilltops to take a gander.

Amos nodded and said, "I reckon if Jeff Davis wants me, he will find me," then rolled over on his blanket and went back to sleep. It was Thursday morning.

As Nehemiah crested a hill walking South, he was surprised to see men working with picks and shovels, far beyond the rest of the soldiers. As he got closer, he thought he recognized the man he had met at the train station.

"Mr. Porter," he said in a booming voice that was loud without shouting. "What're you doing so far out in front? Preparing a road for the Rebels?"

Mose looked up and smiled to see the bear man again. He paused, leaned on his shovel and swept off his hat. "Mr. Nehemiah Woods! I could ask you the same. Are you hunting gray squirrels this morning or Dixie chickens?"

"Amazing how often I shoot at a squirrel and kill a chicken instead," Nehemiah replied with a wink.

Mose laughed, then turned to his left and announced, "I'm taking a break." Nobody objected, although some studied Nehemia with frank curiosity.

Peter Clark asked, "Who's your friend the mountain man, and who is Mr. Porter?"

"Let me introduce you both," Mose said. "Mr. Woods, meet Peter Clark; Mr. Clark, meet Nehemiah Woods of Chillicothe."

They shook hands and walked over to a shady spot under a large maple tree where there was a water bucket with a dipper. After sharing a drink, they sprawled out in the grass.

"Is that a gun or a spear?" Clark asked.

"It's a long rifle. With one of these, nobody can get close enough to use a spear or a bayonet."

"Then maybe you can stick around if things get hot around here," Mose said. "We don't have any guns, and the soldiers back there behind us get itchy feet if they come out this far."

Nehemiah looked surprised and asked, "No guns? What happens if—"

"They don't care what happens to us," Clark replied, angry. "Nobody gives a damn what happens to a black man."

Nehemiah was silent, scowling. Then said, "I lost my son at Shiloh. So I reckon somebody cared."

Then it was Clark's turn to be silent.

Mose said gently, "Sometimes we get all tangled up in our own troubles like a snagged fishing line, hooked on one thing in front of us." He looked at Clark. "Maybe we should stop and think how things look from the other side of the pond. There's things worse than being locked in a mule pen."

Nehemiah looked puzzled, so Clark and Mose explained the arrests, the appointment of Colonel Dickson and the formation of the Black Brigade.

Nehemiah shook his head. "I never went to West Point and never wore a uniform, but it seems to me that any man who is willing to stick his neck out this far in front of the army deserves a rifle to defend himself. I know where to find some that are not being used."

"That's a kind offer," Mose said, "but that might not go well with Colonel Dickson. It seems we are part of an experiment to see if black men are better than logs for catching Rebel bullets."

Clark laughed.

Nehemiah smiled and asked, "Are they at least paying you for all this work?"

Mose nodded. "A dollar and fifty cents a day."

Nehemiah raised his bushy white eyebrows and whistled. "That's a dollar fifty more than the secessionists are getting. And me too, come to think about it. If we can persuade those Rebs to stick around for a while and behave themselves, you can save up enough to buy a rifle like mine."

Nehemiah handed it to Mose, who admired it, aimed it at the horizon, and passed it to Clark, who held it in both hands and just stared at it.

"He's thinking about how he would like to use it on the Special Police," Mose said to Nehemiah. "You better take it back before he does something crazy."

"It's okay," Clark told Mose, handing the rifle back to Nehemiah. "Being out here in front of the army is not entirely bad. The best part of it is we have not seen any of those *Special Police*." He spoke the last words like spitting a curse.

Mose laughed. "When it comes to fightin' men who shoot back, they are not so special, I guess."

Nehemiah chuckled, got to his feet and nodded his goodbyes.

"Can we rely on you to stand in that gap, Mr. Nehemiah?" Mose asked with a smile.

"I will do that if you promise to deliver your people to the Promised Land, Moses."

SHOWDOWN AT FORT MITCHEL
'All his knives laid out for immediate use'

The battery on Mount Adams, from a sketch by R.W. McComas.
Frank Leslie's Illustrated Newspaper, **1862.**

Enthusiasm to defend the city was far from unanimous.

In the first week of the siege, a distant ancestor of Corporal Klinger[125] was caught on the street in a dress, bonnet and shawl. The disguise was not convincing, "as he had forgotten to shave off his heavy black mustache," the *Cincinnati Gazette* reported. He was arrested and fined $5.[126]

Two tailors were arrested a few days later, caught as they worked at sewing machines in their shop, wearing dresses to avoid being drafted for the rifle pits.

Men were caught hiding in cellars, attics, cisterns or under their beds throughout the 12-day crisis.

And some who may have been undecided probably ran for the nearest cellar when they read in the *Times* that "a surgeon has improvised a hospital and has all his knives laid out for immediate use."

Meanwhile, the men in the trenches, batteries and rifle pits managed

---

125   From the TV show *M*A*S*H.*
126   About $150 today.

to make the best of it. They made their muddy camps almost like home, or at least like the neighborhood tavern.

A reporter noted that the Fort Mitchel battery was well stocked with wagonloads of meat and barrels of beer. In Covington, a saloon owner's wife, Mrs. Getz, chased seven soldiers out with a sword when they demanded banned liquor and refused to leave. Or, according to another newspaper, it was the soldiers who chased *her* out of the saloon with their bayonets. Both versions agreed that the thirsty miscreants were arrested.

All week there were steady reports of accidental shootings, some fatal. A boy playing with his gun shot his best friend. Another man, demonstrating his pistol, shot a bystander to death. By the end of the first week, the gun-toting defenders of Cincinnati had shot more of each other than Confederates. But that might soon change.

In the meantime, Wallace and other commanders wondered through sleepless nights if their patchwork army could stand and fight in the nerve-shattering chaos of battle.

Sure enough, at their first skirmish with Confederates, the defenders of Cincinnati crumbled like rain-soaked hardtack.

Henry Heth recalled, "On reaching the vicinity of Newport a force was discovered. I threw out some skirmishers. Before the skirmish line fired a dozen shots, this force broke and ran, throwing away knapsacks, guns and all impedimenta."

Heth and his soldiers might have taken the discarded rifles, but the Austrian guns were "almost useless" according to soldiers armed with the surplus weapons from an armory in Columbus. In one encounter with the Rebels, only six of their 18 rifles worked at all.

Wallace rode out to battle on Old John and spent the day in the saddle when he heard reports of the first skirmish, but it was over by the time he arrived.

The next day, Tuesday, September 9, Wallace and General Wright rode out to inspect the troops. They had eight batteries and forts in a network that arced like an eight-mile shield south of Cincinnati. The rifle pits and batteries of cannons were connected by telegraph lines to Wallace's headquarters in Covington, at the center of the defensive line.

If the Rebels broke through, there were gunboats on the river and cannons in Price Hill and Mount Adams to make a last stand.

But for all the trenches, log walls and gunboats, they had only 15 cannons—an almost laughably small amount of artillery to defend the sixth largest city in the nation. Worse, like many of the infantry, some crews that served the cannons had never been tested in battle or fired their big guns with enemy shells raining down around them.

As Wallace and Wright rode south, they stopped at Fort Mitchel and climbed on the earthworks around the battery. Through German-made binoculars, Wallace could see thousands of Confederate troops camped alongside the Lexington Pike.

At the same time, General Heth was on the rooftop of a home near what is now the intersection of Dixie Highway and Turkeyfoot Road, where he "carefully inspected our lines," Colonel Neff of the Pearl Street Rifles wrote.

They were so close the dueling generals could see each other. Wallace described it in his autobiography:

> From a parapet of Fort Mitchell, I saw through my glass a number of gray-coated gentry mount to the roof of a house. It was easy to surmise what that meant. My opponent was reconnoitering.
>
> An excellent artillery officer, commanding the fort, trained one of the great guns upon the party and begged to fire. I forbade it. There were women and children under the roof; but, if that were not enough, good policy, as it appeared to me, demanded that the enemy should be allowed to see from a distance all he could of what he had to go against.
>
> General Heth, it had been reported to me, was a graduate of West Point. That he had been selected to conduct the expedition was ample evidence of his capacity. I knew fairly well why, having reached his destination early in the day, he had halted instead of at once ordering an assault. The fort commanding the pike had caught his soldier's eye, and, riding to the right and left, he had

taken account of the long line of freshly made yellow breastworks and the masses of people blackening the undulations behind them. It had been more than singular had he failed to be impressed as well as surprised by what he beheld.

The American behind a fieldwork, though ever so slight, and though no soldier, had his established character for courage. And of that, doubtless, the general also paused to take account.

Wallace knew Heth was probing weak points in his lines, so he immediately telegraphed all of the rifle pits and batteries to prepare for an attack. Pickets were doubled. The motley mix of defenders in buckskins, homespun britches, civilian topcoats, coonskin caps, top hats and the uniforms of militias and the Union Army, were on high alert.

As the two generals sized each other up, the skirmishes escalated to small battles. A soldier involved in the fighting, N. A. Pinney of the 104th Ohio Volunteers out of northeastern Ohio, recalled the action:

"Ordered to the double-quick, we were making good time forward when a volley from the woods ahead brought us to a sudden halt. Company A in advance lost one man killed and two wounded. Companies A, F, D and I were immediately filed out to the left and right to be deployed as skirmishers. A ball whizzed over the head of Company D and every man dodged as if he expected to be hit, but never a man broke step out of the ninety greenhorns in line."[127]

An officer waved his sword and shouted that he would cut off the head of any man who flinched. "You are in the presence of the enemy!" he yelled over the gunfire.

The unit found cover in a ravine and shooting continued through the day until they were marched back to Fort Mitchel.

The only man killed was Sgt. William Bleeks.

They passed a retreating regiment, the 101st Ohio, "who presented about as much the appearance of soldiers as a mob of schoolboys out for a holiday," Pinney wrote. As the first shots were fired, the 101st ran back to town.

---

127 Pinney, Nelson A. *History of the 104th Regiment Ohio Volunteer Infantry from 1862 to 1865.* 1886.

Pinney's history of the 104th offers a rare foot-soldier's view of the conduct of the war. His unit's top two commanders were a miserable drunk and a nincompoop, he wrote. When they marched south in October, they were ordered to camp beside Snow Pond, a stagnant sinkhole covered in green scum they called "frog spittle." When horses and men drank so much of the foul water that the bottom was revealed, they discovered the reason so many were sick and dying: at the bottom of the pond were "the decaying carcasses of 13 dead mules thrown in there by the Rebels."

On one occasion, soldiers were so outraged by their colonel's sadistic punishments, 40 of them waited to ambush and shoot him. "And he certainly would have been killed had he not been so drunk that he fell off his horse on the roadside where he was found the next morning."

'Do your duty, men!'

On September 11, gun battles crashed and boomed all day "without relief." Four defenders were killed, one by friendly fire, and three were wounded. Two Confederates were wounded and 16 were taken prisoner.

The battle had begun. There was no more smug talk of a "big scare."

That night, firehouse bells rang in Cincinnati, Newport and Covington and there was chaos in the streets as rumors flew like startled birds. Excited reports said the Rebels were crossing the river at North Bend. Then they were crossing at Maysville. Heth was coming with 12,000. Then 50,000. Then 100,000, gathering recruits all across Kentucky.

The city was about to be plundered by a fearsome Confederate army of "disciplined desperadoes," newspapers reported.

Yet there was no shortage of courage. Cincinnatian Henry Howe was among the men who left their families to go out and confront the enemy—untrained citizens, fathers, husbands, working men, who faced an army of Confederate veterans who had fought against Union Army regulars at Richmond and Lexington, Shiloh and Corinth.

Howe grabbed "a blanket-shawl, a few good cigars, a haversack loaded with eatables, and a black bottle of medicinal liquid—cherry bounce, very choice.

"The good woman was up. The four little innocents were asleep in the bliss of ignorance. ... As I stepped out on the pavement my neighbor did the same. He, too, was off to the war."

As the men looked back over their shoulders, they long remembered a poignant scene they left behind: both wives at their windows, weeping.

They marched to the front on September 10. "The boiling September sun was upon us like a furnace.... Clouds of limestone dust whitened us like millers, filling our nostrils and throats."

The dust-choked men cried for water, but there was "little or none to be had."

Without rest or pause, they were hastily lined up and told, "You are now going into battle. The enemy are advancing! You will receive sixty cartridges. Do your duty, men, do your duty!"

"We waited in expectation of an attack, too exhausted to fight or perhaps, even to run," Howe wrote.[128]

He could have been speaking of the city he left behind. All of Cincinnati was in an uproar, confused, afraid, on edge, worried and frantic. With Heth on the outskirts of Covington, General Wright issued an order to suspend all business—again—until further notice.

'Ripe apples'

The *Cincinnati Enquirer* reported: "Over the River—Throughout the day the city was rife with rumors proceeding from the most stirring drama ever witnessed in this locality. The presence and approach of the enemy was no longer a rumor, it was a fixed fact, and it was moreover whispered that skirmishing had commenced, with casualties on both sides."

Even after a week of frantic preparations, martial law, closed businesses, drums and fifes filling the air, the tramping and shouting of troops marching through the streets; even after thousands of men made the Pontoon Bridge sag and sway, and trainloads of Squirrel Hunters filled the streets—even after all of that, Cincinnati was surprised. The

---

128 Wimberg, Robert J. *Cincinnati, and the Civil War.* 1992.

enemy was actually real, just south of Covington and Newport, near Fort Mitchel.

The sound of rifles could be heard in the distance. Newspapers that had whipped the city into a panic now suddenly advised everyone to "stay calm."

On Thursday morning, September 11, General Heth was just about to give the order to take Cincinnati.

But it was not fear of the defenses that changed his mind. Heth was confident that he would soon be reinforced. Gen. Kirby Smith had ordered another division led by Gen. Humphrey Marshall to "hasten rapidly" to Cincinnati, along with troops coming north from Cynthiana with Colonel Preston Smith. And Gen. Kirby Smith was getting ready to join the battle and do to Cincinnati what Grant would later do to Vicksburg.[129]

Heth had tested the defenses and felt confident they could not withstand a determined assault by thousands of infantry, cavalry and heavy artillery.

But then, as the order to attack was about to be spoken, a rider approached, and everything changed. The rider carried emergency orders from Kirby Smith.

"I was forming my line for an attack when up rode a courier and handed me a dispatch," Heth wrote after the war. "It was a lengthy epistle from General Smith, recalling the permission given [to attack] and positively ordering that no attack be made on Cincinnati."

Heth was flummoxed.

The dispatch said General Bragg had ordered Kirby Smith to be ready to join his attack on Louisville against the Union Army of General Buell. So Smith summoned Heth to immediately return to Lexington.

"Winding up his dispatch," Heth wrote, "he added, 'Cincinnati and Louisville will fall like ripe apples into our hands as soon as the great battle between Bragg and Buell is fought.'"

---

129 During the 47-day Siege of Vicksburg the city was bombarded with artillery for weeks. Civilians moved into caves to avoid the shelling and survived by eating rats, without clean water or medicine. Many died from disease, hunger and wounds, along with soldiers on both sides: 32,363 Confederate casualties; 4,910 Union soldiers killed, wounded, captured or missing.

Looking back, those "ripe apples" must have been bitter for Heth. He had been correct: Cincinnati was the real prize. If Smith and his army had only joined Heth along with other reinforcements, the Queen City could have fallen into his hands just by shaking the tree.

Instead, he was called back to join an assault that never happened. The Confederates forfeited a great victory in Cincinnati for a pivotal defeat at a random place on the map, Perryville. As it turned out, Bragg changed his mind and would not even allow Kirby Smith and his army to support him at Louisville and Perryville, so the recall of Heth was pointless. Smith could have reinforced Heth to win the Siege of Cincinnati—a victory of incalculable benefit to the South, far beyond anything at Louisville.

The man staring down Heth from his perch in Fort Michel knew it. Wallace wrote, "Undoubtedly, if General Smith had marched on Cincinnati after Richmond, Cincinnati would have fallen."

Instead, Heth was called back to Lexington, shaking his head, like Wallace, at the inexplicable blunders of generals.

'Glory, glory hallelujah'

Later that evening, Wallace's scouts noticed "unrest in the enemy camp." By morning, tents were folded, cannons were carried away by mules and Heth's army was gone. Wallace asked permission from General Wright to pursue Heth down Lexington Pike and confirm the retreat. Wright declined.

"They have skedaddled," Wallace told his troops.

In the rifle pits, batteries and trenches, a few men began singing "John Brown's Body," and the Civil War anthem of the North spread across eight miles, a chorus of joyful victory. Cheers broke out in answer from windows, rooftops, riverbanks and streets in Cincinnati.

Colonel Neff recalled: "It reverberated from hill and valley, not dying away but coming back with increased volume and force, an occasion which comes but once in a lifetime, never to be forgotten."

"The agony is over," a *Cincinnati Times* headline said. "Cincinnati is no longer in danger. We breathe easier; the vaults of our banks are safe."

General Wallace led the first troops to return across the Pontoon Bridge as gunboats fired their cannons in celebration. He reviewed his motley army at 12th and Elm streets, saluted them and issued a proclamation:

"People of Cincinnati, Newport and Covington: In coming time strangers, viewing the works on the hills of Newport and Covington, will ask, 'Who built these entrenchments?' You can answer, 'We built them.' If they ask, 'Who guarded them?' you can reply, 'We helped in thousands.' If they ask the result, your answer will be, 'The enemy came and looked at them, and stole away in the night.'"

His stirring words should have been carved into granite as a monument to Cincinnati's original "Spirit of 9/11."

But Wallace, in his heart, knew that Cincinnati had dodged a thousands of bullets and cannon shells. He called the morning of September 12 "The gladdest day of my life."

"I make no disguise of my satisfaction — joy might be the better word — when at daybreak a messenger galloped in to tell me the enemy was gone."

The following days were filled with parades like a Roman Triumph as the proud defenders came home from the Kentucky hills.

As they passed, huge crowds cheered until they were hoarse. Windows were a blur of color from waving handkerchiefs and everywhere were the joyful faces of mothers, sisters and wives who shed tears of gratitude that their men came home safe.

But goodwill toward the Squirrel Hunters soon went sour like milk in the late-summer sun. They were cheered when they came across the bridge. But when they lingered during the next week to enjoy the exotic amusements of the Queen City, newspapers, politicians and citizens agreed: It was time for them to go back to their woods and farms. Eventually, they were paid $13 each for their service and Ohio Governor Tod had the state print thousands of ornate certificates to be awarded in gratitude for their service.

In those first days after Heth's retreat, Cincinnati was jubilant. The city was proud of Wallace, Wallace was proud of the city, and both were very proud of themselves.

Wallace gave special thanks to three men: Colonel Dickson who led the Black Brigade, Colonel Neff of the Pearl Street Rifles, and Colonel R.M. Corwin, who led troops who guarded the fords on the Ohio River.

"The retreat assured, the necessities for keeping the people from their business were gone," Wallace recalled. "The city regiments were formed into column and marched across the river to the Market Square, where they were formally thanked and relieved from duty. It was a splendid triumphal march, with music and banners, through a multitude apparently innumerable on the streets and crowding every vantage-point of sight on roof, window and sidewalk. The soldiers were proud, as they had reason to be; so were the friends and families who welcomed them; so was I.

"Indeed, that was one of the gladdest days of my life. There can be no question, I think, that my services were fully appreciated."[130]

His honor was finally redeemed. But then he added: "...except in Washington."

He was right.

No good deed goes unpunished

Proclamations of praise and gratitude were showered on Wallace like laurel crowns on an Olympic champion. Ohio's governor, the state legislature and the City of Cincinnati passed proclamations to honor him as "The Savior of Cincinnati." They mentioned his energy, determination, courage and ability.

But there was nothing but silence from Washington and the War Department led by General Halleck.

Wallace wrote, "It is to be said here that every point in the scheme for the Defense of Cincinnati had been mine, inaugurated before General Wright could return to the city, and without consultation with him or any gentleman of his staff."

---

130 *Lew Wallace; An Autobiography. Vol. II* - Scholar's Choice Edition. 2015.

Immodest, but true. Unfortunately for Wallace, truth is often tarred and feathered by a lynch mob of lies in the nation's capital.

Halleck gave the credit for saving Cincinnati to General Wright, and then gave Wright the promotion and battlefield command Wallace had desperately hoped to earn. Out of spite, Halleck sent Wallace a miserable assignment: to command Camp Chase in Columbus—populated by angry, undisciplined, paroled Union prisoners who were trapped in limbo, unable to rejoin the war or go home.

The Defense of Cincinnati was a "bloodless success," Wallace said. "What recognition was I to receive for the part I had borne in it? I even flattered myself that of the twelve or fifteen regiments of regularly enlisted men then in camp behind Covington and Newport, a division would be created for me to take to the field, whither I was so desirous of going."

Instead, he was given regiments of angry malcontents at Camp Chase. He suspected "a further intent behind (the assignment) was to drive me out of the army. Enough that I wrestled with it all night before finally resolving to go to Columbus on the duty prescribed."

He left for Columbus on September 15.

Camp Chase was as far from glory as Columbus was from Shiloh. Packed beyond capacity with 6,000 men, it was a Union version of Andersonville, Wallace found. The officers on duty warned him that the inmates were a herd of "beasts," not men. The government acted as if the pariahs who were unlucky enough to be captured did not exist. They were fed—barely—but comforts and clothing were not provided by contractors and bureaucrats who profited from their misery. Disease was killing dozens every day.

As with the treatment of the Black Brigade, Wallace could not tolerate it. As a victim of injustice, he empathized.

When he inspected the camp, he and his horse Old John were surrounded and "walled in" by thousands of bedraggled men. "Such a sight I had never seen or imagined—men long-haired and bushy-whiskered, their faces the color of green cheese; most of them without head-covering of any kind, or coats or shoes; some in dirty cotton

Camp Chase in Columbus, Ohio was a prison for Union parolees and Confederate prisoners of war. *Frank Leslie's Illustrated Newspaper*, 1861.

drawers and wrapped in old blankets in lieu of shirts. Looking down upon them—God help me speak the truth—I could see vermin crawling over their unwashed bodies, while the smell with which the mass thickened the air about me is in my nostrils as I write, it was so pungent and peculiar."

The crowd shouted insults and curses. Someone yelled, "What do you want, anyhow?" They all took up the chant. "WHAT DO YOU WANT? WHAT DO YOU WANT? WHAT DO YOU WANT?"

Trying to stay calm, Wallace waited for the jeers to subside and replied, "I want you to cut your hair, wash your faces, shave, and be the gentlemen you were when you enlisted. I want to put new uniforms on your backs. I want to take you out of this hell hole into fresh tents. I want to put money in your pockets."

The men yelled that he was just another liar, but he asked them to give him a chance to prove he was not. "You have my word," he told them. Despite the risk, stench and squalor, he realized he was glad to be there. "The wretched prisoners had my sympathy and I determined to deal justly with them."

Wallace kept his word. He formed them into companies and regiments and let them choose their officers. He told them to line up for back pay. When the Quartermaster in Columbus refused to provide their pay and uniforms, Wallace sent a burley officer to arrest the man and physically seize the keys to a safe so the men could be paid.

The wretched, hopeless men were transformed.

But then Halleck ordered them all to board trains to fight Indians in Minnesota. That was too much. Infuriated, Wallace arranged opportunities for mass desertions so the men could go home.

He pretended to be surprised but was secretly glad to see them desert before the government could mistreat them again. "I preferred they should go home for, to be perfectly straightforward, my own soul was in rebellion against indignities."

He reported to Washington that it would be a waste of money and manpower to track them down, and Washington reluctantly agreed.

His courageous refusal to follow unjust orders saved him and those 6,000 men from being dragged into the worst mass execution in US history, when 38 Santee Sioux renegades were hanged on December 26, 1862 for rapes and murders in the "Minnesota Uprising."

At the moment of highest risk, when Wallace was nearly crushed by the crowd of inmates at Camp Chase who accused him of being just another liar, he said something that could have been his epitaph:

"I'm a new man, and demand that you hear me. Try me. If I fail my promise, then mob me."

BACK ON THE SHELF

'Keep as quiet as possible'

After closing the abomination called Camp Chase, Wallace tried to rejoin Grant at the Battle of Corinth. Halleck blocked him and Grant refused to have him. He tried to go east to Pennsylvania, where he could have commanded troops at Gettysburg. He was refused again, left to wait at home in Crawfordsville.

But Halleck was not through tormenting Wallace. In a stroke of malicious irony, he assigned Wallace to investigate General Buell. Buell had been caught by surprise at Perryville—just like Grant at Shiloh. And he was disastrously late to the battle—like the accusations against Wallace at Shiloh.

Halleck was itching to send Buell to the guillotine and put Wallace out to pasture. He got both. Wallace was stuck in Cincinnati again as the investigation crawled along for nearly seven months. Buell was exonerated but got the message and resigned from the army a year later.

But Wallace had some revenge. He used the final report to blame Halleck, whose orders had delayed Buell on his way to Kentucky—just as Halleck had handcuffed Grant at Shiloh and squandered victory by dithering on the way to Corinth.

Halleck ordered Wallace to stay in Cincinnati until he was needed—which might come the day after icicles formed on the gates of hell. Wallace volunteered to be demoted and go to Vicksburg at any rank, but was rejected. After complaining about being a prisoner in the city he saved, Wallace was given permission to go home to Crawfordsville, Indiana—a sure signal that his career was finished.

He went home to Susan, and was out fishing on the Wabash River when another old nemesis brought him back into action: In July 1863, Morgan's Raiders struck again, and Indiana Gov. Oliver Hazard Perry Throck Morton was so panic-stricken he called Wallace to the rescue.

Wallace quickly understood that Morton had no intention to fight Morgan. He was given only a thousand raw recruits, all on foot, to catch 2,400 elite cavalry Raiders. "I think I understand you, then," he said to the governor. "Push Morgan into Ohio—the faster the better."

The same governor who supported Cincinnati and Ohio during the siege was now glad to inflict more misery on Ohio if he could keep Morgan's cavalry away from Indianapolis. Morgan had already crossed the border into Ohio by the time Wallace arrived. Mission accomplished.

But Cincinnati was terrorized again.

Mayor Hatch asked for 3,000 men to chase Morgan but gave up the idea when they could not find enough horses. Black citizens were once again rounded up by the police and 600 were forced to work like slaves to reinforce the defenses. New commander Gen. Ambrose Burnside declared martial law, but pressure, lobbying and protests made the list of exceptions grow like his side-whiskers. Exemptions were given to hotels, milkmen, government employees, "eating houses," banks, drugstores, funeral homes....

And with Wallace gone, the city slid backward into cruel injustice as easy as putting on old slippers retrieved from the trash.

Chasing The Fox

Morgan nearly finished what Heth had started by attacking Cincinnati, but decided against it. By then his troops were worn out after riding through scorching days and sleepless nights.

And General Burnside declined to battle Morgan because the surrounding communities might be caught in the crossfire and destroyed.

"The Fox," also known by more colorful names,[131] rode around the outskirts of Cincinnati, spreading fear as he went. One of his officers, George "Lightning" Ellsworth, tapped into telegraph wires along the way to eavesdrop on Union orders and send bogus messages that had Morgan everywhere at once.

---

131   An 1882 History of the State of Ohio wrote of Morgan: "His life had been one of wild dissipation, adventure and recklessness, although in his own family he had the name of being most considerate. The men who followed him were accustomed to a dare-devil life."

Gen. John Hunt Morgan. Library of Congress.

On July 13, the dreaded Raiders crossed the Whitewater River into Ohio and burned a large bridge in Harrison. Panic was set loose. More than 100 volunteers turned out in Oxford, including pastors, lawyers, college professors, barbers and doctors. The same happened in small towns throughout southern Ohio.

Also that day, Morgan got the discouraging news that Lee had lost at Gettysburg.

As he galloped through Glendale at 2:00 a.m. on July 14, some of his men's horses had begun to collapse and die in their tracks; riders fell asleep and dropped from their saddles. It was a fitting metaphor for the worn out, dying Confederacy.

In Deer Park, the family of John Schenk fed breakfast to Morgan, but told him he and his men could not come in their house because one of their children was quarantined with smallpox. It was untrue, but convincing. Morgan and his Raiders ate on the lawn and didn't discover the horses and a family of runaway slaves hidden in the house.[132]

Later that morning of July 14, Morgan's Raiders skirmished at Camp

---

132 Christopher J. Fain on behalf of Ohio History Service Corps. "Deer Park - A Courageous Bluff." Clio: Your Guide to History. January 7, 2022.

Camp Denison was a hospital for soldiers wounded at Shiloh, a bootcamp for troops throughout Ohio and the scene of a skirmish with Morgan's Raiders in 1863.

Dennison and derailed a train in Miamiville, killing a fireman, Cornelius Conway.[133] A group of 18 Loveland militiamen led by Lt. Thomas Paxton was sent to investigate and skirmished with Morgan's Raiders. They shot and killed one of the Raiders, who was buried nearby. According to stories told by the militia, Morgan threatened to come back for revenge if they did not treat the Confederate's body with respect and give him a Christian burial.[134]

Pursuit of Morgan by 4,000 riders under command of Union Gen. Edward Hobson was delayed by burned bridges, but relentlessly followed and was closing fast.

The raiders rode along what is now SR-126 and Branch-Hill Guinea Pike to Mount Repose, where they burned 50 wagons. From there, one group went east into Goshen and rejoined the main group at Williams Corners. From there they rode south to the intersection of what is now SR-131 and SR-132, and then headed south through Owensville and Batavia.

In Owensville, a man fired a shotgun at them from the steeple of a church on Main Street. The Raiders dragged him out, tied his Union flag to a horse's tail and took him along to Williamsburg, dragging the flag in the dust.

---

133 Legend has it that Conway still haunts that spot where he was killed; the ghost carries a lantern.

134 Richard Crawford, Clermont County Historical Society, *Morgan's Raid Trail in Clermont County Ohio, 2000.*

In Georgetown, Elizabeth "Aunt Betsy" King described the raid in an 1884 letter to her friend Ulysses Grant. "While some were searching the stables and sheds for horses, others were going to every house and asking for food. Each one had a basket. The ladies gave them all they asked for, they were all very polite and bowing and lifting their hats when leaving," she recalled.

The raiders "ravaged your old home," she told Grant, robbed a dry goods store and took "all the boots and shoes they could" from a shoe store.

One raider, who was from Ohio, deserted in Williamsburg. Another met a young woman on a farm south of Goshen, when she came out to beg them not to take their horses. He left the horses alone and told her would come back and marry her after the war. He did. John H. Anderson and Katherine Deerwester Anderson are buried together in Evergreen Cemetery in Miamiville.[135]

As the Raiders split into groups, five were killed in a skirmish near the intersection of Woodville Pike and Manilla Road near Goshen.[136]

The Raiders were called terrorists, outlaws, guerrillas and worse. But if they had fought for the Union, history books would glorify them as romantic, dashing heroes. They rode 95 miles in 35 hours—called the longest continuous cavalry ride in history.

As they blitzkrieged through Hamilton, Clermont, Brown, Adams, Carroll, Athens and several other Ohio counties, snipers waited on hilltops. Local militias cut down trees to block roads in the 100-degree heat.

The Raiders rode through Harrison, Springdale, Glendale, Deer Park, Evendale, Sharonville, Blue Ash, Camp Dennison, Miamiville, Loveland, Milford, Goshen, Williamsburg, Owensville, Batavia, Peebles, Georgetown and dozens of other towns and cities in southern and eastern Ohio. Families who saw their giant cloud of dust coming hid their valuables and often brought their horses into their houses.

In Chilicothe, a frightened local militia burned their own bridge.

---

135 Ibid.
136 Ibid.

**The Guardhouse at Camp Denison is now a Civil War Museum
operated by the Daughters of the American Revolution.**

Morgan stopped to burn a newspaper office in Jackson, Ohio—his version of a heated letter to the editor.

Morgan plundered towns for food and supplies and made the locals cook meals at gunpoint. But he was not another Atilla the Hun, as some newspapers claimed. Many men were killed in the running gun battles, and one woman was wounded: Lizzie Compton, a Canadian girl who disguised herself as a man to join the Michigan Volunteers, was shot in the shoulder during a gunbattle in Indiana. A doctor dressing the wound discovered her secret.

Morgan could have escaped. He was swimming his horse halfway across the Ohio when gunboats opened fire. Instead of reaching the other side, he gallantly turned back to stay with his remaining 700 men. About 300 others made it across and escaped to the South.

He was finally captured in Salineville, Ohio, surrounded and outnumbered three to one, under heavy cannon fire. He did not achieve his objective to "burn Indianapolis and take Cincinnati alive." But during the 24-day raid, he caught and paroled 6,000 prisoners, tied

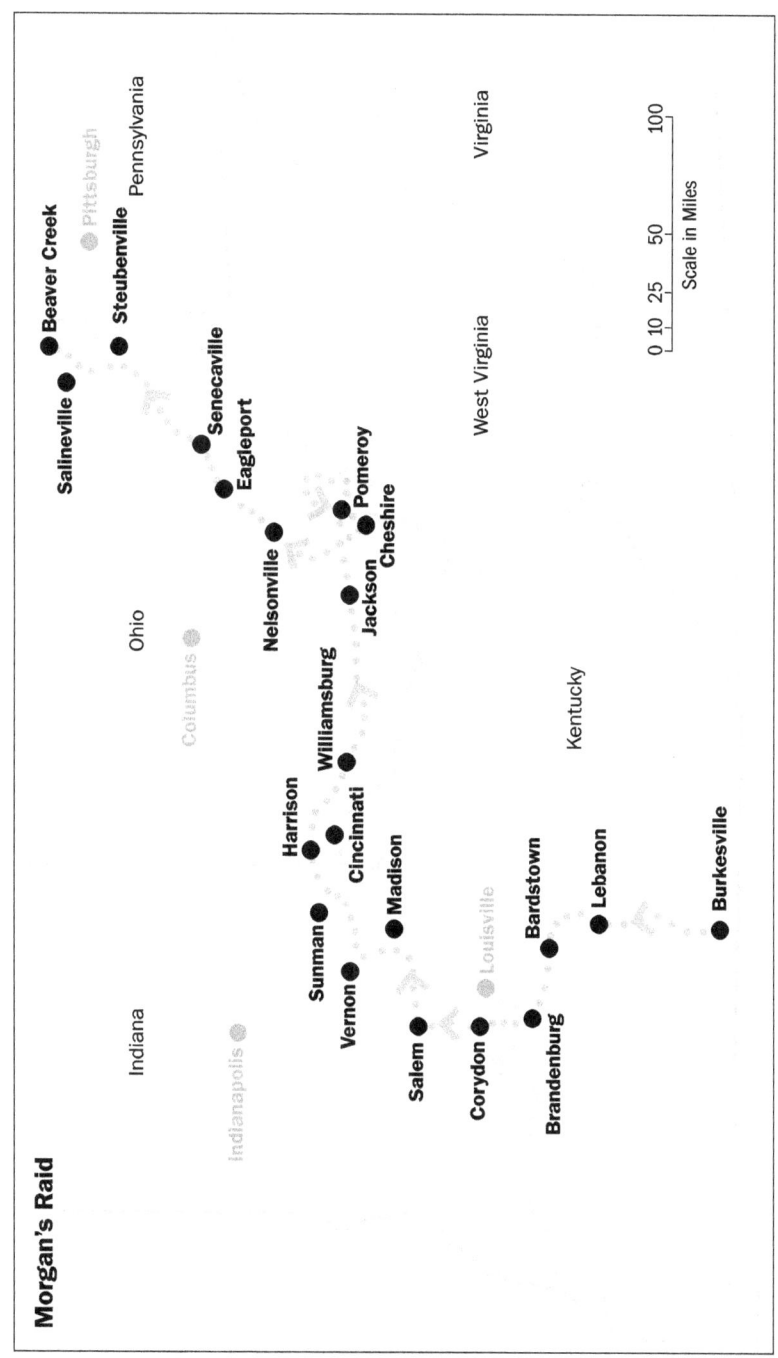

Map 4

down 5,000 Union regulars and 120,000 militia members, burned 34 bridges and wrecked 60 sections of railroad track. The raid delayed Union reinforcements to Tennessee, contributing to the Union defeat at Chickamauga, where Brig. Gen. William Haines Lytle of Cincinnati was killed by a sniper.[137]

Morgan was locked up in the state penitentiary in Columbus but tunneled out with several of his officers, using table knives to dig. They took a train to Cincinnati that night—with Morgan sitting next to an oblivious Union major. Morgan crossed the Ohio River in a small boat and escaped South.

He was killed in battle the following summer near Greenville, Tennessee. Cincinnati finally breathed a sigh of relief. But as much as he was feared in the North, he was beloved by the South, where his raids were celebrated as the last stand of heroic chivalry.

Back in the doghouse

Wallace must have secretly admired and envied Morgan's dashing audacity. The raids were like an echo of his colorful Zouave troops in the early days of the war. After protecting Indianapolis, Wallace was left idling in Crawfordsville. With time to brood and nurse his wounded pride, he wrote letters to demand explanations from Grant about his treatment after Shiloh. He went over Halleck's head to Secretary of War Edwin Stanton, who tried to help Wallace's but gave up after Wallace's prickly letters alienated him too.

Cincinnati Archbishop John Baptist Purcell, one of the most influential Catholics in the nation, was among many who intervened for Wallace with President Lincoln. But Wallace burned nearly as many bridges as Morgan's Raiders. And his military commanders never figured out that they could have saved themselves a herd of headaches if they had just sent him back into battle. Idle hands were the devil's amusement park for Lew Wallace.

Halleck dismissed Wallace's demands for a court of inquiry about

---

137 Lytle was a veteran of the Mexican-American War and a famous poet. His poetry was so popular that Confederates posted an honor guard for his body on the battlefield where he was killed.

Shiloh as just "gas."

General Sherman wrote Wallace a kind letter imploring him to lay low and "keep as quiet as possible"—probably as a favor to his irritated friend Grant. Lincoln was asked to reinstate Wallace. He declined. He was asked to fire Wallace. He declined again.

But finally, the President found a use for the man who saved Cincinnati *and* Indianapolis: save Baltimore.

With elections coming up, Lincoln needed a smart and savvy military commander to make sure the city would vote for abolition of slavery. Baltimore was the nest of Copperheads that hatched plots to kill Lincoln, but the President didn't want to be embarrassed in an election year by using bayonets to manhandle voters, Wallace was told.

Wallace persuaded the governor of Maryland to request federal troops at all the polling places, and then used them to intimidate pro-slavery voters. The election came out just as Lincoln hoped it would: for abolition.

Wallace tamed Baltimore with martial law, following his blueprint from Cincinnati. He shut down some newspapers, tried to hang four men as spies and opened a prison for female spies and smugglers.

Lincoln finally asked Wallace to back off. No doubt Lincoln's ears were burning from the scorching complaints of wealthy Baltimore residents—especially after Wallace converted the city's opulent Maryland

LAST SLAVE-CHAIN IN MARYLAND.

Slave chain found on Margaret Toogood when she was rescued and set free by Lew Wallace in Maryland. Courtesy of Oberlin College, Ohio.

Club from a haven for secessionists to a shelter for homeless slaves who had been set free by emancipation.

When a slaveowner followed a freed teenaged girl to Baltimore, kidnapped her and took her back to his plantation, Wallace sent cavalry to bring them both back. They found Margaret Toogood shackled with a four-pound chain around her neck that Wallace immediately had removed. He put the owner in prison at hard labor until the man agreed to pay her $500 (almost $10,000 today).

Last chance for glory

In 1864, while the eyes of the nation were on the cataclysmic battles between Grant and Lee at Richmond and Petersburg, Washington, DC was almost captured by Confederate Gen. Jubal Early.

General Early led 17,000 men through the Shenandoah Valley behind Union lines. The path to Washington was undefended, wide open to attack.

Except for Wallace.

As he had in Cincinnati and Indianapolis, Wallace mustered all the raw troops he could find and came up with a paltry force of just 2,300—mostly wide-eyed recruits, clerks, quartermasters, cooks, wagon-drivers and other non-combatants who hoped to serve safely behind the lines.

The crisis began one year after the Battle of Gettysburg, in July 1864. Wallace was commander in Baltimore and heard news of Early's approach. Halleck refused to believe it, so Wallace slipped out of the city at night to find out for himself.

He discovered that Early was indeed on the march and had orders from General Lee to take Washington. There was no hope for reinforcements from Grant in time. Wallace decided there was only one choice: Delay the Rebels and buy time for Grant to send help.

Halleck still insisted to Grant that no help was needed, but Grant ignored him as he should have at Shiloh, and sent reinforcements to Wallace. But because of Halleck's stalling they would take days to arrive.

Meanwhile, Wallace took a stand. Brig. Gen. James B. Rickets arrived

Bayonet charge, *Harper's Weekly*, 1862.

with 2,700 men, bringing the total of Wallace's troops to about 5,000, facing more than 17,000. Early had 24 cannons; Wallace had two, including a 24-pound howitzer. But because of his foresight, he was able to take the high ground, with the Monocacy River in his front, forcing Early to cross narrow bridges under enemy fire.

And he was blessed with an overconfident enemy who wasted time. Early was too late.

Wallace knew his mission was almost suicidal. "Had I a right, morally speaking, to subject those under me to the perils of a battle so doubtful, if not so hopeless?" he worried. "I saw my role distinctly. It was to hold the enemy back until the reinforcements reached me."[138]

As the Battle of Monocacy began on July 9, General Early launched attack after attack, but the Union defense held. Wallace described Rebels yelling like yelping wolves, while his men stood and fired at a distance of less than 100 yards. In the middle of the battle, his biggest cannon, the howitzer, was disabled by a jammed shell because an untrained artilleryman had loaded the shell and powder out of order.

138   Wallace, Lew. *Lew Wallace; an Autobiography* ... New York ; London, Harper & brothers, 1906.

Wallace was forced to retreat, but by then the day had ended, and he had bought enough time for Grant's reinforcements to protect the Capital. The Union lost 1,300 men; Early lost 900.

Wallace called the battle "the most trying and, in point of service rendered, the most important of my life." He had acted without orders, support or approval from Washington, in defiance of Halleck.

Yet Monocacy became "The Battle that Saved Washington."

If losing Cincinnati would have devastated the Union, losing the Capital could have lost the war. Like Cincinnati, Baltimore was scared and ready to surrender. Wallace pictured Lincoln running out the back of the White House while a Confederate officer kicked down the front door.

A few weeks later, even Grant finally admitted he was wrong about Wallace. Over dinner in Baltimore, he told Wallace, "If I had known then what I know now, I would have ordered you where you were marching when stopped."

It was the best exoneration Wallace would ever get for his long march at Shiloh. Grant finally had admitted that his staff was wrong to stop Wallace and turn him around. But it was said privately. The public stain on Wallace's reputation remained.

BOOK V:
NEW MEXICO TERRITORY

1879

Geronimo (right) and his renegade Apaches. 1886.

JORNADA DEL MUERTO II
'This way of living does not suit me'

"What do you reckon will become of that notorious desperado known as the Kid?" Duck asked the governor.

After leaving the town of Lincoln and their clandestine meeting with William Bonney/Kid Antrim, they had ridden northwest to desolate Fort Stanton, which sat like the Army's orphan on the cactus-barbed edge of Mescalero Apache land. At the fort, Wallace gathered the latest reports about Indian troubles and asked many questions about the role of suspended commander Col. Nathan Dudley in the Lincoln County War.

Governor Wallace was not pleased by what he learned. The reports of increasingly violent raids by renegades were grim and descriptive. And some troops who had been with Dudley during the Lincoln shootout were much *too* eager to defend their former commander or blame him, as if they were already preparing their alibis for a court-martial.

In reply to Duck, Wallace only grunted. They rode on. Duck had just about given up on getting an answer when Wallace cleared his throat and spoke in his opaque literary style, as if he were writing a letter or a book.

"This way of living does not suit me," he said. "Some men find an unaccountable fascination in the danger and outlawry of the frontier far beyond my understanding."

Duck considered that. It was an answer of sorts. And then he had an epiphany: *He's already tugging on strings in Washington to find a replacement governor and get back to the so-called civilized world.*

Duck thought about that. Then turned to Gillespie and asked, "What about you?" Gillespie rode slightly behind Duck and the governor, pulling a pack mule that replaced the wagon left behind at Fort Stanton. They were traveling lighter on the return to Santa Fe.

"There's killin' and then there's killin'," Gillespie replied. "I'm with the governor, I guess. I like this life out here, but I have no patience with men who glorify lawlessness. We've seen our share and, Lord knows, done our share of killin', but it's not something to boast about any more than I would boast about stepping on a spider... which is what I feel like doing when I look at the Kid and his gang. What about you, Duck?"

Duck reined his horse slightly to ride alongside Gillespie. "Remember that Apache at the meet up?"

"Yep."

"And that salamander who called himself Copperhead or Sidewinder or some-such?"

Gillespie nodded.

"Well, I always figured men like them was missing something, like God had some parts left over when they were set loose in the world. Whereas most of us get soul-sick when killin' is required, they draw some kind of perverted satisfaction. I think about all the good, God-fearing young men who died on Cemetery Ridge." He nodded at Gillespie and added, "And the Hornet's Nest. How come *they* are gone and these varmints are still breathing the same air I have to use? I saw drummer boys killed who had not even reached the age of ten."

He pulled out his tobacco pouch, began to roll a smoke and added, "I figure there must have been some kind of oversight by St. Peter to let those mad dogs slip by. So if I get the chance I will help him correct it."

Gillespie laughed and shook his head. "Governor, are you really gonna give that back-shooter amnesty for testifying?"

Wallace looked back at them but didn't reply. Duck thought he saw the hint of a smile. Instead, Wallace said, "Boys, I think I will take the stage from Carrizozo to Santa Fe and leave you to your own peripatetic inclinations. Those '*varmints*' we call a legislature do more damage than carpenter ants in a library. And Ben-Hur is about to enter a chariot race that I am eager to witness."

Duck raised his eyebrows at Gillespie, with a look that asked, "What?"

"I think he means we're on our own," Gillespie replied.

"No, I comprende that 'peripatetic inclinations' part. Who's this Ben Her woman who races chariots?"

"It's that book he's writing," Gillespie chuckled. "Something about an innocent man named Judah Ben-Hur who is wrongly accused and spends the rest of his life trying to prove his innocence and redeem his reputation."

"Ahh, I see," said Duck, nodding as he looked pointedly at Wallace, who pretended not to hear them.

After a while, Duck said to Wallace, "You know, Governor, that Lincoln County prosecutor is as worthless as a Jeff Davis dollar. He will hang the Kid no matter how he testifies. He might just be ornery enough to hang him *before* he testifies."

Wallace replied, "Ezra, your perspicacity has a remarkable acuity today. The answer is yes."

"Yes to what?" Duck asked.

Gillespie said, "He means yes he knows that."

"But he can't do any governor-like stuff about it from Santa Fe."

Gillespie gave him a look.

"Ohhh. I see the light," Duck said. "The Kid will be left to the hemp-collar justice the dime novels like to go on about."

"Seems only fitting for a dime-novel desperado like the Kid," Gillespie said. His lips smiled but his eyes were like flint.

Revenge of El Sapo

Leaving the governor at the stage depot in Carrizozo, they rode southwest around the Sierra Blancas Mountains, aiming to loop down around the Black Mountains and then angle northwest to Silver City. Duck had a small, neglected ranch there called Thorn & Thistle, and a woman in town named Lucille.

"You ever get that itchy feeling at the back of your neck like someone's leaning over your shoulder?" Duck asked as the two rode along the northwestern fringe of the Apache reservation, trailing their pack mule.

"You mean the one you get when someone is following about a mile back?"

Chiricahua Apache leader Victorio.

"I make it about six or eight riders. Over your left shoulder, behind that ridge of foothills."

"Could be friends of Victorio or Geronimo."

"Meaning no friends of ours."

Gillespie pulled up his horse, handed the reins to Duck and dismounted to adjust the cinch on the pack mule, giving himself a chance to take a closer gander at the ridge. In the afternoon sun, he could just make out thin whisps of dust rising against the sky. It could be a dust devil. But it was not. He could feel it.

It was quiet in the heat of the day. He could hear the mule's steady breathing. The hard thump of a hoof on packed earth as it shifted a foot. There was a slight breeze through the creosote bushes and desert broom, carrying that sharp, clean smell of sage. And somewhere off to the west the call of a hawk that was probably not a hawk. More likely a scout with eyes on them, signaling to the rest that the two white men had stopped.

His skin prickled and it was not just the sun. Gillespie thought about it. The idea of being taken by Apaches made his knees go soft.

They could take a man apart and make it last for days. They worked with fire like artists, drawing out a symphony of agony like a musician sawing on a fiddle. Or they might invite ants, scorpions or snakes to the party. He'd heard of a soldier who was tied down and tortured with a *Gila monster*. Those ugly lizards never let go once they got their teeth into you.

But they were rare, he reminded himself. Snakes, ants and scorpions were plentiful, unfortunately.

The breeze whispered secrets to the creosote bushes. The sun had nothing to say. The nearest town was many miles behind. Fort Stanton was even farther than that. But a few miles to the west were the San Andres Mountains, where they might find a small canyon or at least a pile of fallen boulders to hole up and make a stand.

"Do ya think they will settle for the pack mule if we cut her loose?" Duck asked. "I hate to leave her, she's a good old girl. But she might buy our lives."

"I don't see another choice. Ride like hell and hope they all stop. Or at least a few. There are three bottles in the packs. If we leave two, that might slow 'em down for a few hours. If we ride like scalded dogs, maybe they won't...."

He let the thought trail off. Neither wanted to give words to the rest of that sentence.

Gillespie reached in, grabbed a bottle of Governor Wallace's favorite bourbon, tossed it to Duck and grabbed three cans of beans to stuff into his shirt. They took a moment to top off their canteens from a water bag the mule was carrying, then opened the stop to let the rest pour out on the ground. No sense making it easy for the riders behind that ridge. And it was a small kindness to the mule.

"How are you fixed for cartridges?" Duck asked.

"I'm bringing an extra box of forty-fours."

He remounted slowly, casually, and they cantered off, picking up the pace, but not yet ready to put a strain on their horses. If they were right, dust clouds behind them would soon show them if they were still being followed. If not, they could loop back for the mule.

After about 15 minutes of riding, Duck pulled a spyglass out of his saddlebag, waved it at Gillespie and both slowed to a stop so he could take a look back. The land was as flat as a ballroom floor, nothing to see for 40 miles in that direction but bruised-purple mountains on the horizon, writhing in the heat shimmer.

Gillespie waited. Duck steadied the glass. His horse seemed to know, and stood as still as a tombstone. Gillespie used the pause to make sure his Henry rifle was loaded to the maximum: 15 rounds in the magazine, one in the chamber.

"Two of 'em are staying to make friends with the governor's Old Forester."

Duck wiped sweat from his eyes with a shirtsleeve and refocused. "Two... no three, still coming. By the dust, I'd say they are coming hard."

"I am insulted," Gillespie said. "They think us worthy of no more than three?"

"Impertinent," said Duck, catching Gillespie's humor and imitating the governor. "Then again, that's good whiskey. I'd be half a mind to stay there too. And if I knew I was coming against two of the most deadly shootists in the West, I'd turn around and ride back to the reservation."

Gillespie laughed. They turned their horses and rode, first at a canter, then spurring on to a gallop across the treeless desert under a sky so clear and deep blue it looked like you could dive in and swim through it. Like the Big Lake Gillespie remembered in Michigan. The foothills ahead looked almost on top of them, which meant they were still miles away.

Duck and Gillespie's horses were bigger, gaining more ground with each stride. But the Indian ponies were sturdy and fast and would take any amount of abuse. They would run as hard as they could until they burst their hearts and died, still running.

Gillespie's mare, Agnes, felt strong and willing, almost eager, as if she was tired of dawdling and enjoyed a chance to show him what she could do. Duck and his gelding Benito were falling back a bit so Gillespie reigned in slightly, banking reserves for a sprint.

He threw a quick glance over his shoulder and was relieved to see that the three riders were no closer, maybe a bit farther behind. They still had at least a mile on them, so he and Duck slowed their horses to a canter to give them a rest.

By alternating gallop and canter, they could cover more ground and spare the horses for a flat-out sprint to the finish. They would let the Indians gain a bit, then pull away again. They rode like that for most of an hour.

As they approached the foothills in the late afternoon, riding west, dark mountain shadows painted the ground like the edges of an unexplored continent. The land began to slope upward, and rocks as big as a man's head littered the desert floor among the sun-blackened, scaley brush.

By pushing their ponies without mercy, the pursuers had gained a half-mile. Duck and Gillespie instinctively scanned the rising land ahead for a place to take cover. They saw it at about the same time and looked at each other, both nodding in the direction of a cluster of rocks. The small ones were as tall as a horse, the biggest ones could hide a sod house or a chicken coop.

And it was upslope enough to give them the advantage of high ground—a lesson both had learned through bitter experience in the recent War of Rebellion.

"Open ground on each side so it won't be easy to flank us," Duck shouted as they spurred their horses to a gallop. "I'll cover, you tend the horses."

Gillespie nodded and gave Agnes a nudge to get ahead so he could dismount and take the reins from Duck in a hurry. As it turned out, he had time to tie the horses to a stunted palo verde tree behind the biggest boulder before joining Duck behind the smaller rocks that were still almost head-high.

"You want a good look at these hombres?" Duck asked, breathing hard from the ride.

Gillespie knew what he meant. Duck was a sharpshooter near the end of the war and was surprisingly accurate to well over 400 yards. At that distance, it was hard to make out much of a man's features.

"I don't need a look. Let 'em know it will be healthier to keep their distance."

"Let's hope they don't have good rifles like the Sioux had at Little Bighorn," Duck said. He wet a finger for the breeze, settled in and took aim with his left hand wrapped in his bandanna. The Henry had no fore-stock and could get blistering hot in heavy shooting.

"You mean 'that damned Yankee rifle that can be loaded on Sunday and fired all week'?" Gillespie said, quoting Confederate Col. John Mosby.

Duck was concentrating, focused on his target, and only grunted.

The three riders were coming fast and started shooting on the full gallop, which was quite impressive. The whanging of bullets off rocks in front and behind Duck and Gillespie showed they could shoot well.

"How do they do that?" Gillespie mused. "I can hardly roll a smoke at a walk on horseback."

Duck fired once with a piercing crack that seemed to split the desert air. One of the Indian ponies went down in a swirl of dust and kicking legs.

"Aww, did you go and shoot a horse?" Gillespie said.

"No," Duck replied. "The rider. Don't be impertinent."

As the other two riders wheeled their horses and retreated out of range, Gillespie saw the third pony scramble to its feet and stand there, heaving air. It slowly walked back to the other horses. The rider did not.

Gillespie borrowed Duck's spyglass and took a closer look. The man looked as still and lifeless as the rocks scattered around him. But Gillespie was more interested in something else. He slowly scanned the ground and found it. "Springfield," he said. "Muzzle loader."

"If that's all they have, we're in luck," Duck answered.

Then a bullet ricocheted off a boulder behind them, followed by a deeper boom.

"That was a Sharps, I'd say," Duck said. "Good range. Big round. Deadly in the right hands."

He aimed again and fired a round that kicked up dust about 30 yards in front of the riders. They didn't flinch or move. But Gillespie knew

Duck wasn't trying to hit them. His intention was to make them think they were safely out of range, so they might get careless.

Gillespie took another long look with the glass, then handed it to Duck. "Do you see what I think I see?" he said.

Duck focused, started to say something, then put the glass to his eye and looked again. "Well, if it ain't our friends El Sapo the Toad and Serpiente the Snake. Why didn't I save us a lot of trouble and just shoot them both?"

"You might get your chance yet."

The riders waited and watched until the mountain shadows crept out past Duck and Gillespie. The two men had dismounted and sat cross-legged on the ground, passing a bottle.

"Let me see if I can provoke them," Duck said, finally losing patience. He went to his saddle and opened a leather tube attached to his rifle scabbard, drawing out a metal cylinder nearly as long as his rifle barrel. He dusted both ends with his bandanna and clipped it on his rifle: a 4-power scope built for a Whitworth sniper rifle, adapted to his Henry repeating rifle.

Gillespie watched, curious. "Those are accurate to what, 800 yards?"

"A bit less with the .44 cartridge," Duck said. "But next to the forty-seven dollars my Henry cost, it was the best ten dollars I ever spent."[139]

"If it gets us out of this, I will double that ten dollars," Gillespie said.

"You're on. Get the horses ready."

When Gillespie returned, Duck took careful aim and squeezed the trigger.

As Gillespie watched through the glass, half a fifth of the governor's best Old Forester exploded in a shower of glass as it was being passed between the men. Toad was blinded by splinters of glass and alcohol as the man they called Snake held his bleeding left hand and rocked back and forth, shouting curses.

The Indian ponies, startled by the unfamiliar sound or stung by flying glass, bolted.

---

139 Many Union soldiers bought a $47 Henry that fired 15 times a minute compared to the $16 Springfield that could fire three times in a minute.

"Lucky," Duck said. "Neither one looks fit to pick up that Sharps. In the right hands, that big gun is deadly to a thousand yards."

"Then let's ride," Gillespie said.

Showdown in Las Cruces

The rest of their ride to Silver City was uneventful. Duck speculated, "It might be a long time before Garter Snake asks for three fingers of whiskey. I don't think he has that many left."

The ride past Massacre Peak to the south and the Black Mountains to the north reminded Gillespie of the description he had read of a New Mexico desert journey written by the governor's wife, Susan Wallace:

"Five hundred miles across plains level as the sea, treeless, waterless … Under ceaseless sunshine, against pitiless wind."

"Now the sun comes up, we see they are kingly mountains, wrapped in robes of royal purple and wearing crowns of gold. The atmosphere is so refined and clear, they appear close beside us; but the driver says they are forty miles away. Noon comes on, hot and still, with a desert scorch. We journey over a road surprisingly free of stones; across a blank and colorless plain, bounded by mountain-walls which stand grim and stark like bastions of stone."[140]

Susan Wallace.

---

140 Wallace, Susan Elston. *The Land of the Pueblos.* 1888.

After a week's rest in Silver City, Duck and Gillespie rode southeast to Las Cruces on the Rio Grande to meet some Mexican Federales. Victorio was raiding both sides of the border, and the governor wanted them to explore ways to cooperate and keep him from using the border to evade pursuit.

Las Cruces—"The Crosses"—was a young town, settled in 1848, south of the black lava wasteland of Jordana Del Muerto. The meeting went well, and Duck and Gillespie were in the livery stable, saddling their horses for their ride back to Santa Fe. The interior of the barn was shadowed against the open doors, where bright morning sunlight made the dusty street outside look almost white as snow. The barn smelled good: honest manure, hay, horses, saddle leather and hard work.

Duck was about to put his Henry in the saddle scabbard. Gillespie was checking the load on his Colt .44 pistol. He opened the gate and let the fat .44 cartridges spill out into his palm for a quick inspection. No grit. They were clean. He was just finished reloading when they heard the jingle of spurs and looked up.

Two men were silhouetted in the doorway. As they stood there, pausing to let their eyes adjust, Duck and Gillespie noted their shapes, their sizes and the twin braids hanging from under the hat of the taller man on the right. Duck said one word: "Toad."

At the same instant, the smaller man recognized the men who had mocked him at the meeting with the Kid and reached for his gun. Too late. Gillespie fired first. His .44 slug hit Cottonmouth square in the upper chest and threw him back over his bootheels into the street, where he landed with a thud and puff of dust. A quick second round caught him below the belt as he fell.

At almost the same time, two rifles made a deafening blast so close together it was like one sound, filling the barn and spooking horses that began to whinny and rear and kick their stalls.

He heard Duck lever another round and braced for the shot that didn't come. He watched as Toad went down in a heap, falling like a tree, slowly at first, then all at once. The Mescalero's shot had gone high, but not by much. Splinters and dust floated down from a hole in a wooden beam just over Duck's head.

Gillespie and Duck said nothing. They approached the bodies with guns drawn, slowly, moving from the shadowed darkness to the light. Cottonmouth squirmed and frothed red spittle from his mouth, his eyes full of hatred as he gurgled out his last curses, deflated and died. The left hand was still wrapped in a dirty, bloodstained bandage.

The Mescalaro looked impassive, as always, his face as blank as an empty sheet of paper—with one round, red-black hole in the left center of his forehead. It made a punctuation mark above the rune-like scars and small, scabbed cuts from broken glass that decorated his face. His eyes were windows into darkness. No message of murder, now—just the glaze of death. Tied to his belt was a long streamer of light chestnut hair. A woman's hair. Maybe a little girl's hair.

"I recall this hombre now," Duck said. "He was one of the warriors with Victorio in '77, when they raided so many homesteads. Lots of children were taken. We heard tell of a pair that sold them in Mexico. From the poster I saw, I reckon this pair."

Gillespie nodded and said softly, "Toad has croaked."

Duck looked to his left. "And the snake is introducing himself to his new friends in hell."

Gillespie turned back to the horses and Duck asked, "What now?"

"Find my badge. I think we finally have someone important to impress."

"Local law?"

"Uh-huh."

The next week, the *Las Cruces Citizen* carried a brief item that was not uncommon in local news:

Colt .44 Justice

Two men were killed in an affray in Los Cruces last week. Horace Carter, said to be originally from Louisiana, reputed to be a Confederate deserter, was wanted for abduction, arson and murder. The other victim was an Apache known only as Toad and El Sapo.

Mr. Carter and Mr. Toad were believed to be part of the gang of thieves and desperadoes who stole more than 40 horses from the Mescalero Apache Reservation near Lincoln and rustled 1,000 head of cattle from the Coughlin Ranch in the past three months.

Both men were killed in a gun battle, by two agents of Territorial Governor Wallace. The agents declined to give their names and asked that the small reward be used to bury the dead men.

Sheriff Pat Garret said he could vouch for the agents and no charges would be brought.

For years these banditii have struck like an incubus in the Territory, thieving, burning and murdering, running with a gang of the worst outlaws ever seen in this blood-soaked landscape....

EPILOGUE

The study designed by Lew Wallace as "a pleasure house for my soul" was his refuge for creativity. He wrote *Ben-Hur* under a giant, spreading beech tree that stood where his statue is today (left). The tree died the same year he did, struck by lightning.

WARRIOR AT PEACE

'What do you think Cincinnati worth?'

Lew Wallace after the war. 1893.

Europe watched the American Civil War like lawyers on the sidelines of a bitter, violent divorce, looking for a chance to scoop up something of value.

England considered an alliance with the Confederate States of America to get its hands on all that prime Southern cotton. According to some historians, that alliance was just a few days from being drafted when General Lee surrendered at Appomattox Courthouse.

France saw an opportunity to exploit the chaos to expand its colonial empire in Mexico, perhaps reaching into the southwestern Confederate states. France already had 28,000 troops in Mexico, to chase President Benito Juarez from Mexico City and declare its own transplanted emperor: Archduke Ferdinand Maximillian Joseph of Austria, a crony of Napoleon III.

Lew Wallace was idle in Crawfordsville again, despite his success at Monocacy. But he was watching the events in Mexico during 1864, and became alarmed enough to write to General Grant with a warning and a proposal.

The warning was that Mexico and France might aid the Confederates and offer them a refuge across the border to keep their rebellion simmering for decades.

The proposal: Wallace would go to Mexico, find out if the threat was real and find a way to prevent it.

Grant agreed and soon found out Wallace was right. The commander of the Confederate Army in the Southwest was Gen. Kirby Smith—the same Kirby Smith who had nearly taken Cincinnati. He was negotiating with Maximilian, just as Wallace had predicted. Maximillian was very interested, but most Confederate troops and commanders under Kirby Smith refused to join Mexico and France against their own country, divided as it was. Memories of the Mexican-American War and the Alamo in 1836 were too fresh and bitter.

General Smith became an exile in Mexico, then Havana. But he finally swore an oath of allegiance to the Union for amnesty and became a college professor, teaching botany in Tennessee.

Wallace had now saved Cincinnati, Baltimore, Washington and probably at least three southern states: Texas, Arkansas and Louisiana.

After that, he served as judge at the Andersonville War Crimes Trial, and also in the trial of the assassins who killed Lincoln.

In 1865, he was offered $100,000 to become a general in the Mexican Army to help Benito Juarez. France finally left Mexico in 1867, and Juarez returned to Mexico City. But Presidente Juarez reneged on the deal with Wallace, who came home discouraged and deep in debt.

By 1867, he was back in Crawfordsville, practicing law, broke, frustrated and bored.[141] He ran for Congress twice, and lost both races.

But in 1878, President Rutherford Hayes appointed him as the Territorial Governor of New Mexico, where he crushed the Lincoln

---

141 He referred to the practice of law as "that most detestable of occupations."

County War, captured Billy the Kid and worked on his greatest book, *Ben-Hur*, in a secluded room in the governor's mansion, writing by candlelight, sometimes all night.

He also waged a bloody war against Victorio. As Susan Wallace wrote, "Very few know or care to know that in the Apache War, ending October 1880, more than 400 white persons were scalped and tortured to death with devilish ingenuity."

Unable to get help from Washington, Wallace mocked people in the East who were safe enough "for the indulgence of rose-colored theories about the Indians."

Victorio was finally killed in Chihuahua, Mexico, where he was tracked down by a combined force of the Mexican Army and U.S. Cavalry led by Col. Edward Hatch and his Buffalo Soldiers. Victorio died along with 77 of his ruthless band in October, 1880 at the Battle of Tres Castillos. He was replaced by another Apache raider, Geronimo.

In 1881, President James Garfield read *Ben-Hur* and liked it so much he sent a note of praise and gratitude to Wallace. That led to an appointment as ambassador to Turkey, where President Garfield hoped Wallace would find material for another book.[142]

When he arrived in Constantinople to meet the Sultan, Wallace asked an interpreter to "say to his imperial majesty that as representative of the American people I desire to take his majesty's hand."

After a pause of disbelief, the interpreter finally stuttered the message. The Sultan, too shocked to refuse, extended his hand. "It was the first time in the history of the Ottoman Empire that a Sultan had shaken anyone's hand, much less a Christian and foreigner."[143] Sultan Abdul Hamid II soon became a great admirer of Lew Wallace and tried to hire him to modernize his nation's military.

Wallace left Turkey in 1885, and finally came home to Crawfordsville to stay. He volunteered to fight in the Spanish-American War in 1898, but was politely rejected at age 70. He designed and built a writing

---

142 Garfield was shot by an assassin in July 1881 and died almost three months later from an infection.

143 Morsberger, Robert Eustis, and Katharine M. Morsberger. *Lew Wallace, Militant Romantic*, McGraw-Hill Companies, 1980.

A detail on the frieze at the Lew Wallace study shows the face of Ben-Hur as envisioned by the author.

study in 1895 that is a National Historic Landmark. It had retractable skylights, walls of bookshelves, electric and gas lights, running water, a gas fireplace, a moat and reflective pool stocked with fish and a 35-foot ceiling.

Today it's a museum to display the artifacts of an amazing life: his Civil War uniform tunic, guns, cannon balls, pieces of his homemade violins, artworks, gifts from the Sultan of Turkey, sculptures, fishing tackle and one of his patented inventions, the first telescoping "pocket fisherman" fishing pole.

One of his final legacies to the country he loved and served was his return to the Shiloh battlefield. He went back twice, in 1895 and 1903, to ride the route of his ill-fated march in 1862 and help to preserve the hallowed ground as a National Park.[144]

In 1875, Wallace's good friend, Col. Charles Whittlesey of Cincinnati, wrote a paper for the Historical and Philosophical Society.[145] The veteran of Shiloh and the Defense of Cincinnati quoted General Sherman

---

144 Wallace took along a surveyor to measure the route. A march of 14 miles a day was average for an army. "Yet that day we moved 18 miles, under disadvantages seldom encountered."

145 Became the Cincinnati Historical Society, now the Cincinnati History Library and Archives.

from his memoirs to prove Wallace was right and Grant was wrong about Shiloh:

Sherman wrote, "General Grant visited me about ten a.m. where we were holding our ground and said that on his way up he stopped at Crump's Landing and ordered Lew Wallace's division to cross Snake Creek so as to come up on my right."

That made it clear: Wallace had chosen the right road to cross Snake Creek. Grant knew it. Sherman knew it.

Whittlesey also quoted seven ranking officers on the march with Wallace that day, who all recalled that he followed orders explicitly. Whittlesey wrote: "It would be very difficult to produce a statement wider of the truth than that which attributes the defeat of the first day at Shiloh to the tardiness of Wallace's division. The battle was lost before he was ordered to move." He accused Grant and his staff of "an effort to shift responsibility at the expense of historical truth."

But it was too late. The accusations had become embedded in history

Lew Wallace, writing under his beloved beech tree. Courtesy of the General Lew Wallace Study & Museum, Crawfordsville, Indiana.

**Sculpture of Christ by Lew Wallace. Courtesy
of General Lew Wallace Study & Museum.**

like a bullet too close to the heart to be removed, carried by Wallace
for the rest of his life.

He died in 1905 at 77.

His statue stands in Statuary Hall at the US Capitol—the only
novelist there.

"I know of no happier way of passing time," he said of writing, "none
which takes me so completely out of this world and affairs of the present,
a perfect retreat from the annoyances of daily life."

He indulged his lifelong dream of being an artist, creating beautiful
paintings and sculptures.

One was a bust of Christ.

His wife Susan was raised as a Quaker, but Lew Wallace confessed
that until 1875, "I had no conviction about God and Christ." He
described his attitude as "indifference to the Tomorrow of death."

But when confronted by a well-known agnostic on a train that year,
he was embarrassed by his own ignorance of the Bible and decided to
investigate. The result was *Ben-Hur.* It contained no sermonizing, no
formal religion, but became one of the greatest Christian books of all time.

"Long before I was through with my book, I became a believer in God and Christ," he wrote.

He was not a churchgoer. But his faith was strong and deep, springing from the well of personal discovery.

Reflecting on his achievements that could fill a dozen lifetimes, he said "I shall look back upon Ben-Hur as my best performance."

The public agreed. The book has never been out of print, and has sold more than 50 million copies. A stage play version ran from 1899 to 1921, seen by 20 million people at 6,000 shows around the world.[146] Three movies were made, including the famous 1959 version starring Charleton Heston that still holds the record for most Oscars, 11. The story is as timeless as its message of redemption: Jesus died to set us free.

As a painting, the life of Lew Wallace would fill a mural that could cover all four 25-foot walls in his Crawfordville temple of creativity. There would be scenes from the Mexican-American War, Fort Donelson, Shiloh, Baltimore and Monocacy, with cannons, muskets, wounded soldiers, Andersonville Prison and his beloved warhorse, Old John.

There would be sylvan landscapes along the sunlit Kankakee River of his boyhood; fishing lures, fiddles and afternoons writing under his favorite beech. Law books, ceremonial swords, favorite hats and pens and blueprints for inventions would be scattered about.

Another wall might show Wild West outlaws, gunfights, renegade Apaches and the grand Palace of the Governors in Santa Fe—followed by the Sultan and his fabulous riches in Turkey, chariot races, Ben-Hur, Aztec warriors from his book *The Fair God,* and library shelves crowded with his favorite reference books and literature.

The Lincoln assassination trial, Mexican Juaristas, Abraham Lincoln and at least three other presidents; Confederate generals, US Grant, William Tecumseh Sherman—even his nemesis Henry Halleck might make an appearance, spinning his web in the shadows.

Susan would be in an honored place with his son Henry and his grandchildren. And his sculpture of Jesus.

---

146 The chariot race was recreated with horses on treadmills; Christ was imagined as a beam of light.

Somewhere in a corner there would be long lines of Squirrel Hunters, soldiers and members of the Black Brigade, returning across the Pontoon Bridge in triumph, carrying rifles, picks and shovels, greeted by cheering crowds waving colorful handkerchiefs from rooftops and windows, celebrating the Defense of Cincinnati.

There might also be a curious scene of two retired generals in a dark corner of a hotel bar in Cincinnati, long after the war, sharing a drink, laughter and a treasure of secrets known only to men who have had their hands on the levers of history and moved, by inches, the trajectory of the future.

At the Burnet House bar

Back in 1868, as fate would have it, Wallace met his Confederate doppel-gänger in Cincinnati at the Burnet House: Gen. Henry Heth. They were the same age. Both were hellraisers who bristled at incompetence and sometimes ignored foolish orders. Both had served in New Mexico and the West. Both were excellent horsemen, unsung heroes, and had streaks of impulsive recklessness, resulting in reprimands by the top generals of their time (Grant rebuked Wallace, Lee scolded Heth).

Wallace told the story in his autobiography:

"I happened to be again at the Burnet House and was informed that General Heth was also a guest. I sought him out and invited him into the basement, where, in that day, private conversations were generally conducted with the bar in sight.

"He was a frank, candid, quiet gentleman and, 'the great unpleas-antness' over, neither of us could see why a discussion of the 'siege of Cincinnati' should not be enjoyed."

Wallace asked the question that had kept him awake so many nights in September 1862: "Do you believe you could have taken the city?"

"Yes," Heth answered with a soft but confident drawl.

"Why didn't you?"

"My column was in motion to attack when I received an order from General Kirby Smith to rejoin him in haste, as Bragg was retreating from Kentucky. But for that I would have got in behind you at a place on the west which you had left undefended and unguarded."

"It was a narrow neck between the river and the foot of the large hill on the south and right, was it not?"

"Yes, that was the place."

"Perhaps it was well enough you did not try it."

Wallace described hidden guns at the foot of Race Street, plus six gunboats. "Besides that, within an hour I could have covered the hills on your right hand with 50,000 sharpshooters. It was just the place for my irregulars to show their handicraft."

Heth sipped his bourbon and smiled. He was not impressed. He had already seen some of those irregulars run from battle. "I knew what you were doing in Cincinnati and the Kentucky towns. My men were going in and out all the time."

The two retired generals shared secrets about spies on both sides and had a good laugh at how they had tricked each other. Then Wallace wondered: "Now, if you had taken Cincinnati, tell me, won't you, what would you have done with it?"

"I will answer Yankee-like," Heth said with a grin. "What do you think Cincinnati worth?"

"In money?"

"Yes."

"Probably $5 million."

"More than that."

"Well, say $10 million."

"It is a great city," Heth prodded. "A great city, and rich, and the people think a great deal of it. And if I had proposed to its authorities to sack it from end to end or that they should redeem it with $15 million, [147] or such a matter, which do you think they would have preferred?"

Wallace might have replied with one of his favorite guiding principles:

"May a man tell what he can do until he tries? That, I take it, is the soul of the Americanism."

Heth would have laughed and understood.

---

147   About $555 million in 2023.

GENERAL LEW WALLACE.

Author of "The Prince of India," "Ben-Hur," etc.

Lew Wallace in 1893. Illustrator unknown. Possibly a self-portrait.

ACKNOWLEDGMENTS

This story began more than 20 years ago, near midnight on Cemetery Ridge at Gettysburg, where a group of trespassers who called themselves the Cincinnati Irregulars passed a flask and shared profound thoughts on a haunted battlefield.

My first thanks go to those friends, and especially Greg Delev, the organizer and instigator. The Cincinnati Irregulars went on to Antietam, Shiloh, Charleston and Gettysburg again. I have been fascinated, inspired and amazed ever since by that stirring chapter of American history.

Thanks also to Tom Meeks, associate director of the General Lew Wallace Study and Museum in Crawfordsville, Indiana, whose years of scholarship and devotion make him one of America's foremost experts on Lew Wallace. The museum is a wonderful day trip for anyone interested in our history and one of America's greatest heroes. It was a real treat to spend time with Tom and the spirit of Lew Wallace, who must have been greatly amused as he listened to us from his favorite writing chair.

Jill Beitz, manager of Reference and Research Services at the Cincinnati History Library and Archives in the Cincinnati Museum Center tipped me off to the story of the Oxford spy Lottie Moon. She graciously introduced me to some fantastic resources.

My neighbor Don Dunton heard I was working on a book about the Civil War and generously shared his father's lifelong collection of Civil War books and *Civil War Times* magazines, all containing articles, stories and information that cannot be found anywhere else.

Jason French, curator of collections at Behringer-Crawford Museum in DeVou Park, Covington, gave me a tour of their outstanding Civil War collection and told me about the attempt to assassinate Abraham

Lincoln in Cincinnati. The museum sits near one of the few remaining artillery positions from the Defense of Cincinnati, Battery Hooper.

Thanks also to the late James Ramage, a Civil War scholar at Northern Kentucky University, whose lecture on the Siege of Cincinnati got me interested in the topic when I was working as a columnist at *The Cincinnati Enquirer*. Ramage was a leader in preserving Battery Hooper along with so much of our local treasure of history.

Rick Roesel's collection of Civil War rifles and sidearms was very helpful. And thanks for the reading tips from Bernie O'Bryan, the world's greatest Lew Wallace impersonator.

Special thanks to my uncle, Col. Dick Bronson, a Vietnam veteran and artilleryman who walked the battlefield at Shiloh with me and my son James, explained the positions and fields of fire, and introduced me to our ancestor Andrew Gillespie, who fought a few miles south in Corinth, Mississippi with the 12th Michigan.

Thanks to my wife, Kathy, who was patient through months of research and writing when I was not always good company, lost in my time machine, stuck in the 1860s, sometimes as salty as Sherman in Atlanta.

Finally, thanks to Lew Wallace and all the veterans like him who sacrificed their "todays" so we could have our "tomorrows." Except for his combat heroics, paintings and just about everything else admirable, I recognized a few things we had in common: bad student, troublemaker, opinionated, romantic, follower of Christ, avid reader and writer.

He said, "I would rather write books than be rich."

Amen to that.

QUOTES FROM LEW WALLACE

"My greatest personal satisfaction was due to discovery of the fact that in the confusion and feverish excitement of real battle, I could think." – Autobiography.

"In the very beginning, before distractions overtake me, I wish to say that I believe absolutely in the Christian conception of God. … I am not a member of any church or denomination, nor have I ever been. Not that churches are objectionable to me, but simply because my freedom is enjoyable, and I do not think myself good enough to be a communicant." – Preface to *Ben-Hur*.

"I am glad that I have had the opportunity to travel and learn a little of other lands, but if my life has taught me anything, it is that our own is the best, the freest, the happiest one beneath God's sunshine—worth living for and worth dying for, too, whenever the need arises." – Letter.

"I want a study, a pleasure-house for my soul, where no one could hear me make speeches to myself, and play the violin at midnight if I chose. A detached room away from the world and its worries. A place for my old age to rest in and grow reminiscent, fighting the battles of youth over again." – Letter to Susan in 1879.

"To be able to laugh at himself is pretty good evidence that one has reached the philosophic state of life; to invite others to join him in the laugh is a final test conclusive of the fact." – Autobiography.

"To catch a boy and hold him fast one has only to set the delicate machinery of the wonder-box in him at work." – Autobiography.

"In the nature of things freedom and slavery cannot be coexistent. I could not bring myself to defend the institution of slavery, my sympathies would side with the fugitive against his master. In all nature there was nothing more natural than the yearning for freedom." – Autobiography.

"I want to bury myself in a den of books. I want to saturate myself with the elements of which they are made, and breathe their atmosphere until I am of it." – Letter to Susan, 1885.

BOOKS, WORKS CITED

Baker, La Fayette Curry. *The United States Secret Service in the Late War*. 1894.

Beemer, Charles G. *"My Greatest Quarrel with Fortune."* 2015.

Cincinnati, Literary Club. *The Literary Club of Cincinnati, 1849-1999*. 2001.

Cozzens, Peter. *The Darkest Days of the War*. UNC Press Books, 2017.

Dodge, Theodore Ayrault. *A Bird's Eye View of Our Civil War*. 1883.

Elrod, Matthew. *The Impact of the Civil War on Northern Kentucky and Cincinnati, 1861-1865*. ProQuest, 2006.

Foote, Shelby. *The Civil War: A Narrative*. Vintage, 2011.

Force, Manning Ferguson. *From Fort Henry to Corinth*. 1881.

Garrett, Pat Floyd. *The Authentic Life of Billy, the Kid*. 1882.

Geaslen, Chester F. *Our Moment of Glory in the Civil War*. 2007.

Groom, Winston. *Shiloh, 1862*. National Geographic Books, 2012.

Hansen, Harry. *The Civil War*. Penguin, 2010.

Heth, Henry. *The Memoirs of Henry Heth*. Praeger, 1974.

Morsberger, Robert Eustis, and Katharine M. Morsberger. *Lew Wallace, Militant Romantic*. McGraw-Hill Companies, 1980.

Morton, Joseph W. *Sparks from the Camp Fire*. 1892.

Pinney, Nelson A. *History of the 104th Regiment Ohio Volunteer Infantry from 1862 to 1865*. 1886.

Pratt, Fletcher. *Civil War in Pictures*. 1962.

Shaara, Jeff. *A Blaze of Glory*. Ballantine Books, 2013.

Shaara, Michael, and Jeff Shaara. *The Civil War Trilogy*. 1999.

Stephens, Gail. *Shadow of Shiloh*. Indiana Historical Society, 2013.

Wallace, Lew. *Ben-Hur*. 1880.

Lew Wallace; an Autobiography ... New York ; London, Harper & brothers, 1906.

Lew Wallace; An Autobiography. Vol. II - Scholar's Choice Edition. 2015.

The Boyhood of Christ. Health Research Books, 1996.

The Fair God. 1898.

The Prince of India; Or, Why Constantinople Fell. 1893.

Wallace, Susan Elston. *The Land of the Pueblos*. 1888.

Widmer, Ted. *Lincoln on the Verge*. Simon & Schuster, 2020.

Wimberg, Robert J. *Cincinnati and the Civil War*. 1992.